Russian Legal Culture Befor
After Communism

In late Imperial Russia and, again, in the immediate aftermath of communist rule, legal scholars were confronted by similar challenges in their efforts to modernize the country's system of criminal justice. Inspired by some of the fundamental principles of classical liberalism, notably those designed to protect individual legal rights and freedoms, they endeavoured to promote juridical awareness and respect for law. For post-Soviet specialists, an integral part of this process has involved the recovery of an abandoned pre-Revolutionary legacy. Valued for their example as humanists and activists, 'past masters', such as Judge Koni, Nikolai Tagantsev, and one of Russia's most celebrated nineteenth-century thinkers, the moral philosopher Vladimir Solov'ev, have also earned posthumous recognition for the actuality of their ideas concerning the 'right to a dignified existence', the moral responsibilities of the judiciary, and the legal rights of the accused.

This book bridges two eras of legal reform. It examines competing theories of crime and the criminal, together with various prescriptions for punishment respecting personal inviolability. More broadly, by charting endeavours of the juridical community to promote legal culture through legislative reform and education, it throws light on aspects of politics, society, and mentality in two turbulent periods of Russian history.

Frances Nethercott is a Lecturer in Russian history at St Andrews University, UK. She specializes in intellectual and cultural history. Her previous publications include *Une Rencontre Philosophique: Bergson en Russie, 1907–1917*, and *Russia's Plato: Plato and the Platonic Tradition in Russian Education, Science and Ideology, 1840–1930*.

BASEES/Routledge series on Russian and East European studies

This series is published on behalf of BASEES (the British Association for Slavonic and East European Studies). The series comprises original, high-quality, research-level work by both new and established scholars on all aspects of Russian, Soviet, post-Soviet, and East European Studies in humanities and social science subjects.

1 **Ukraine's Foreign and Security Policy, 1991–2000**
Roman Wolczuk

2 **Political Parties in the Russian Regions**
Derek S. Hutcheson

3 **Local Communities and Post-Communist Transformation**
Edited by Simon Smith

4 **Repression and Resistance in Communist Europe**
J.C. Sharman

5 **Political Elites and the New Russia**
Anton Steen

6 **Dostoevsky and the Idea of Russianness**
Sarah Hudspith

7 **Performing Russia**
Folk revival and Russian identity
Laura J. Olson

8 **Russian Transformations**
Edited by Leo McCann

9 **Soviet Music and Society under Lenin and Stalin**
The baton and sickle
Edited by Neil Edmunds

10 **State Building in Ukraine**
The Ukranian parliament, 1990–2003
Sarah Whitmore

11 **Defending Human Rights in Russia**
Sergei Kovalyov, dissident, and Human Rights Commissioner, 1969–2003
Emma Gilligan

12 **Small-Town Russia**
Postcommunist livelihoods and identities: a portrait of the intelligentsia in Achit, Bednodemyanovsk and Zubtsov, 1999–2000
Anne White

13 **Russian Society and the Orthodox Church**
Religion in Russia after communism
Zoe Knox

14 **Russian Literary Culture in the Camera Age**
The word as image
Stephen Hutchings

15 **Between Stalin and Hitler**
Class war and race war on the Dvina, 1940–46
Geoffrey Swain

16 **Literature in Post-Communist Russia and Eastern Europe**
The Russian, Czech, and Slovak fiction of the changes 1988–98
Rajendra A. Chitnis

17 **Soviet Dissent and Russia's Transition to Democracy**
Dissident legacies
Robert Horvath

18 **Russian and Soviet Film Adaptations of Literature, 1900–2001**
Screening the word
Edited by Stephen Hutchings and Anat Vernitski

19 **Russia as a Great Power**
Dimensions of security under Putin
Edited by Jakob Hedenskog, Vilhelm Konnander, Bertil Nygren, Ingmar Oldberg, and Christer Pursiainen

20 **Katyn and the Soviet Massacre of 1940**
Truth, justice, and memory
George Sanford

21 **Conscience, Dissent and Reform in Soviet Russia**
Philip Boobbyer

22 **The Limits of Russian Democratisation**
Emergency powers and states of emergency
Alexander N. Domrin

23 **The Dilemmas of Destalinisation**
A social and cultural history of reform in the Khrushchev era
Edited by Polly Jones

24 **News Media and Power in Russia**
Olessia Koltsova

25 **Post-Soviet Civil Society**
Democratization in Russia and the Baltic States
Anders Uhlin

26 **The Collapse of Communist Power in Poland**
Jacqueline Hayden

27 **Television, Democracy and Elections in Russia**
Sarah Oates

28 **Russian Constitutionalism**
Historical and contemporary development
Andrey N. Medushevsky

29 **Late Stalinist Russia**
Society between reconstruction and reinvention
Edited by Juliane Fürst

30 **The Transformation of Urban Space in Post-Soviet Russia**
Konstantin Axenov, Isolde Brade and Evgenij Bondarchuk

31 **Western Intellectuals and the Soviet Union, 1920–40**
From Red Square to the Left Bank
Ludmila Stern

32 **The Germans of the Soviet Union**
Irina Mukhina

33 **Re-constructing the Post-Soviet Industrial Region**
The Donbas in transition
Edited by Adam Swain

34 **Chechnya – Russia's 'War on Terror'**
John Russell

35 **The New Right in the New Europe**
Czech transformation and right-wing politics, 1989–2006
Seán Hanley

36 **Democracy and Myth in Russia and Eastern Europe**
Edited by Alexander Wöll and Harald Wydra

37 **Energy Dependency, Politics and Corruption in the Former Soviet Union**
Russia's power, oligarchs' profits and Ukraine's missing energy policy, 1995–2006
Margarita M. Balmaceda

38 **Peopling the Russian Periphery**
Borderland colonization in Eurasian history
Edited by Nicholas B. Breyfogle, Abby Schrader and Willard Sunderland

39 **Russian Legal Culture Before and After Communism**
Criminal justice, politics, and the public sphere
Frances Nethercott

Russian Legal Culture Before and After Communism

Criminal justice, politics, and the public sphere

Frances Nethercott

Routledge
Taylor & Francis Group
LONDON AND NEW YORK

First published 2007
by Routledge
2 Park Square, Milton Park, Abingdon, Oxon OX14 4RN

Simultaneously published in the USA and Canada
by Routledge
711 Third Avenue, New York, NY 10017

Routledge is an imprint of the Taylor & Francis Group, an informa business

First issued in paperback 2012

Typeset in Times by Wearset Ltd, Boldon, Tyne and Wear

British Library Cataloguing in Publication Data
A catalogue record for this book is available from the British Library

Library of Congress Cataloging in Publication Data
A catalog record for this book has been requested

ISBN13: 978-0-415-54314-9 (pbk)
ISBN13: 978-0-415-31770-2 (hbk)
ISBN13: 978-0-203-59181-9 (ebk)

For DMN

Contents

Acknowledgements

Research on this project originated some time ago in an interdisciplinary project carried out with Dutch colleagues at the University of Nijmegen (1998–2001) funded by the Dutch Organization for Scientific Research (NWO). Entitled *Civil Society and National Religion: Problems of State and Society in the Philosophy of Vladimir Solov'ev*, it examined the relationship between 'civil society' and 'national religion' in Russia, past and present, through the prism of Solov'ev's thought. My contribution focused on Solov'ev's ideas on law. Regular workshops and seminars with colleagues and doctoral students provided an ideal, indeed privileged, forum for the refinement and development of ideas and have produced some excellent dissertations by members of the group.

Since collaborating on the Nijmegen project, I have benefited from several awards allowing me to further my research on criminal justice in the late Imperial and post-Soviet periods more broadly. The Carnegie Trust for the Universities of Scotland and the British Academy funded my more recent research trips to St Petersburg and Moscow in 2004 and 2005, and in 2006 an award granted by the Arts and Humanities Research Council (AHRC) gave me the opportunity to concentrate on the final stages of the first draft. In this regard, I would also like to express gratitude to my home University, St Andrews, for accepting my bid for research leave 'out of turn'. My thanks to Geoffrey Hosking and Richard Sakwa for supporting my application to the AHRC and other grant bodies, to Hamish Scott for his critical insights, to Peter Sowden at Routledge, to Hannah Dolan, production editor, and to my anonymous reviewer for the many valuable comments on an earlier version of the book.

Parts of the current study and related topics have been presented at various international conferences, just two of which I would like to mention here: 'Vladimir Solov'ëv: Reconciler and Polemicist', an international conference held at the University of Nijmegen in 1998 organized by Evert van der Zweerde and Wil van den Bercken; the interdisciplinary symposium, 'Gewohnheitsrecht – Rechtsprinzipen – Rechtsbewusstsein', Munster, 2004. Special thanks to the organizers Alfred Sproede and Werner Krawietz for seeing the possibilities of the subject matter and to other participants, especially Nikolai Plotnikov (Bochum) for initiating collaboration on the problem of *lichnost'* (person/personhood) in Russian intellectual culture. While, as such, no part or chapters of this book have been published elsewhere, materials from it have been used for one shorter article, 'Discipline or Punish? Russian Criminal Justice in the Era of Reform', *Rechtstheorie*, 35 (2004) and a 'lexicographical' essay, 'The Concept of *Lichnost'* in Russian Criminal Law Theory, 1860s–1900s', for the Russian–German project *'Person' und 'Subjekt' im deutsch-russischen Kulturtransfer. Untersuchungen zum Begriffsfeld der 'Personalitat' in interkultureller Perspektive* at the Ruhr-Universitat, Bochum, sponsored by Volkswagenstiftung.

Last but not least, I would like to thank friends and interlocutors in Russia, Holland, and Great Britain: special thanks go to Irina Shubenkina and Dmitry Sergeev at the library housed in the Institute of State and Law, Moscow, Leonid Mamut, and Anatoly Naumov, Institute of State and Law, Alexander Mikhlin at the Research Institute of the Ministry of the Interior, Katia Dmitrieva, Natasha Chist'yakova, Larissa Kozlova, Alexander and Olga Dobrokhotov; Evert van der Zweerde, Machiel Karskens, Pauline Schrooyen, Manon de Courten, and Anton Simons; Constance Blackwell, Alan Caskie, Owen Downes, Penny Ellingham, Clare Fallon, Lindsay Fraser, Georgia Gavin, Stephen Gaukroger, Bruce Lenman, Frances Lynch, Iseabail McCleod, David Mitchell, Christina Outram, Stana Nenadic, Joanne Soroka, and Jonathan Sutton.

Note on transliteration

I have used a modified version of British Standard transliteration, which affects some proper nouns familiar to a Western audience (Yeltsin, Dostoevsky, but Tolstoi, rather than Tolstoy, and Solov'ev, rather than Solovev, Solov'ëv, or Solovyov). Unless otherwise stated, translations are my own.

Abbreviations

GiP	*Gosudarstvo i Pravo*
Pgd.	Petrograd
SEER	*Slavonic and East European Review*
SEET	*Studies in East European Thought*
SPb.	St Petersburg
VE	*Vestnik Evropy*
VF	*Voprosy Filosofii*
Zh. Min. Yust.	Zhurnal Ministerstva Yustitsii

Introduction

> The place of the individual in a criminal trial aptly reflects his position in the state more generally (…). [R]espect for the rights of the citizen by the judiciary is a necessary precondition for the state to carry out its educative mission successfully.
>
> (Pavel Lyublinsky, 1906)[1]

This book combines a history of Russian criminal justice in the era of Reform with an analysis of theories of crime and punishment formulated in anticipation of a more humane penal system. While the history of Alexander II's judicial reform, which tentatively introduced trial by jury, is generally well documented, less well known is the body of theoretical work written by juridical thinkers and practitioners of law exploring the causes of crime and the social role of punishment. Albeit remote from the day-to-day dealings in the courtroom or the harsh realities of the penitentiary as brilliantly evoked in the novels of Dostoevsky, findings intended for intellectual debate within the profession or for instructional purposes in the classroom present a useful tool for reconstructing the development of Russian legal thought. More broadly, they afford insight into some of the key issues of Russian intellectual culture during the twilight years of tsarist rule.

Explanations for the disappointing outcome of judicial reform resulting in the backlash of reaction and conservatism associated with the reigns of Alexander III and Nicholas II usually focus on fundamental incompatibilities between the modernizing world view of reformist thinkers and the reaction of autocracy, which, if it authorized the new legislation in criminal procedure, was reluctant to see its powers diminished.[2] This argument is valid, of course, but it has limitations. First, it overlooks contingencies such as the financial and organizational hurdles, which thwarted endeavours to set up a more uniform network of prisons thereby bringing Russia's penal system in line with Western models as envisaged by reformers and, indeed, endorsed by the state. Second, it does not account for the fairly lopsided manner in which judicial reform was actually carried out. If the 1864 statutes, which introduced new regulations concerning detention and access to an attorney, offered promising parallels with the concept of habeas corpus, substantive law and the penal code remained basically unchanged. This generated an uncomfortable coexistence between Reform-era innovation in procedure premised on the ideas of personal inviolability and its corresponding assumption of equality before the law and pre-reform legacy (not to mention post-reform social reality) that was based on estate privilege. This situation had serious consequences for first-generation reformers in their role as 'legislators', since, from the outset, it obliged them to operate with two sets of conflicting logic. As the era of reform progressed lack of coherence between procedural and substantive law worsened, though the terms of the dichotomy were unexpectedly inverted: forward-looking ideas introduced into the arena of procedural law were gradually rescinded by imperial decree in response to mounting social and political tensions, and ultimately blocked by the promulgation of emergency rule in the wake of Alexander's assassination. Paradoxically, it was during Alexander III's reign, inaugurating the era of 'counter reform' (a term originating in the contemporary oppositional press) that the project to compile a new criminal code was finally authorized, and it was a process in which reform-minded juridical thinkers were invited to take a leading role. Granted, the task of redefining the code consisted in little more than the laborious whittling away at the inherited legislation, with innovations inspired by contemporary West European criminal law incorporated in controlled measures. Ambitions for a complete overhaul of the existing legislation were thus reduced to a series of partial revisions. However, by the turn of the century, the project to modernize criminal legislation had managed to secure more durable gains, on paper at least: albeit only partially enacted, a new more streamlined code marking a definitive departure from the cumbersome legacy of the Digest of Laws compiled during the reign of Nicholas I was finally ratified in 1903.

One could argue that the drafting of a new legislation was more of a theoretical exercise than the intellectual endeavours of reformers in their role as 'teachers' and enlighteners. In the university auditorium and, especially, in their research, they had more leeway to test out their ideas or explore points of difference with peers. As 'interpreters', committed to instilling a legal consciousness and encouraging trust in the law, the lecture-based textbooks they produced together with their scholarly articles and monographs constituted a canon of national juridical literature, which, over time, became staples in the university curriculum up to the Revolution, indeed, even into the early Soviet period. Since the collapse of the Soviet Union, some of these works have been resurrected as classics of pre-revolutionary legal culture serving as models to emulate in endeavours to overcome a more proximate Soviet legacy. As part of more ambitious efforts to save a cultural patrimony that was mostly squandered by the Soviet regime, contemporary juridical scholarship is as much engaged with adding to the gallery of remarkable Russian thinkers the names of those who have been largely overlooked or merely footnoted as source information as it is with addressing the modern climate of criminal activity. Indeed, some juridical thinkers working today openly admit the importance of 'past masters' as role models. The integrity they ascribe to persons such as Judge Koni and Nikolai

Tagantsev as intellectuals and public figures committed to the ideals of 'legality' during the reigns of Alexander III and Nicholas II is for many just as relevant as the content of their scholarly output designed for the classroom and academic peers.

Analysis of the ways Russian legal scholars theorized crime and punishment and the conceptual apparatus they used is, as intimated earlier, revelatory of the formation of a community of discourse and of a corresponding sense of corporate identity that was gradually consolidated through a set of shared values and beliefs. At the core of reformist thinking was the question of individual rights (*prava lichnoi svobody*). Initially, inspired by classical liberal philosophies of law, Russian theorists transposed the concepts of rights (*prava*), freedom, and duties to the arena of crime and punishment in a projected modern, rule of law state. Early Reform-era specialists, such as Vladimir Spasovich, his pupil, Nikolai Tagantsev, and Nikolai Sergeevsky recognized that in order to consolidate the Russian science of criminal law, a metaphysical grounding of crime and punishment was indispensable. Inspired by the classical texts of German idealism such as these had filtered into the work of German legal scholars active during the first half of the nineteenth century, they likewise upheld the idea of the autonomous legal subject (*pravovoi sub'ekt*) as the bearer of rights and freedoms. The principle of personal inviolability pertaining to the 'purely individual rightful lot of the citizen – his person, property and possessions' (*sfera chisto-individual'nykh pravovykh blag grazhdanina – ego lichnost', zhilishche i imushchestvo*) would, they believed, provide the building blocks for the development and protection of the individual's rights in his capacity as citizen (namely the right to form associations) and, eventually, in the realm of politics as well.[3]

The meanings that accrued to what was, with one or two exceptions, a relatively stable lexicon articulating the idea of *lichnost'* in the arena of crime and punishment generally reflected the social political world views of given authors – from liberalism to socialism, loosely understood. But, they were also nuanced in response to competing schools of philosophical–juridical thought in Western Europe. Correspondingly, in Russia, early reform accounts privileged formal juridical conceptions of *lichnost'* qua legal subject as the perpetrator of a crime and rigorously separated the realms of inner and outer freedom, with only the latter falling within the province of law. However, the emergence of broadly conceived collectivist world views affording a new perspective on the individual as a socially determined being generated the idea of a *sotsial'naya lichnost'* in criminal politics, a branch of criminal law originating in positivism and which, from 1907 on, became a compulsory course in the university curriculum. Thus, the fundamental assumptions of the classical school – free will and moral responsibility, crime as a breach of norms – were openly challenged by a slightly younger generation keen to restore the idea of the criminal as flesh and blood reality in the dock. With its emphasis on the struggle undertaken by society to contain crime, the criminal was now viewed primarily through the prism of social–economic relations and perceived as a victim of poverty, ghettoization, and degenerative disease.

From roughly the turn of the century, we can retrace the ways in which otherwise opposed schools of criminology – the classical and positivist – were each beginning to incorporate the moral dimension – albeit differently conceived – into their studies of the criminal and criminality. This period witnessed the revival of Kantianism and the religiously inspired debate on the moral–political, metaphysical and aesthetic meaning of 'personality'. As an integral part of Silver Age culture, these ideas formed the backbone of new philosophies of law and in some cases filtered down to inform developments in criminology and various prescriptions for combating crime. The parameters of legal positivism were also shifting, producing a hybrid of sociological and psychological theories of criminal behaviour that were likewise receptive to the moral dimension. This new path in positivism was, in part, due to the highly influential, yet 'multi-directional' work on intuitive theory of law developed by Leon Petrazhitsky at home, and in Germany, it was due to Georg Jellinek, whose broadly conceived legal positivism ('law as a minimum good') was paired in the literature with Vladimir Solov'ev's theory of law and morality.

One of Russia's best-known and original philosophers Solov'ev (1853–1900) plays a pivotal role in this book for a number of reasons, even as his interest in law and criminal justice stemmed from premises that were, to say the least, maverick in the eyes of his contemporaries.[4] Unlike the classical or positivistic approaches adopted by his professional peers – some of whom he knew well, thanks to his collaboration, during the last decade of his life, on the editorial board of the 'liberal' journal the *European Messenger* (*Vestnik Evropy*), Solov'ev's appeal to trust in the law was explicitly informed by his position as a moral philosopher and Christian thinker. While his early forays in legal matters, notably his appeal to Alexander III to pass a stay of execution on his father's, Alexander II, assassins, drew openly on the language of charity, he later re-couched his basic conviction that the death penalty and life sentences were morally wrong in moral/juridical terms, in light of which he set down his proposals for a more humane penal code. Solov'ev's mature work on the philosophy of law and criminal justice, which he developed in articles first published in the *European Messenger* and *Questions of Philosophy and Psychology* in the 1890s, formed important chapters in his last major works, *Justification of the Good* and *Law and Morality*, both published in 1897.[5] His call to admit the 'right to a dignified existence' and his resolute defence of the 'moral integrity of the person', which, he argued, should be accounted for in the elaboration of positive laws, inspired a number of philosophers of law and theoretically minded jurists thereafter in their efforts to frame a social–legal order. More specifically, his arguments operated as a catalyst of change in liberalism and its philosophical foundations.

Despite major theoretical differences separating schools of criminal law theory, they were all united by a common concern to explore the subjective side of crime (a blind spot in the Criminal Code). Placing the civic rights of the accused in the spotlight and raising questions about the degree to which these may be diminished in the event of a conviction, in turn, underscored a second feature cutting across theoretical differences, namely a shared commitment to institute restorative justice – in deed, and not just in name. If, as most accepted, the function of punishment was to protect the state, which they conceived – against the autocratic grain – as a complex body of institutions, they also sought to ensure the social reintegration of the offender, whether conceived as an autonomous (and abstract) *pravosposobnyi sub'ekt* or a physical being. This almost universally held ambition was tested on one of the most vexed topics within criminal law theory – the death penalty. However, while theoretical discussions proved largely inconclusive (two major exceptions being the arguments put forward by Solov'ev in his later work and by the neo-Kantian, Sergei Gessen), as a consciousness-raising issue, it played an important role in the development of *obshchestvennost'*, a term that loosely translates as public awareness and the public sphere. Initially the topic of ivory tower speculations among a fairly self-contained intellectual elite during the 1880s and 1890s, when in fact very few executions were carried out, it was really in the wake of the 1905 revolution, as the state engaged in ruthless reprisals rooting out political enemies whom it executed in a wave of summary executions, that calls for abolition filtered into the broader public sphere. For the historian, this episode is instructive in two ways: if, on the one hand, state executions exposed the fragility of the rule of law in Russia, on the other, as an object of debate, the death penalty worked as a powerful mobilizing force, galvanizing public opposition to repressive state measures.

Although the problem of this book – theories of crime and punishment, rights and justice – which are examined with reference to a relatively restricted corpus of literature would appear to be rather speculative and self-contained, it does in fact engage a host of offshoot topics that have a wider social–political resonance. Russian liberalism is one of these. Most, though not all, juridical thinkers encountered in this book espoused broadly conceived liberal values of freedom of speech and association, civil rights and duties, and rule of law in their commitment to impart the value of legal culture (*zakonnost'*) to a wider readership. After 1905, some of the authors whose works I discuss – Tagantsev, Kuz'min-Karavaev, Anatoly Koni – had a brief spell in Duma politics. As public figures (*obshchestvennye deyateli*) and Kadets, they were particularly active during the first two stormy sessions of parliament.[6]

A second topic concerns the way that the history of punishment is instructive of changes in social expectations and mentality. Some of the best-known, indeed, most influential studies in the field – those by Michel Foucault, Norbert Elias, and more recently, Richard Evans – have linked the history of punishment to the history of the state and, more diffusely, to the civilizing process.[7] Throughout most of Europe, the argument goes, it was with the emergence of the nation state during the nineteenth century that violent, ritualized punishment was gradually phased out: 'It ceased to be the public stamping of the sovereign's personal authority on the body of the offender.'[8] Evans argues that one of the most powerful ways to gauge mentality is through an examination of the death penalty. If, in the late medieval and early modern periods, attitudes to death, cruelty, and suffering were 'rooted above all in social experience (…) built on the fabric of everyday life',[9] by the nineteenth century, they were couched both in juridical terms and, more forcefully, in terms of what nowadays we would call a 'human rights' concern. Thus, as a public spectacle it became increasingly unacceptable, both socially and morally and, if anything, was perceived as an unwarranted display of force by a weak state desperately clinging to its last vestiges of power.

In some key respects, late Imperial Russia subscribes to this pattern of attitudinal change: the emancipation of the serfs in 1861, the creation of the zemstvo as a form of local self-government, besides judicial reform, all stimulated new social expectations and sensitivities among the educated elite. The work of Solov'ev is, again, especially instructive in this connection. At one level, his contribution to the philosophy of law and his prescriptions for a system of criminal justice that would respect 'human dignity' act as an interface to debate among his immediate professional peers while anticipating further developments in criminology after his death. More broadly, however, his association with liberal reformers on the *European Messenger* from the late 1880s and his role as a champion of human rights allow us to view him as a bridge between the community of juridical specialists and the wider social sphere. In the first instance, this applies to the pre-Revolutionary era, where some of his ideas helped shape the debate on death penalty. But his thought is equally pertinent to the post-Soviet context: the implications for criminal justice of his commitment to the Christian-inspired idea of a dignified existence as a basic human right were again cited in renewed debate on the death penalty in the Gorbachev and Yeltsin eras when it was placed on the government agenda as part of the leadership's pledge to recognize the international convention on human rights. For this reason, the debate generated by the death penalty is examined in two time spans in this book: first, in late Imperial Russia, and, second, in the decade since the collapse of the Soviet Union, where, by way of a coda, the legacy of pre-revolutionary juridical culture more generally is explored, together with attempts by a few modern-day scholars to situate some of its achievements as 'intellectual resources' in contemporary issues of criminal justice.

1 Fathers and sons of legal reform

> For all peoples of the new Christian world there is a single goal: the unconditional recognition of the worth of a human being, of an individual person, and his comprehensive development.
>
> (Konstantin Kavelin, 'Survey of Judicial Practice in Ancient Russia', 1847)

The pioneers of judicial reform were, to borrow George Fischer's term in his classic study of Russian liberalism, *Kulturträger*, men who lived by the goals of 'human dignity and civic culture'; they campaigned in their pledge for social change.[1] They believed in human freedom as a fundamental value and dreamed of a system of justice in which a person's rights would be fully recognized. As 'activists' (*deyateli*), they fell, broadly speaking, into two main groups: on the one hand, bureaucrats and official servitors, who worked implicitly towards these goals as the authors of judicial reform within the Ministry of Justice, and on the other, 'men of the pen' – intellectuals usually held in suspicion within government circles but who enjoyed moral authority among their peers for their more forthright comments on the progress and achievements of the reform. Two good examples of this second breed of reformers, differences in age and temperament notwithstanding, are the criminal lawyer Vladimir Spasovich (1829–1907) and the philosopher Vladimir Solov'ev. Both men remained outside the system, having resigned their university posts under duress.[2] In their work as *publitsisty*, they channelled their views on social justice and legality through the medium of essays, reviews, conference transcripts, and in the public stand they took on specific issues – Spasovich in his role of defence lawyer in some of the showcase trials of the 1870s, and Solov'ev in various petitions to the tsar. More characteristically, however, the fathers and sons of reform moved through a variety of professional occupations, from bureaucrat, advocate, scholar, to *publitsist*, or even a combination of these. Of the pre- and early-reform generation, Konstantin Kavelin (1818–1885) perhaps best exemplifies this type of 'bureaucrat-*intelligent*', bridging the two categories of reformers just mentioned. Jurist and historian, Kavelin worked in the Ministry of the Interior and was a university professor and a *publitsist*; his controversial essay in 1847 on Russian social–juridical and political development famously polarized the existing ideological differences between Slavophiles and Westernizers. But it was as co-author, together with Boris Chicherin and N.A. Mel'gunov, in 1856, of a seven-point 'Liberal programme' calling for freedom of conscience, press, and transparency in the administration of justice that he set down the ground rules for reforming the nation's state and social institutions.

By the late 1850s, exchange of ideas among like-minded reformers were taking place in a variety of informal contexts. The salon, once the natural home for polite society (*obshchestvo*) to practise the art of civilized argument during the reign of Nicholas I, was no longer a privileged oasis of free thought for members of a free-thinking gentry; rather, it had become a more inclusive and informal meeting ground bridging the worlds of academics, non-conformist thinkers, and men in state service committed to social and institutional change. Moreover, as 'polite society' began spreading its base to encompass members of different social estates, public awareness (*obshchestvennost'*) was forged increasingly outside the private foyer in various *kruzhki* (student and/or revolutionary circles), or, indeed, even at the workplace, and found some controlled outlet for expression in the press.[3] At the Ministry of Justice, the Assistant Minister to Panin, Dmitry Zamyatnin, encouraged discussion groups on legal questions, and in 1858 founded the *Journal of the Ministry of Justice* to provide a platform for theory and informed discussion of current judicial practices. Besides original contributions by Ia. G. Esipovich and I.I. Ivanov, both authors of textbooks in law, and Spasovich, the journal published translations of works by leading European scholars.[4] Carl Joseph Mittermaier, professor at Heidelberg University, is especially important in this regard. One of Germany's leading campaigners for the abolition of the death penalty, Mittermaier played a key role in Russia's reform of criminal justice, both as a teacher to visiting Russian students, such as Spasovich's pupil, the future Professor of Criminal law at St Petersburg University, Nikolai Tagantsev (1843–1923), and as an outside expert invited to comment on draft proposals of the judicial statutes. As a proponent of the law for life's sake' approach, Mittermaier was actually a rather controversial figure in his own country that was then dominated by the 'classical' Tubingen School. But his belief that the judiciary was dealing with 'a living phenomenon' and not a 'geometric formula' echoed perfectly the aspirations of young Russian students of law, bored by rote learning of the Digest and the mechanical application of the book to individual cases.[5]

The articles submitted to the Ministry's *Journal* became the object of great interest and animated debate. Students of law in Moscow and St Petersburg formed discussion groups, learning to read critically and develop informed interpretations of laws and their theoretical premises. Indeed, the 1860s saw a sharp increase in the number of students matriculating in law, making up more than half the total number of students registered at Russian universities by the end of the decade. As Konstantin Arsen'ev, the journal's first assistant editor (1858–1863), recalled in a memoir note: 'From our milieu there was practically no one who would not associate himself in one way or another with the work of the new judicial institutions.'[6] A graduate of the Imperial School of Jurisprudence, Arsen'ev (1837–1919) is yet another fairly typical example of 'state servitor cum intelligent', combining a career as an attorney with a prolific output as a *publitsist*. He worked tirelessly to defend the role of the Bar against mounting attacks by critics and restrictions imposed by the government and to safeguard the role of the zemstvo in local administration. He also used *publitsistika* as a powerful tool in his campaign for religious tolerance and freedom of the individual.[7]

The *European Messenger* (*Vestnik Evropy*) and Russian liberalism

The history of this periodical, which dominated reformist *publitsistika* from its launch in 1866 up to the October Revolution, is instructive in several ways. It provides insight into the development of Russian liberalism and, more specifically, legality across three generations, especially in terms of the way these ideas took shape through polemic with rival journals, and were defended during the 'era of counter reform' (*vremiya kontrreform*), a term that originated on its pages.[8] In addition, the journal played an important role in the last decade of Vladimir Solov'ev's life, acting as a soundboard as he developed his ideas on law and morality. Solov'ev's contacts with colleagues such as Spasovich, Judge Koni, and Arsen'ev were also crucial to the refinement of offshoot issues such as 'human rights' and criminal justice, which he privileged as illustrations in both his polemical and theoretical writings of the period.

During the 1850s, Kavelin's weekly Sunday 'salon', a regular gathering of academics and erstwhile colleagues with whom he had worked in the Ministry of the Interior, was one of the most important forums in St Petersburg for fine-tuning ideas on the impending reforms. Regular visitors included the original core group of '*vestniki*' (a term derived from the Russian name of the journal, *Vestnik Evropy*): Spasovich, the self-styled 'private man of letters'; the literary historian Aleksandr Pypin; and Boris I. Utin, a specialist in comparative law.[9] The journal's editor from its launch in 1866 to 1908 was Mikhail Stasyulevich, a medievalist, a position he combined with his work as a leading Petersburg publisher. All were former lecturers at the University whose appointments more or less coincided with Kavelin's own, if not at his instigation, but who resigned in 1861 (or, like Spasovich, dismissed some time afterwards) in protest against the blatant infringement by the government of the principles of autonomy and collegiality promised in the reforms. Although not present at its inception, Arsen'ev, who joined the journal in 1867 to work as a literary critic, later became one of its leading spokesmen, chiselling out a 'political' position for the journal through his monthly review and chronicle sections (*Vnutrennoe Obozrenie'/Iz Obshchestvennoi kroniki*) which began to appear in 1882.

In 1868, the journal's original editorial policy, which concentrated on history, was broadened to cover history, politics, and literature – the term 'politics' used in a very vague sense to mean 'work, issues, knowledge' (*trud, delo, znanie*). From then on, it rapidly attracted copy from eminent scholars, including the historians Sergei Mikhailovich Solov'ev (Solov'ev's father), N.I. Kostomarov, and V.I Ger'e, as well as popular literati such as A.M. Ostrovsky, Ivan Turgen'ev, and N.V. Uspensky. Later, in the 1880s, the well-known satirist, M.E. Saltykov-Shchedrin, also developed close ties with the journal. Albeit a generalist periodical, the *European Messenger* contributed significantly to the growth of a legal consciousness making the nitty-gritty of scientific debate accessible to a wider audience. Through its reviews, book notices, and (rather unexpectedly) minutes of meetings held at the St Petersburg and Moscow Juridical Societies, the journal provided a staple of information on the more punctual aspects of criminal justice theory and practice.[10] It also attracted copy from respected authorities in the field like Nikolai Tagantsev, Nikolai Sergeevsky, Dmitriy Dril', and Anatoly Koni, the 'brilliant liberal' (*blestyashchii liberal*) as Lunacharsky called him. As a judge and procurator, Koni was famed for his oratory skills in court. The brilliance with which he succeeded in obtaining an acquittal in the trial of Vera Zasulich in 1878 secured his reputation as a defender of rights among reformers, though it also turned him into an object of suspicion in the eyes of certain bureaucrats.[11]

The *Vestniki*'s engagement in legal matters was an all-inclusive one. Discussions were driven by a passionate dislike of dead-letter applications of the Statutes and by an endeavour to inculcate respect for human worth, irrespective of which side of the dock the person might be. An early 'sensationalist' piece in the journal's history on the topic was an article by Arsen'ev ('The political trial: 1869–1871') in which he looked at the social and ethical significance of political crime arising from the famous 'Nechaev conspiracy' and his secret organization 'The People's Reprisal'. Arsen'ev accepted that any revolutionary activity is criminal and therefore punishable. But he also insisted, controversial for that period if commonplace wisdom today, that, in the first instance, it was crucial to understand the underlying causes of terrorism and endeavour to combat these through a system of humane and constructive measures permitting greater scope for individual initiative and social autonomy (*glasnost'*, *samodeyatel'nost' obshchestva*). The struggle against crime could not, he reasoned, rely solely on repressive measures; rather, what was needed was the more difficult and challenging undertaking to heal society by encouraging more freedoms (*glasnost'*) in speech and the press, by developing social awareness (*znanie*) and by exercising greater social controls on the activities of the state (*vlast'*). The state, he argued, was responsible for preventing crime and could do so by consolidating a civic culture, thereby putting into practice what it had merely rubber-stamped in the Reform programme, namely the legally sanctioned rights and freedoms of the individual. That terrorism was on the increase was sure proof that the new legislation had failed to address these issues in a meaningful way. Arsen'ev's reasoning, however, appeared to usurp the wisdom of autocratic infallibility. Thus, for daring to suggest that the government was politically short-sighted, even backward in its use of outdated retributive justice, his proposals in this piece incurred the journal's first official warning of closure.[12]

Politically, the journal came to occupy the middle ground between more radical publications, such as the *Contemporary* (Sovremennik) and *Notes of the Fatherland* (Otechestvennye Zapiski), banned in 1884, and the conservative nationalist journals, such as the *Russian Herald* (Russkii Vestnik), *Russian Review* (Russkoe Obozrenie), *Moscow Bulletin* (Moskovskie Vedomosti), and Aksakov's *Rus'* on the right. As chronicler, Arsen'ev spelled out the liberal credo:

> Freedom of the press, freedom of conscience, personal inviolability – here are the three goods, the demand for which is felt ever increasingly as, on the one hand, respect for man grows, for his worth, his right to independent thought, while, on the other civil solidarity receives its due recognition.[13]

If, however, in the 1870s, liberals defined their 'political' position by highlighting their differences with respect to the progressive left, by the 1880s their socio-political principles were being tested by rivals on the right who, in the wake of Alexander II's assassination, were becoming increasingly aggressive. A round of attacks and parries published in the spring and early summer issues of 1882 forced the *Vestniki* to dot the i's and cross the t's of their political programme. Challenged by the editorial board of *Rus'* that had thrown down the gauntlet – 'What has been written under the banner of the liberal party? What is its programme? What political or social principles do they preach? Nothing but hot air!' – Arsen'ev responded, addressing point by point the issues raised by his critics, and, in doing so, pieced together a mosaic of 'liberal' principles.[14] Beyond those of freedom of press and conscience, and the inalienable rights of the person, which both camps nominally shared, he singled out the right to education (and, notably, the right for a 'Realist' to go on to higher education[15]) and tackled some in-depth questions about local self-government and agrarian reform. On this last point, Arsen'ev took his cue from the zemstvo liberals. Like them, he called for an 'all-estate' *volost'* as an independent whole, governed by freely elected representatives, so as to avoid artificial concentration of power in the hands of one or another social group. The economic question was in his eyes all-important for assuring national well-being (*narodnoe blago*), and he listed a number of recommendations: the retention of communal (*obshchina*) ownership (to prevent loss of land on a large scale); greater cooperation between the government and zemstvo in overseeing the transfer of land to peasants, especially in poor soil areas; the introduction of a credit system for resettlement in new areas; abolition of the internal passport system; and abolition of collective responsibility for taxation and redemption payments – the notorious system of *krugovaya poruka*, a system of fiscal control designed to subordinate the individual to the community. In addition, Arsen'ev called for the lowering of redemption fees in areas where these exceeded the income derived from the repartitioned land, abolition of the poll tax, greater fairness in the distribution of the tax burden (namely higher taxes for the wealthy), and cuts in non-productive government expenditure. He did not, however, insist on the right to individual possession of land. Instead, he adopted what was regarded in Russia as a safeguard against impoverishment, namely the allocation of land within the commune.[16] On the issue of social order, he made a bid for popular representation based on electoral procedure in the zemstvos and municipalities. Interestingly, he did not use the word 'Constitution', but he took over the enemy term '*sochinitet'stvo*' (implying active participation by the people as opposed to policies taken solely by the state on their behalf) to compose an Aesopian style fable of his own:

> The election of representatives is a first step, decisive and important as it is. What comes after this – is hard to say at this moment in time. What we can say for sure is this: the matter (*delo*) cannot avoid the '*sochinitetel'stvo*', which our nationals are shouting down. '*Sochinitetel'stvo*' requires that we find new means for new ends. It is a necessary element of state life. It plays the same role in politics as it does in art.

Arsen'ev never revised this programme as such, but, as polemics with conservative nationalists sharpened in the climate of Alexander III's Russification programme, he did come back to several of the points raised. Accused of engendering atheistic radicalism and nihilism, his riposte in defence of the journal's policy consisted in drawing on the 'liberal' value of religious tolerance.[17] Similarly, he defended the interests of the advocacy and the new jury system – another 'beloved institution of the liberal party', as detractors coined it.[18] For Arsen'ev, these two achievements of the reform had become the symbolic sacrificial lamb of the Counter-Reform era as independence of the law courts was eroded, and the introduction of land captains in 1889 quickly made many parts of the judiciary redundant.[19] Ultimately, however, all Arsen'ev could do was reiterate the liberal credo – freedom of the individual as the foundation stone of civic freedom – to parry the national conservative insistence that inner freedom was compatible with authoritarian governance and a strictly hierarchical social order.

> Freedom (...) must be vested in such a form that an individual may not avail himself of it in order to harm others, and that everyone might use it in the interests of the whole. If anarchy as an excess of freedom is dangerous for society, no less dangerous is stagnation as an excess of order.[20]

Although Arsen'ev clearly espoused 'liberal' principles, nowhere, during the 1870s and 1880s, do we see him actively endorsing the term as such. Indeed, when challenged by rival editorial boards of the *Russian Herald* and *Rus'*, he was careful to point out that a 'Liberal Party ... in fact, does not even exist', an observation that was later taken up by V. Vodorozov in his Brokgaus-Efron entry, 'Liberal Parties'. In this survey of the liberal movement in Russia, Vodorozov argued that it was more appropriate to speak of a 'tendency' whose representatives had promoted the introduction of the Great Reforms and then defended them 'against attacks of a conservative and reactionary character'.[21] To be branded 'liberal' was, in fact, a harsh indictment leaving a journal's contributors susceptible to the scrutiny of the censors and the editorial board exposed to repeat warnings of closure. In 1889, for example, a report by the Ministry of the Interior referred to the *European Messenger* as 'run through with bad will towards all government measures'.[22] The *Vestniki* therefore tended to bracket the liberal label in inverted commas, 'for want of a better expression', a strategy that also allowed them to take distance from the pejorative connotations the term was acquiring among national conservatives and social democrats alike. The former associated liberalism with the corrupting influence of a secular West driven by material gain. Lev Tikhomirov, for example, went so far as to claim that the liberals were in league with terrorists, feeding on their anti-religiosity and 'theoretical materialism'.[23] Progressive revolutionaries, by contrast, offered backhanded compliments: in their vocabulary, the 'honesty' and 'clear sighted intellectual rigor' of liberalism implied 'ineffectiveness' (*bessilie*). Their cause was therefore doomed to failure, a prognosis made by Chernyshevsky as early as 1858 and echoed by Plekhanov, the 'Father of Marxism' in 1911.[24]

> From the theoretical narrowness of the liberal concept of freedom as simple absence of prohibition flows the weakness of liberalism in practice, lacking as it does any solid support in the mass of the people who place no value on rights of which they cannot, for lack of necessary means, make use.[25]

The unflattering connotations that accrued to the term 'liberal' in Russian *publitsistika* found parallels in works of contemporary fiction producing some lasting, if unfortunate, stereotypes. Typically, the liberal was caricaturized as a convert to bourgeois values and Manchester economics, a landlord with a taste for frivolous European culture (French mainly), but lacking any meaningful understanding of the reality of contemporary Russian life:

> Obsolete and retrograde dregs … the so-called 'educated society' of old is a motley collection of everything that has separated itself from Russia, that has not understood Russia and has become Frenchified – that is what a Russian liberal is, and that is why he is reactionary.[26]

Paradoxically, this cruel typecasting – in this instance, by Dostoevsky – was not just the work of hostile opponents for whom bourgeois individualism was synonymous with an alienating, inhumane Western civilization, it was equally the fruit of literary licence taken by novelists with distinctly liberal sympathies. The otherwise self-styled liberal, Ivan Turgenev, who spent much of his life abroad, famously made a nihilist, Bazarov, the protagonist of his novel *Fathers and Sons*. Denigrating all traditional values, Turgenev's 'anti-hero' exhibited the nihilist's scorn for the term 'liberal' with some flair, lumping it together with other 'useless, foreign words – aristocracy, progress and principles'.[27]

Generally speaking, studies of Russian liberalism show that attempts to draw neat parallels with West European equivalents yield little: as a rule, the inalienable rights defined in 'classical liberalism' were restricted in the Russian context to religious confession, press, assembly, association, and free speech. One has to look quite hard for a consistent defence of property rights (with its three attributes of right of possession, utilization, and disposal) or the free market, not to mention political rights. It has been suggested that this silence with respect to the right of property was the consequence of a long-standing suspicion of private ownership. For many, possession of land implied privilege rather than right and oppression rather than equality of opportunity. There were, however, notable exceptions to this attitude: one was Chicherin whose view of property has been argued to resemble Western liberalism quite closely: 'Property stems from the nature of man as a rational and free being. It is the first expression of freedom in the physical world.'[28] Another exception to the rule was Chicherin's intellectual antipode, Solov'ev. If Chicherin argued that widening property rights was tantamount to the strengthening of freedom, Solov'ev defended 'the right to a dignified existence' in the light of arguments pertaining to the moral foundations of the economy. First published in the *European Messenger* in 1896, Solov'ev incorporated his essay into his last major work, *Justification of the Good*, the following year.[29]

In his discussion on the economy, Solov'ev did not start from the immediate realities of the Russian countryside, but he took issue with the cluster of factors traditionally covered by the 'economic question', namely production (in terms of capital and labour), distribution of wealth and exchange of values, the free market, as well as the liberal definition of the 'natural' inalienable' right to dispose of one's wealth as one sees fit. In addition, he took up the problem of inheritance in relation to equality of opportunity. As he would do so often, Solov'ev mounted his argument on two fronts, directing it against conservative plutocrats and socialists alike, both of whom, in his eyes, attributed unwarranted importance to material well-being: 'Man is not in the first instance a producer of material goods and exchange values, but something far more important (…) It follows that society is far more than an economic association.'[30] From this perspective, he also criticized the liberal 'laissez-faire, laissez-passer principle': far from enhancing the priority of the individual over the commonwealth, it was, he believed, an economy sadly lacking in a moral foundation, one operable uniquely in an atomized, dead society.[31] Solov'ev was endeavouring to make explicit something which, to his mind, remained obscure in the liberal credo, namely that both the right to spiritual/religious freedom and the right to property (economic freedom) should be morally grounded.[32] To a degree, his understanding fitted well with the so-called 'self-developmental' tradition of Kant and Hegel, which stressed a view of the individual as an end to be achieved. In this light, property is an attribute of personhood; it is important as a means allowing the person to form himself/herself in relation to other selves and the world of things. Yet, Solov'ev went further than this by explicitly resetting the economy in a social ethical framework. While he subscribed, as all true liberals would, to the Kantian categorical imperative (consider each person an end and not a means), he extended this classical definition to include the very soil we labour. This should also, he believed, be cherished as an end and not a means. Next, he added an all-important new element to the list of fundamental civil rights: the notion of dignity. Society, he argued, has an obligation towards its members 'to recognize and guarantee each one the right to a dignified existence, both for himself and for his blood ties'.[33] Thus, unlike the laissez-faire view (which, apart from Chicherin, was rarely argued for in Russia), Solov'ev demanded state involvement in the economic life of the community. Extreme poverty, he believed, makes it impossible for a person to live in a truly human manner, and therefore the state or society has an obligation to provide each of its members with a certain minimum of well-being.[34]

Solov'ev and the *Vestnik*

In one of the last pieces he wrote, *Three Conversations: War, Progress and the End of History*, Solov'ev contributed his own memorable pencil sketch of the typical liberal–political thinker, gently mocking his belief in progress, and his theory that '*la politique*' and '*la politesse*' are derived from the same root. One of the most humorous moments of his portrait occurs when Solov'ev renders the politician's foolproof recipe for good civil behaviour in terms of a mock Kantian categorical imperative: wash regularly so as not to be disgusting either to yourself or to others; pray – a couple of times a day (with feeling); fast – it is good for your health; do not meddle in other people's affairs; give generously to the poor that you encounter; and give regularly to the Church (the celestial body will take care of the sums).[35]

Solov'ev's defection in the mid-1880s from Ivan Aksakov's *Rus'* to join ranks with the editorial board of the journal, the *European Messenger*, was an episode in his life that vexed some of his contemporaries (notably those he had abandoned), while it would puzzle others. Not least among the latter was the group of intellectuals whose company he sought. By far older than Solov'ev, they were, as I have mentioned, mostly professionally engaged as jurists, historians or former university professors at one time or another in government service. United in their commitment to the spirit of the Reforms, which, indeed, to a considerable degree, they had initiated, they were more practically minded than metaphysical in outlook. For his part, Solov'ev defended himself against what he regarded as a misplaced accusation by erstwhile colleagues that he had become a 'liberal-Westernizer': he asked his critics 'Tell me where there is a camp, still true to the original Slavophile principles, to which I might belong?'[36] The point of his rhetoric in this particular instance was, of course, to silence his detractors rather than to divulge his reasons for choosing the new company he had. But where he was more explicit about this (in a letter to Stasyulevich, in 1888), he downplayed a point of difference that was arguably too important for him to have done so:

> As far as politics and social questions in Russia are concerned, I feel – and have felt for some time now – an affinity with the line of the *European Messenger*, and I don't see why our differences with respect to questions about

> the supernatural realm should prevent us from working together on immediate objectives.[37]

In many ways, Solov'ev's contributions to the *European Messenger* made him a fairly typical 1890s' liberal. With political issues more or less taboo, liberal reformers were obliged to concentrate on social–economic questions. Accordingly, Solov'ev addressed the right to education, the right to work, the right to material security, and the right to form social or cultural organizations. His articles on the 1891–1892 famine, for example, were received by his colleagues as an important moment in the battle to raise social awareness and to encourage a sense of social responsibility. Thus, in view of the difficulties involved in defining 'Russian' liberalism, and the widespread ambivalence expressed towards the Western economic model, one could argue that to question Solov'ev's alliance with liberalism at all is perhaps to miss the point. It is possibly more accurate, if not simpler, to suggest that he was associated with a number of intellectuals around a journal with a broad editorial programme covering history, literature, and current affairs. Individual contributors, Solov'ev included, took a stand on specific issues as they arose – the economic consequences of the emancipation of the serfs, local government, nationalism – using certain recognizable, if select, liberal precepts as props in building their arguments.[38] Indeed, it is interesting to note that, in some respects, Solov'ev's concerns came closer to those of the zemstvo liberal, Dmitry Shipov, than to those constitutional dreams of the *Vestniki*. Shipov, a monarchist and anti-constitutionalist, wanted to reinvest social and political practice with a moral – Christian – foundation; purely legal management of social relations, he warned, leads to an irreversible separation between instances of power and the people. Shipov openly acknowledged his indebtedness to the Slavophile pathos of 'union' (*edinenie*) between tsar and people, a moral bond, which could then dispense with legal ties and restrictions.[39] But while Solov'ev, like Shipov, hoped to build society on a moral (and Christian) foundation, unlike Shipov, he recognized the intrinsic importance of legal, social, and economic questions, and it was this that, arguably, gradually earned him a place in the more secular company of Spasovich, Stasyulevich, and others, despite certain misgivings on their part and differences in temperament. If he quickly became the adored 'Benjamin' of the group – a 'life companion' (*sotrudnik zhizni*), as Stasyulevich called him,[40] he was decidedly a bit of a misfit in their midst.

Intellectually, Solov'ev had a lot in common with his new colleagues: a taste for historical and literary reflection with Pypin and a love for poetry with Aleksei Zhemchuzhnikov – a man some 30 years Solov'ev's senior. Spasovich, a pivotal and hugely influential figure in the history of Russian criminal law, shared his expertise in juridical matters with Solov'ev as well as his enthusiasm for Shakespeare and Mickiewicz. But, as a self-confessed 'anti-cleric, anti-nationalist, anti-statesman', Spasovich would appear to have little in common with Solov'ev, the religious thinker, poet, and self-styled mystic, who hoped to ground the institutions Spasovich avowedly despised in truly Christian principles. Solov'ev's preoccupations with the Kingdom of God rather than the organization of temporal power were at odds with the views of his new collaborators. His arguments on a 'nation's self-denial' in the name of 'universal religious principles', and mainstream *Vestniki* accounts of 'national self-determination', issued from different principles and nurtured different goals. His explicit call for a 'Christian politics' was in a different key from liberalism, even if religious tolerance was a crucial part of the liberal commitment to social justice. In the end, while Koni and Spasovich remained uncertain as to whether Solov'ev did actually regard himself as a prophet, he was for sure a 'mystic' (Spasovich) and one occasionally given to writing 'abracadabra' (Arsen'ev).[41]

Paradoxically, although the *Vestniki* regarded Solov'ev as an 'Old Slavophile', this particular evaluation was not intended to keep him at bay; on the contrary, it was a sign of endorsement, because, like Solov'ev, they too expressed a deep respect for the original Slavophile stand on freedom of speech and conscience: 'No less than Konstantin Aksakov', wrote Koni, 'he stood for freedom of life and the spirit, freedom of the press.'[42] For the *Vestniki*, this betokened a nascent liberalism within the Slavophile movement itself.[43] Indeed, in view of their sympathies with the original Slavophiles, one might wonder why Solov'ev did not answer his detractors about his supposed betrayal by asking, 'what is a liberal-Westernizer?' For Spasovich, the fact that Solov'ev separated ethics from religious dogma and the authority of the Church, and that his own religious quest did not exclude the ideas of secular progress, entitled him to the accolade of 'humanist-Westernizer'. Inversely, the fact that the *Vestniki* asked what made the Slavophiles 'liberal' suggests that they, too, saw the importance of presenting liberalism not as a poor imitation of the Western model but as a movement that was authentically 'Russian'. Thus, while they may have found Slavophile messianism suspect, they shared Solov'ev's nostalgia for original Slavophilism that had advocated freedom of conscience and true patriotism. Indeed, it was precisely these motifs, together with Solov'ev's call for a dignified existence, which was to find a niche in liberal discourse after 1900. Solov'ev's view that the state is beneficial as a means of serving people in their rights and making possible a richer life, but that it must allow the person freedom with regard to civil rights and private conduct, foreshadowed the principles of the Kadet 'welfare state liberalism', as Andrzej Walicki has termed it, which emerged after 1900 and which, as has often been pointed out, was just a hair's breadth away from socialism.[44] Suspicious that private ownership could lead to an unbalanced distribution of wealth, the Kadets pursued an agrarian policy of large-scale expropriation of private land with compensation for its owners. In other words, both for Solov'ev and the Kadets, human dignity should be assured by state action; ideally, the state should be the bearer of egalitarian principles.

Studied, then, as a 'political thinker', Solov'ev's maverick views throw light on the nature of Russian liberalism at the turn of the century. As a call for social change and progress based on respect for human freedom and carried out peacefully through legal institutions, all sorts of additional epithets could be, and indeed were, attached to liberalism – old, conservative, left, right, zemstvo, democratic, welfare state, progressive, new. Granted, these epithets may be explained in terms of generation differences as George Fischer in his classic study suggests. But one could also argue that the 1890s were marked by a coexistence of several 'liberal stands'. The Slavophile nostalgia of zemstvo leader and monarchist Shipov (and N.A. Khomyakov) was quite different from Chicherin's *Rechtsstaat* brand of liberalism, which, according to some accounts, was still dominant at the end of the century.[45] The profile of the *Vestnik Evropy* collaborators alone shows quite well that to speak of a passage from one kind of liberalism to another is not entirely accurate. The core group of five who launched the journal – Stasyulevich, Kavelin, Pypin, Spasovich, and Utin – may, certainly, be described as 'Old liberals', namely men of the 1860s who had taken an active part in the reforms and whose demands were the traditional liberal demands of legality, publicity (*glasnost'*), freedom of the person and society (*samodeyatel'nost'*) through enlightenment, and constitutionalism (in a vague sense of good governance). But they could equally be labelled 'progressive' or 'new', both in the sense that they were mostly 'professionals' of non-gentry origin and also in terms of their engagement in questions of a social and cultural nature.[46] Indeed, this last point is of particular significance when it comes to a reflection on the place of Solov'ev in the liberal movement. In the 1890s, the liberal movement suffered major 'political' setbacks. The rulings on land captains in 1889 and the zemstvo policy of 1890 meant that the zemstvos lost their autonomy and were absorbed as cogs into the state administrative machine.[47] The coronation speech of Nicholas II (1894), in which he referred to the political representation of society as 'senseless dreams', was another symbolic blow to liberal hopes of reform; it announced a change in the winds that more or less obliged the 'liberals' henceforth to concentrate their efforts on social cohesion by creating organizational and cultural networks, certainly to banish any dream of constitutionalism. It was, notably, in this context that the debate on education and questions of enlightenment (*prosveshchenie*) generally became very important. Education was regarded as a sure means to awaken a sense of responsibility in the individual, to encourage an understanding that religious tolerance, legality and *obshchestvennost'* were intrinsic values, and crucial for transforming the tsar's passive subjects into responsible citizens of a Russian (*Rossiiskii*) nation.[48]

Individual rights and citizenship

If, in the eighteenth century, the notions of 'citizen' and 'citizenship' meaning equality of all and equal responsibility before the law had enjoyed currency, by the late nineteenth century they had, if anything, turned into a bad joke.[49] The simple, self-evident claim – civil freedom is inseparable from personal freedom – that Arsen'ev defended as the chronicler and, in a sense, 'spokesman' of the *European Messenger* was dragged over the coals by conservative rivals in defence of a legal order that persisted in conflating 'political and civil freedoms'. Granted, conservatives claimed to acknowledge 'freedom of the person', but they confined it, in the eyes of liberal critics, to inner autonomy or spiritual self-determination (according to which logic even a slave could be called 'free'). It followed that this kind of freedom should have no place in society, let alone serve as its foundation stone. For conservative thinkers, society should be structured hierarchically with the instruments of force and authority and maintained through discipline and 'stratification' (*razsloenie*).[50] Thus, by the close of the century, the existence of a journal entitled *The Citizen*, the political stance of which was archly conservative and whose editors took vicious delight in ridiculing any reform initiative, was no doubt experienced by some as an instance of fairly crude irony.[51]

Rather than push for 'citizenship', which, in any case, had no real anchorage in Russian society or had lost whatever hold it had since Catherine the Great's day, it was arguably more prudent to call for an awareness of the person (*lichnost', chelovek*) and, by association, insist on 'human' rights rather than 'civil', let alone 'political'. The Reform and Counter-Reform periods offer numerous examples, both in specialist juridical literature and more generalist 'philosophical' *publitsistika*, where projects for the 'rule of law' (in the way of guarantees and regulation of civil freedoms) were centred on the concept of a 'personal principle' (*lichnostnoe nachalo*).[52] However, if Russian 'liberals' were committed proponents of 'personhood', they were also careful to avoid the idea of individualism not least because its Western 'bourgeois' connotations might leave them open to attack by radical revolutionaries and conservative nationalists alike. Russian radicals disdained the idea of the individual *tout court*, because it had no place in their revolutionary project for a classless society, and conservatives were wary of it, because individual initiative threatened to undermine the protective, patronage role of the state. But even among liberals, especially among those whose intellectual-cum-philosophical trajectory had taken them from Marx back to Kant (the case of some leading 'Silver Age' thinkers active after the turn of the century), it also prompted responses which were, to say the least, ambivalent. As Laura Engelstein notes:

> Individualism was both an ardently desired prize and a threat to cultural values that distinguished their world from the 'out there', a place that often seemed better, but also spiritually impoverished; private property and the marketplace (whether in goods or culture) seemed deeply troublesome attainments; and the rigors of bourgeois morality struck them as narrow and vein.[53]

In view of this guarded attitude towards individualism among Russian intellectuals, one difficulty (for an outsider, that is) is to unravel the interplay between the juridical terminology of the day in which *lichnost'* was (and is) a term commonly used to refer to the individual human being qua citizen, and the anti-individualistic associations it carried in the moral philosophy of the day, without forgetting its even deeper associations with nineteenth-century intellectual movements such as romanticism with its focus on self-fulfilment and personal feelings. One of the most outspoken anti-individualists during the Silver Age of Russian culture was the philosopher and *publitsist* Nikolai Berdyaev. In his work, he consistently drew sharp distinctions between, on the one hand, the concept of man as an empirical-cum-biological being, designated by the Russified, and ill-sounding loan word 'individ'/individuum, and the person (*lichnost'*) with freedom as his/her most salient quality, on the other. If Berdyaev's rather romantic idea of personal autonomy sat poorly with the more widespread acceptance of the autonomy of the will in a Kantian vein (among juridical thinkers, certainly), in which concern for the welfare of others was also at stake, his disdain for bourgeois values was fairly typical: whatever the context in which conceptions of *lichnost'* were couched and accordingly nuanced, from the religious–philosophical–social to the ethical, the majority of first-generation and Silver-Age intellectuals and professionals were more engaged with the problem of 'human dignity' and moral worth than they were with material well-being. The partial exception to this generalization concerns the juridical definitions of *lichnost'*. While new theories of crime and punishment that emerged at the turn of the century attest the discovery of the accused as a moral being, prior to that, as I discuss in the next chapter, reformers had, first of all, to confront the stubborn vestiges of estate-governed definitions of inalienable rights. Paradoxically, in their efforts to instil a modern legal consciousness and to modernize the practice of criminal justice, they needed to expel the moral dimension of the individual, precisely that feature of the accused traditionally spotlighted by the judiciary in its condemnation of crime.

2 Reforming criminal law (1864–1903)

For reasons quite historical/We have a lack intense/Of that quality diabolical,/Juridical Common sense./Too lofty is our sense of right/in this broad-natured nation/To fit within the confines tight/Of legal codification.

[B. Adamotov (B.N. Almazov), *Dissonances*, 1863][1]

Suspicion of formal legal remedies as implied in Almazov's comic verse cited here is often considered to have been a distinctive feature of the peasant world reluctant to change its ways. But, in fact, it cut across society as a whole and, albeit for vastly different reasons, was just as much a mark of radical thought seeking to defy the status quo as it was telling of government practice that was determined to maintain it. It was therefore imperative for juridical reformers to gain public trust in the law and in the judiciary as an independent professional body. Open justice, reformers believed, would enable the people to see for themselves that crimes, whether for reasons of personal vengeance or political gain, were being dealt with fairly.

The new legislation on criminal procedure introduced in 1864 in order to complete, and where necessary, revise the existing body of criminal legislation contained in the fifteenth volume of the *Digest of Laws* of 1832 seemed to answer the reformers' goals of transparency and rationalized procedures in the administration of justice. Article 1 of the Statute on Criminal Procedure read: 'no one is liable to a judicial enquiry having not been called to account in accordance with the convention defined by the regulations of this Statute'; Article 14 stipulated that 'no one may be punished for a crime or infraction falling to the competence of the judicial department other than by the sentence passed by the court in accordance with the law'.[2] The statutes ruled against arbitrary arrest 'and other denials of personal liberty' and also made provisions for legal defence in criminal trials as part of the general shift from inquisitorial to accusatorial procedures in court. In addition, the reform instituted penal statutes for minor infractions to be applied by Justices of the Peace – a decision later described by Konstantin Arsen'ev as 'one of the best legislative acts of the period'.[3] By speaking of 'nationwide privileges' (*privilegiya vsenarodnaya*), the new criminal justice system suggested an end to a history of privileges granted to the nobility instituted during the reign of Catherine the Great and practised ever since. Personal inviolability for ordinary crimes was, henceforth, to be safeguarded by due process of law and procedure; arbitrary denial of personal liberty and arbitrary search or violation of the secrecy of correspondence were prohibited.

The success of the reform of criminal justice was rapidly compromised by several mutually reinforcing factors, which we may categorize as contingent and attitudinal. In addition, the new legislation itself contained inbuilt caveats that would effectively erode the personal inviolability of the accused in the event of suspected political crime, thus undermining, virtually from the start, the principles of open justice espoused by reformers. While the inalienable rights of the accused as a 'human person' (*chelovecheskaya lichnost'*) were formally acknowledged on paper, the preponderant privileges of the police and administrative authorities empowered to prevent 'political' crime and mete out punishment accordingly presented a major obstacle for those pledged to the ideal of an independent judiciary. The note to article 1 of the Statute on Criminal Procedure read: 'Measures taken by the police and other administrative authorities for the prevention and suppression of crime in the manner established by the laws do not come under judicial proceedings'; 'the police see to it that no one undertakes anything contrary to proper obedience to lawful authorities. It suppresses in the very beginning all innovations contrary to the laws' (Art. 119).[4] In the event of suspected political offences, then, the police continued to enjoy rights of preliminary detention independent of the rules and procedures of the courts. However, given it was relatively easy to turn suspected critics of the state (notably, members of the radical, even moderate intelligentsia) into political criminals and banish them into administrative exile, traditional suspicions of the law gradually transmuted into suspicion of widespread political crime: *mutatis mutandis*, provision for the civil rights and freedoms of the accused continued to be ignored. This, together with lasting prerogative of the tsar to overrule procedure left the reform programme as a whole susceptible to what Laura Engelstein has aptly called autocracy's policy of 'deliberate misrule'.[5]

Irrespective of these inbuilt inconsistencies, the reform programme as a whole was, quite simply, an unfortunate casualty of the wider socio-political conjuncture. The hostility of conservative-minded thinkers to reform seemed rapidly vindicated by the episodic violence and acts of terror sweeping through the countryside as the peasantry gave vent to disbelief and profound disappointment at the caveats listed in the Emancipation Act. But it was an attempt on the tsar's life in 1866 by the student, Karakozov, that stalled further work on reform, refuelling arguments to the effect that the role of the state was to preserve law and order by any means. For critics, here was proof that 'rule of law' was, in fact, thinly veiled anarchy. Plans for a major overhaul of the existing criminal legislation to complement the 1864 Statutes were thus abandoned; instead, in 1866, a revised edition of the 1845 Penal Code was published. Thus, within the space of a mere three years, as Alexander II set on a course of rescinding the liberties he had generously distributed to enlightened bureaucrats at the start of his reign, optimism for the success of a reform celebrating scientific principles as the basis of formal legal remedies began to fade. As a regime of police surveillance (*politseiskii nadzor*) was gradually put in place – its powers that had been slightly diminished by the 1864 statutes restored – Russia reverted, all but in name, to the custodial model of 'Police State'.

Over the next decade, reformers witnessed further backtracking into diehard habits as the government took on the urgent task of curbing social unrest and acts of terrorism. A series of 'provisional' measures empowering the authorities to deal as expeditiously as possible with the augmenting numbers of political crimes were introduced. In 1871, the privilege of preliminary arrest, which the police already enjoyed, was extended to the Provincial and District Gendarmerie Boards – an ordinance that, as Marc Szeftel puts it, 'inaugurated a development which led to the final abolition of almost all guarantees against arbitrary arrests in the case of political offences'.[6] Measures of this kind took yet another dramatic turn in the wake of Alexander II's assassination, inaugurating the era of Counter-Reform. On 14 August 1881, an 'extraordinary temporary law' was passed in which provision was made for 'extraordinary protection' (*chrezvychainaya okhrana*) in areas of the Empire, where serious or worrying disruptions were occurring, and martial law (*voennoe polozhenie*). Renewed every three years, this 'temporary ruling', which suspended normal legal procedures, effectively became a permanent part of the legislation of the Empire. Trials were transferred to courts martial, where cases were dealt with summarily in closed sessions. Local authorities were empowered to pass administrative sentences of up to five years' exile, and police control was considerably extended.[7] Arrests could be made on grounds of suspicion, and the right to search private domiciles was unrestricted (a person could be held under arrest for up to four weeks). Under the state of reinforced protection (*usilennaya okhrana*), political crimes and cases involving violent action against public authorities – murder or attempted murder, infliction of wounds, injuries, heavy blows, or arson – could be transferred to military jurisdiction and judged according to procedures effective in wartime, that is, by laws and procedures not bound by the rules of the Statute of Criminal Procedure concerning the legal status of the individual regarding personal inviolability. In addition, the ruling of August 1881 provided for 'administrative deportation' (*vysylka administrativnym poryadkom*) of persons deemed 'harmful to the state and public tranquillity'. In view of the blanket permission given to the police to arrest on grounds of suspicion, differentiating between ordinary and political crimes was, at best, subject to error, and at worst, a tempting abuse of authority. The upshot was that many common criminals were tried in military courts on counts of murder, rape, or theft.[8]

If trial by jury and open courts were the most visible achievements of the judicial reform, and often cited by historians as a sign of radical departure from pre-reform legislation and practice, they were possibly its most vulnerable gains. In 1867, the Minister of Justice, Zamyatnin, one of the chief architects of judicial reform, was replaced by the conservative, Count Pahlen. Uncomfortable with the idea of an independent judiciary, and the subversive potential it might enjoy, Pahlen effectively (if unwittingly) eroded its newly acquired accolade of impartiality in court proceedings. According to Wortman, Pahlen initially encouraged open court procedure as a way of outlawing revolutionaries and thereby undermining their cause in the public eye. But the outcome of the trials of the 1870s beginning with the Nechaev conspiracy in 1871 through to the trial of 193 Populists in 1877, when defence lawyers (including Spasovich and Utin) successfully acquitted 90 political criminals, proved Pahlen wrong.[9] Capped by Judge Koni's remarkable defence of Vera Zasulich a year later, which provoked Pahlen's resignation, the popular success of these trials did not amount to a victory for open justice, however. The government's response consisted in placing open courts under suspicion as foyers harbouring anti-regime sentiments, a gesture which, at the same time, vindicated its decision to abandon legal channels in endeavours to combat revolutionaries. Thereafter, the government resorted to the tried and tested methods of administrative exile, military justice, and closed court sessions for the 'most serious crimes', thereby downgrading the role of jury – possibly the most significant achievement of the judicial reforms – to overseeing minor cases. Even though Pahlen's successors in the Ministry – D.N. Nabokov, N.A. Manasein, and, in particular, N. Murav'ev, who oversaw the new Criminal Code project in 1895 – were all, as Wortman puts it, 'committed to ensuring the integrity of legal procedure', their influence in the government was small and certainly not enough to alter the reputation of the judicial system as profoundly unreliable.[10]

The final steps in this long retreat from an independent judiciary came a decade later in the shape of the famous ordinance of 12 July 1889 instituting land captains. These powerful and not uncommonly corrupt figures enjoyed combined administrative and punitive powers in the zemstvos. In the eyes of critics, the land captain symbolized the uncomfortable fusion of two legal worlds – one dealing with non-political crimes, where personal inviolability was supposedly sovereign, and the other operating with loosely defined discretionary powers. As judge-arbitrator and chief investigator of petty crime (*zemskii uchastkovyi nachal'nik*/*ispravnik*), the required impartiality of the former was effectively undermined by the potentially wide girth for bullying or bribery frequently practised by the second. According to eyewitness reports, it was not uncommon for land captains to use their position to have odd jobs, such as mending a fence, relocating the *banya*, done gratis.[11] Thus, with the original provisions for inalienable freedoms of the accused (for ordinary crimes) ignored, growing paranoia within officialdom that most crimes were politically motivated and the decision to privilege the administration over the judiciary in the business of sentencing at zemstvo level for petty infractions, the use of law and the legal system served to reinforce traditional practice, and the tsar's power of discretion (*proizvol*) to pardon or punish remained an enduring feature of pre-Revolutionary legal culture.

In view of these circumstances, reforming criminal justice became a very modest undertaking involving the tedious whittling away at an existing body of laws and the piecemeal incorporation of modifications and minor alterations. Successive editions of Bludov's Code of Criminal and Corrective Punishments

(1857, 1866, and 1885) consisted in small amendments, which sustained, rather than challenged, the strict, yet cumbersome original classification of punishments. And despite efforts by well-respected legal scholars and high-ranking statesmen to impart greater coherence to the body of laws, the results exhibited an almost wilful resistance to a clear unifying principle.

Reform era criminal law in the mirror of the pre-reform age

The modern definition of a crime as an action in breach of the law (*zakon*) first appeared in Speransky's 'Digest of Laws' (*Svod Zakonov*) of 1832 and was incorporated into the Penal Code of 1845, where it remained in force casting its shadow over subsequent revisions until 1917:

> Any breach of the law (*zakon*) which impinges on the inviolable right (*neprikosnovennost prava*) of the supreme power, and the powers established by the latter, or which affects the rights or security of society or individuals (*chastnye*) is a crime.[12]

Speransky provided the template for the compilation and systematization of Russian law in early 1830s, but it was his successor, Count Bludov, charged with the direction of the supplements and revisions to the Digest until the onset of Alexander II's Reforms, who oversaw the 1845 publication of a separate Penal Code, the 'Code of Criminal and Correctional Penalties' (*Ulozhenie o nakazaniyakh ugolovnykh i ispravitel'nykh*).[13] The Code listed 150 types of crime, including those of a religious nature. Yet, despite the variety of crimes specified, many of the distinctions used were little more than thinly veiled synonyms for crimes against the state as attested by frequent reference to infractions committed against the treasury, state, and administration (*kazna, gosudarstvo, upravalenie*). Of around 2,035 articles, only 320 (roughly 16 per cent) detailed crimes involving loss inflicted on an individual (life, property, health).[14] Rigidly hierarchical, the inventory of crimes reflected the thinking and ingrained practices of 'ancien régimes'. Not only was the state well armed against 'political' enemies, real and imagined, the hierarchy of legally recognized (*zakonnyi*) 'personal' rights, their degree and number determined by one's social estate was, arguably, designed as much, if not more so, to incriminate as to protect: any attempt to call on rights (*prava*) not admitted by the law (*zakon*) was regarded as a prosecutable criminal act. Obviously, those most disadvantaged by this ruling were the intelligentsia and non-Orthodox religious minorities.

The principle that all are unequal before the law underpinned a complex scale of punishments ('the penal staircase' – *lestnitsa nakazaniya*). Arranged in a descending order of severity corresponding to the gravity of the crime committed, the type of penalty inflicted – death penalty, various categories of exile (from hard labour (*katorga*) to resettlement and the frequent practice of administrative exile), imprisonment, or fines – was also dictated by the social estate of the accused. As a rule, privileged estates comprising the nobility, clergy, honorary citizens, merchants of the first and second guilds were exempt from corporal punishment.[15] Building on the ten basic penal categories established in Speransky's Digest of Laws, Count Bludov introduced what one might call two 'generic' forms of punishment: punitive and corrective (*nakazaniya ugolovnye/nakazaniya ispravitel'nye*). However, if, in theory, such a distinction betokened the welcome, albeit timid, beginnings of modern juridical thinking (irreversible loss of rights in the former case and eventual reintegration into society in the second), in practice it merely betrayed a highly formalized judicial practice in which the distinction was one of degree rather than of nature. Thus, just as punitive sentences – the death penalty, exile and hard labour, exile to Siberia, exile to the Caucasus – differentiated between social estates, with non-privileged estates subjected to a public lashing (*plet'*) in prelude to death or exile, correctional offences were, similarly, broken down into various terms of exile for all estates, entailing loss of rank, property, and the right to work in government service. For the most serious corrective offences, the privileged classes were 'exiled for resettlement' (a new category introduced in the 1845 code that permitted engagement in trade and industry), while equivalent grades of punishment for non-privileged classes subject to corporal punishment carried various terms in 'correctional convict detachments' (*ispravitel'nye arestantskie otdeleniya*). Punishment for petty crimes applied to all classes and comprised various forms of confinement, fines, and loss of certain rights.[16] Granted, correctional punishments for non-privileged estates was generally weighted towards terms of confinement in a variety of institutions, such as the workhouse, prison, fortress, and the *smiritel'nyj dom*.[17] But this does little to alter the overall system of punishment and its social impact: with the more traditional and cost-effective practice of hard labour and administrative exile continuing to be prescribed for many cases, including so-called 'correctional offences', the upshot was a two-tier system of penalties on paper, but with differences between them arguably too subtle to notice. As the leading specialist on the prison question, Ivan Foinitsky noted, out of 260 categories of crime, only 54 were punished by a term in prison, workhouse, fortress, or reform house.[18]

Well into the Reform era, stubborn remnants of past practices seemed to frustrate hopes of modernizing the system of justice. For example, running through the inherited scale of punishments was the idea of loss of freedom and personal rights (*porazhenie prava*). Successive editions of the 1845 Criminal Law Code listed three categories of loss originally modelled on 'degradation' in the Napoleonic Code: loss of all rights (*lichenie vsekh prav sostoyaniya*); loss of special rights and privileges (*lichenie vsekh osobennykh prav*), both personal and acquired; and loss of certain rights and privileges. Itemized as 'political, civil, family and property, rank, honour and good name', with levels of deprivation corresponding to the severity of the sentence passed (death penalty, *katorga*, resettlement), clearly lacking here was any distinction between inner, 'moral', and outer 'civic' freedoms.[19] Failure or, indeed, refusal to differentiate between the moral and civic spheres had damaging and lasting consequences for the offender, because on completion of his sentence, he effectively became a social pariah, his rights and freedoms never fully restored. Contemporary critics likened what amounted to the 'perpetuity' (*pozhiznennost'*) of punishment and wide volume of rescinded rights (*pravoporazhenie*) practised in both pre- and post-reform Russia to ancient customs: deprived of his rights, the criminal was reduced to the level of a wild beast (*dikii zver'*). On this point it was noted that, in other countries, such as Germany and England, loss of rights tended to be temporary and pertained to the right to vote or the right to hold certain public positions. The French, for example, had replaced the idea of 'mort civile' with 'degradation civique' entailing loss of all political and some social (*sic*) rights, namely the right to carry arms, medals, serve in the army or on a jury, as well as some family rights, namely the right to exercise marital authority while serving one's sentence.[20] Certain traditional forms of punishment were also difficult to eradicate, a case in point being the public rituals that accompanied the sentencing process, whereby the accused was symbolically deprived of his 'civic' status pertaining to his social estate. In the pre-Reform period, public shaming had served as a token enactment of corporal punishment for members of privileged estates sentenced to 'political' or 'civil death' (*politicheskaya smert'/grazhdanskaya kazn'*), two categories introduced by Empress Elizabeth Petrovna in 1754 in lieu of the death penalty. Albeit rarely carried out, the brutality involved in the shaming ritual was, according to some accounts, life threatening: 'Those condemned to political death are to be flogged with the knout, have their nostrils torn out, be chained in fetters, and sent to Rogervik and other places.'[21] Well-known instances of public shaming in the early Reform period (by then a case of symbolized rather than physical annihilation) were those of Chernyshevsky, condemned to civil death and ignominiously dragged through the streets of St Petersburg, and the student Ishutinyi, one of Karakozov's accomplices, sentenced to political death (Karakozov was executed).[22] Nominally, the ritual of public shaming was preserved in the Judicial Statutes (1864) and Penal Code (1866) for those condemned to death as a substitute for the death penalty.[23] But, the problem, as contemporaries noted, was that if political death could be conceived of as a form of pardon, civil execution, which, in terms of its public enactment, was virtually identical, could not; it was the fulfilment of the sentence passed for conviction of a serious crime. Moreover, in the post-Reform era, it became a curious form of 'free-standing' punishment in its own right for non-political crimes such as adultery or theft, especially in provincial *gubernye* towns.[24]

For reformers, the fact that the practice of public shaming had slipped through the reform net was nothing short of a mystery, especially given that, for most estates, corporal punishment, with its dual purpose of demoralization through pain – if not, de facto, a masked form of capital punishment – had been abolished. With its humiliating sequences of degradation enacted, indeed 'staged' before a crowd of onlookers, it was surely very difficult to conceive of punishment in terms other than moral retribution. To suppose that, by inflicting shame and humiliation for the benefit (so to speak) of the public, this somewhat carnivalesque scene might be rationalized in terms of its symbolic function betokening the loss of civil rights was grossly misplaced: 'Shame and the irreversible loss of one's honour is what stands out before all other impressions. Such is the practical, public, and personal significance today of the ritual of public execution.'[25] Punishing one's sense of personal honour instead of one's 'civic, individual freedom' was, reformers argued, a telling indictment of Russia's poorly developed civic culture. By contrast, across continental Europe, with possibly the exception of Spain where the 'argolla' (chain) was still used, the practice had been struck off the books before or around the mid-nineteenth century: Prussia in 1851, Austria in 1852, and in France as early as 1818. In Belgium, it was abolished in 1867.[26]

In the early 1870s, the future Minister of Justice, Nikolai Murav'ev, reported his findings of this practice after a tour of the regions, to the west of the Urals and the two capitals, in a damning piece entitled 'The Ritual of Public Punishment'.[27] Complex rituals of simulated torture and execution, he observed, were carried out before an audience, usually in the central square on market day. The prisoner would be brought out in an open dray cart before an audience of local townsmen and villagers, the nature of his crime writ large on a board attached to his chest. Taken on to a raised scaffold, he would then be tied to a pillory (*pozornyi stolb*) and held there, usually for about ten minutes, while the sentence was read out. (In the case of murder of a parent, the offender's head would be covered with a shroud.) A prison official dressed as the executioner gave the spectacle the needed realism, while an attendant priest supplied ceremonial solemnity through a prayerful admonition (*uveshchenie*) marking the religious renunciation of the offender's former civic life. Thus, stripped of all rights as a member of the community (symbolically, yet powerfully dramatized by the breaking of one's sword into half in the case of privileged estates), the offender was then sent off on his last journey into exile.[28]

If this kind of punishment was intended as a deterrent in the style of Voltaire's 'encourager les autres', with the tsar as the supreme arbiter of prosecution, for a rural audience that typically regarded the criminal as an 'unfortunate sinner' standing before God, the ritualized 'shaming devices' symbolically removing the offender from the sphere of earthly justice (*zemnoe pravosudie*) must have lent the sentencing procedure an aura of divine 'retribution' (*vozmezdie*) and redemption. At first, the crowds would jeer at the offender, outraged by the nature of his crime, but, once condemned, the offender struck the moral conscience of the onlookers and elicited their pity as one of God's poor 'unfortunates' (*nechastnyi*) in his final moments of acute spiritual pain. At this point, as Murav'ev notes, it was not unusual for people in the crowd to throw coins onto the scaffold, which the criminal would then stuff into his shirt and take with him to Siberia.[29] The gesture was intended both as a way of expiating their own sins (none of us is guilt free) and as an expression of hope for the condemned man's eventual salvation. In other words, the point of the exercise was easily missed; rather than indignant horror, shaming was just as likely to win the sympathy of the spectators.

Staging one's loss of civic status in public, therefore, produced a curious cocktail of formal procedure and rural concepts of criminality, which was detrimental to the modernizing process in two ways. At one level, it undermined trust in the legal bodies through which the state channelled its authority:

> Russian people were reluctant to believe in the unconditional rightness of the judicial verdict, to trust its infallibility. Thus, it was not unusual to hear from amongst the crowd comments of the type 'maybe he wasn't guilty. Did he get a fair trial? It's easy to slander a person, and, who knows, he might be totally innocent after all?'[30]

At another, it exposed the common denominator to both code and custom, namely an inability to differentiate between what is unlawful and what is immoral.

Accommodating custom

Late-nineteenth-century accounts by ethnographers and historians of legal practice in the peasant commune attest just how little headway the modern idea of crime as an infraction, and punishment as deprivation of 'outer' freedom', had made. In the peasant world, crime was conceived of as a sin or an offence (*obyda*) irrespective of whether the victim be another person, animal, or property. Punishment was both retribution (*vozmezdie*) and an opportunity to exercise forgiveness and charity. In a study of peasant legal customs, the historian of law, Dmitry Dril', described in some detail the function of the peasant assemblies (*skhodki*), and the manner in which the elders addressed matters affecting the community, from distribution of land and stocks to grievances. His findings showed how quite primitive notions of morality and legality fed into one another and that the main stumbling block for developing a unified legal system across town and country was the neglect in the peasants' mental world of autonomy as the basis on which to build a civic culture:

> No distinction is made between so-called questions of law, and questions of morality, between the inner side of an act, and its outer manifestation (…). Such blurring of distinctions is the direct outcome of the communal structure in general, in which there is no room for the private (*lichnoe*) sphere (…) On the contrary, everything is done communally (*soobshcha*), and, it follows, every individual action is only significant when it is in the general interest of everyone. There is simply no room for the private sphere, independent from the whole: in communal-tribal (*rodovyi*) society the concept of the separate individual (*lichnost'*) simply does not exist.[31]

Rural concepts of criminality, as Cathy Frierson has shown in her various studies of peasant culture, were strongly affected by other codes of behaviour within the peasant community. The importance of family and community as part of the peasant's immediate universe meant that criminal acts committed within the community were deemed more serious than those committed on a stranger, or indeed on the landlord or the state as property owner. A peasant might be prosecuted for 'dishonouring a calf' belonging to a neighbour, but taking fruit from an open field was not regarded as a crime, because fruit growing freely in a field is the gift of God. That the state or lord might lay exclusive claim to it was something the peasant could not (or would not) comprehend: 'God grew the forest for everyone.'[32] 'A mouzhik', wrote the ethnographer, A.N. Engelhardt,

> is unaware of laws; he just respects some kind of 'divine law'. For example, if you, having caught a mouzhik with a cartload of stolen grain, take the grain away from him and then pin to his chest 'don't steal', well, that is perfectly understandable; if a koulak, having bought hemp, discovers dampness, then yells at the mouzhik 'don't cheat', that is fine too. It is all fair play in God's eyes (*po-Bozheski*). But if the law according to which a cartload of stolen straw merits three-and-a-half months in prison, well, that is not fair.[33]

A similar observation was made by the poet and memoirist M.A. Dmitriev: 'The people have no difficulty in understanding a crime directed against another person (murder, robbery), but crimes against the state go completely over his head. He only understands crime as a sin.'[34]

If customary law appeared almost wilfully subjective, a rebuttal of a system of justice based on abstract norms, it did, nevertheless, exhibit a number of criteria, which seemed to operate as constants when deliberating the nature of an offence and the appropriate punishment. Frierson identifies these as personal injury, sin, premeditation, and the membership status of the offender or victim within the community. But she also, and rightly, stresses that if considerations pertaining to premeditation and degree of personal injury suggest some parallels between customary law and formal law, the most striking difference was the way rural justice was ultimately affected by local interests. The upshot was that two individuals charged with the same crime could be punished differently depending on the circumstances and on the general interests of the community as a whole.[35]

Community sentencing could take the form of shaming, often for adulterers or petty thieves who were made to march through the village carrying or wearing the goods they had stolen and jeered at by an audience of censorious neighbours. Compensating for a crime with vodka also featured frequently in community sentencing.[36] Granted, as the reform progressed, evidence suggests that in minor civil disputes, peasants showed a growing willingness to take matters to the *volost'* courts and played custom and code off against each other as suited.[37] However, more serious criminal wrongdoings, such as theft, continued to be handled outside the formal system, at the village assemblies. The most serious crimes of all, notably horse theft and sexual crimes, would be rectified in the form of *samosud* – literally 'judging by oneself'. *Samosud* justice was usually practised when the offender was caught in flagrante delicte. These spontaneous acts of summary justice whereby peasants took matters into their own hands, settling scores through brutal physical punishment, shaming, or exacting compensation, continued unchanged throughout the post-Reform era.[38]

Obviously, for the peasantry, equating freedom with universal rights sat awkwardly with a system of communal tenure (*obshchinoe vladenie*) wherein the village allocated strips of land to households, rarely to individuals. Correspondingly, to define crime and punishment in terms of broadly speaking enlightenment principles was arguably rather futile when, for a large part of the population, property betokened (undeserved) privilege, rather than a guarantee of man's freedom.[39] But this did not deter pre-revolutionary scholars from arguing that the solution to legal backwardness in the countryside lay with cultivating a practice of respect for the person. By the turn of the century, studies of the peasantry had moved further in the direction taken by Dril', the 'peasant question' increasingly being treated as a 'legal' issue, free of the populist pathos that had governed the intelligentsia's approach to the peasantry in the 1870s. Ivan Strakhovsky's study, *Peasant Rights and Institutions* (1904) for instance, was cited in the literature as an important example for its innovative approach to the issue of peasant mentality as well as for his attacks on the discriminating practices of criminal justice. Strakhovsky urged that the peasant be regarded as a person vested with rights 'without which all cultural and economic development is unthinkable'. His emphasis on the civic status of the peasant housed stark criticism of residual pre-reform penal practice, namely the continued use of corporal punishment, and of current legislation generally, which still failed to register right to property and freedom of movement.[40]

It has been suggested that Russia's prevailing estate hierarchy made it virtually impossible to unify legal procedure; rather, it produced the classic 'customary law legal situation', an odd concoction of formal and customary practices, which, as Gareth Popkins notes, is commonly found in colonial and post-colonial contexts.[41] Inversely, however, one could argue that, for all their differences, aspects of the legal and moral code in the peasant world – as these were practised, less in terms of the underlying *Weltanschauung* of course – dovetailed with the moral formalism embedded in the inherited Code of punishments. Both regimes of code and custom enforced traditionally sanctioned religious and public morals, one in the name of tsar and God, the other for the sake of the immediate community and God. If breached, the culprit faced moral condemnation that was generally crudely enacted through physical or symbolized humiliation and torture. Both seemed marred by a linguistic fudging of law and morality (moralizing), and both were prone to arbitrariness or the pressures of extra-legal interests. Of the two orders, custom ironically contained more provision for the perpetrator of a crime by dint of his status within the community, than did the inherited code, which, as reformers complained, privileged the objective side of crime. Russian reformers, then, were confronted by a tradition of legality – of code and custom – which epitomized the 'combined underdevelopment of discipline and law'.

Modernizing law in the age of counter-reform (1882–1903)

If, as Richard Wortman notes, reform is not the beginning but 'the culmination of processes of change taking place within officialdom', then, certainly, the year

1864 was an important landmark achievement in the transformation of the Russian judiciary as a professional group.[42] But, in terms of modernizing the law of the land, it signified, rather, the beginning of a series of attempts and hesitant stops and starts, yielding the first modest results only in the closing years of the century.

In 1881, the new tsar, Alexander III, commissioned a review of the Criminal Code enlisting the counsel of some of the foremost and respected reform-minded scholars and statesmen, including Tagantsev, Foinitsky, and Neklyudov, who began work on the project the following year.[43] Progress on the Code quickly lost momentum, however: while the commission's recommendations to reduce the sentence for non-political murder to 15 years hard labour were approved in 1884, draft proposals concerning penalties for theft and arson, completed in 1886, were not. Much the same pattern of stops and starts continued thereafter. In 1894, a commission to review statutes of the Code of Criminal Procedure, by that time under Murav'ev's tutelage, was created as part of a wider initiative to revise the Criminal and Civil Law Codes, but, once again, it yielded results that can only be described as disappointing.[44] Albeit benefiting from the expertise of Koni, Tagantsev, Foinitsky, and Sluchevsky, efforts to clear the hurdle of a dual order of justice in rural affairs were frustrated by a recalcitrance masked as reasonableness. Murav'ev himself pledged 'solidarity and unity' between the Ministry of Justice and 'other institutions in service to the Emperor'. He reasoned, 'Not dissension, nor isolation between powers, rather their solidarity based on rational principles and complete autonomy (*samostoyatel'nost'*) within their own sphere, provides the solid basis, one that would be indestructible and beneficial for a civil society (*grazhdanskii poryadok*).'[45] However, with the definitive version of the *sudebnaya chast'* on matters of arbitration finally ready in 1899, a carefully worded explanatory note to the statutes argued the logic of 'render unto Caesar':

> It would be appropriate to review the distribution of judicial affairs at the local level (ie as run by the departments of the Ministry of Justice and the Ministry of the Interior) with a view to preserving the principle of jurisdiction to the organs of the Ministry of the Interior those matters which touch the immediate interests and requirements of the rural community, but at the same time alleviate these bodies of tasks of a purely juridical nature, which are not directly concerned with the daily running of the community, and which may be charged to the judiciary.[46]

In the eyes of contemporaries, this timid concession to judicial authority did little to alter the underlying dual system of managing law and order, a situation that elicited one wry observation – 'ainsi que deux soleils, il n'y a pas deux justices' ('Like two suns, there is no such thing as two justices').[47]

A project for the new Criminal Code was published in the Ministry's Journal in 1895. Subjected to some rigorous, and indeed, constructive criticism in the liberal press, the new draft proposal contained some quite far-reaching bids for change to penal practice that clearly reflected a modern vision of criminal justice, familiarity with practices in Western European countries, and an ease with the principles of contemporary juridical science.[48] That said, not unlike the outcome with respect to arbitration, the compromise that reformers, as commissioners, were forced to wrestle with in their dealings with Senate and Ministry servicemen is evident once again when one takes stock of the elements that passed into the definitive 1903 Code and those that did not. The proposal for suspended sentences was rejected outright, an idea that figured prominently in the scientific juridical literature of the day as part of wider endeavours to introduce restorative justice, but which obviously represented too radical a departure from existing legal practice in Russia. Proposals that did weather the storm either took their cue from Bludov's 1845 Code or built on modifications that had been successfully assimilated into subsequent editions. For example, the issue of complicity (*souchastie*), present in the pre-Reform code, was now tied to the concept of 'individual responsibility' that had been introduced in the Reform era revisions as a measure to stop the practice of 'transferred responsibility', whereby, for example, an editor of a journal might be indicted on behalf of his entire editorial board for an action he might not have had a direct hand in.

Establishing motives, differentiating between premeditated crime, manslaughter, attempted murder, misdemeanours, and infractions was, of course, a crucial component in modern criminal justice, enabling the courts to determine degrees of guilt and hand down the appropriate sentence. With these goals in mind, the commissioners of the 1895 draft managed to streamline the original six categories of non-imputability (*nevmenyaemost'*), on various grounds of mental health and age limit, to three: intellectual underdevelopment, nervous disorders, and states of unconsciousness, all of which could now be corroborated by scientific or medical evidence.[49] Complementing this refinement in levels of 'non-accountability' was a stock of terms referring to different levels of involvement in a criminal act (from unintentional manslaughter to premeditated murder), as well as to different types of illegal activity: crime, misdemeanour, and infraction (*prestuplenie*, *prostupki*, *narushenie*) inspired by French and German models (crimes, Verbrechen; délits, Vergehen; infraction/contraventions, Ubertretungen).[50] Correspondingly, the generic definition of a criminal act saw a subtle, yet hugely significant modification. Newly defined as 'an action forbidden at the moment it is carried out by law under threat of punishment' (*deyanie, vospreshchennoe vo vremya ego uchineniya zakonom pod strakhom nakazaniya*), the added temporal specification reflected the authors' intention (Tagantsev's, notably) to prevent sentencing 'by analogy', a much-abused practice already in Imperial Russia, but which was to become legion in the Soviet period.[51] Finally, Bludov's original ten categories of punishments were reduced to eight, and the formal and, anyway, fairly meaningless division between punitive and corrective punishment was dropped. The revised penal staircase now consisted of the death penalty; *katorga* (penal servitude from a minimum period of four years to life); exile; incarceration in a reformatory institution (*ispravitel'nyi dom*); incarceration in a fortress; prison; short-term arrest; and fine. In addition, these sentences, barring the last two, entailed loss of estate privileges for the nobility, clergy, and merchants, a measure that, again, betokened the underlying message of 'equality before the law' that reformers were seeking to drive home.

The disappointing outcome of this second phase of 'reform' is well known and usually points an accusing finger at Nicholas II for constantly stalling or obstructing any progress made. Revisions of the Criminal Law Code, which were finally completed in 1903 and sanctioned in 1904, were then held on ice. The official reason given was that it was better to wait until the Code of Procedural Laws (including the *sudebnaya chast'* dealing with court practices) had been verified as well. But, it was obviously more a case of reluctance, fear, and ingrained conservatism on the part of Nicholas II to pass softer measures against crime in the face of increasing social unrest. Thus, revisions to the Criminal Code were ultimately compromised by the degree to which law continued to be an instrument of autocratic rule. In the eyes of committed reformers, modifications to Bludov's 1845 code introduced since 1864 only thinly veiled a lingering formalism and arbitrariness, which merely added to the bureaucratic red tape.

On a balance sheet of gains and losses, the poor performance in the reform of criminal justice may be viewed as the result of blocked initiatives, compromise, and contingencies. Public shaming rituals were eventually dropped in 1881, nearly 20 years after the reforms had been launched. In the same year, executions were also banned from the pubic eye, henceforth to be carried out behind prison walls in the presence of a few invited dignitaries, townsmen, and a priest, a measure suggesting both a response to changes in public perception of the function of punishment and an attempt by officialdom to prevent further martyrdom (and therefore an example to follow) of revolutionary activists. Various forms of corporal punishment were, in fact, phased out both before and after Alexander II's reforms. During the reign of Paul I, for example, corporal punishment was abolished for criminals over the age of 70 (1798). Alexander I abolished the knout in 1810 and nostril slitting (*vyryvanie nozdrei*) in 1817. In 1871, the use of rods was abolished, and thereafter, the most severe form of corporal punishment was lashing (*plet'*) used for both sexes until 1893, when it was abolished for women. However, branding (*keimenie*) and birching (*rozga*), though removed from the statutes in 1866 as a form of punishment, remained a staple of Russian disciplinary measures in the army and for convicts throughout the Reform era. Birching, for example, was widely used to discipline uncooperative recruits and as a 'corrective measure' for prisoners, exiles, and those sentenced to hard labour, the *katorzhnye*. Indeed, modifications to the 1885 edition of the Penal Code in fact extended the practice to offenders convicted of crimes against the state. In addition, for members of non-privileged estates with minor convictions, birching served as a substitute for incarceration in order to ease the strain on overcrowded prisons. While, of course, this practice could be explained pragmatically, it was strangely at odds with the principles of reform.[52]

On the surface, state measures in the 1880s to modernize the penal system by phasing out certain institutions of incarceration such as the workhouse and *smiritel'nyi dom* (a legacy of Catherine the Great) did seem to meet the expectations of reformers. But, in reality, prison reform was stillborn. An edict of 15 February 1879, announcing the centralization of prison administration was an encouraging sign that the prison system would, at last, be streamlined: it was to be broken down into four main categories: 'hard labour prison' (*katorzhnye tiur'my*), 'prison', 'house of correction', and detention centres (*arestnyi dom*). But, lack of finances meant that few maintenance and reconstruction projects were ever completed. Thus, restricted in the number of concrete measures it could take, the Central Prison Administration resorted to a peculiar type of advice literature, issuing thousands of circulars containing guidelines on the latest regulations for the daily running of the prison. In the 1880s and 1890s, a relatively high proportion of these were of an educational kind, urging the importance of religious and general instruction for the internees, but, it would seem, to little positive effect: a circular of 1891 suggested that in the event of prisoners tearing out pages from the Bible to use as cigarette papers, the cost of the book should be deducted from their labour earnings.[53] Not only, then, did the pressures of expediency that generated a number of sentencing anomalies disrupt the admittedly somewhat inscrutable logic of the Scale of Punishments, they also thwarted the progress of reform. Calls for a more humane penitential system designed not so much to punish as to educate through disciplined labour and daily routine were undermined by equal doses of pragmatism and theoretical short-sightedness. Despite some partial revision of the legislation and the introduction of procedural laws that cut across estate divisions, the result was an unfortunate compromise that satisfied no one. With one kind of formalism substituted for another, reforming the justice system was, as Tagantsev put it, like 'dressing a piece of rotten dead flesh'. Granted, legal procedures at the close of the nineteenth century had moved a long way from the quite fanciful logic that one sometimes came across in the sixteenth and seventeenth centuries, when, for example, no distinction was made between animate and inanimate objects (in 1593, a church bell was reputedly charged with treason, flogged, and deported to Siberia[54]) or, indeed, from notions still current in the early nineteenth century such as 'collective guilt' and, inversely, what one might call 'proxy' or 'transferred' guilt. Such practices not only obscured awareness of one's individual responsibility but seemingly denied the existence of the individual *tout court*. Even with punishment defined as 'deprivation of freedom' in the late Imperial era, reformers felt that modern-day Russian legislation was a proverbial house of cards – an impressive but flimsy edifice lacking a conceptual core and blatantly compromised by political interest.

Legal culture in the age of reform

Whatever the motives prompting the state's reaction to worsening social disorder – a genuine concern to preserve security and order or to safeguard its own authority, the consequences of its shift in stance from reform patron to watchdog, and, particularly, its constant tampering with procedural laws are clear enough: on the one hand, it reinforced the already deep-seated – and, it would seem justified – suspicion of 'the law' among the Russian population; on the other, it succeeded in making a mockery of the liberal ideal of the normative function of justice. Intellectuals, both on the right and on the left of the 'liberals', variously dismissed the call to respect the law by reformers as sheer fantasy, unpatriotic kowtowing to Western masters (and proof of the reformers' bourgeois proclivities, to boot), or simply unworkable in a country that had become inured to the law of force and the blatant discrimination between the social estates. The radical intelligentsia, following Marx, dismissed law as yet one more privilege of the already unjustly privileged bourgeoisie. And so it scarcely mattered what changes were introduced, because they merely highlighted class differences.[55] The Slavophiles and their successors in the 1860s, conservative nationalists, reached similar conclusions, albeit for quite different reasons. The Slavophiles opposed formal justice (identified with Western practice) with a higher 'inner justice' practised spontaneously, so the argument went, by the Russian people. Accordingly, the relationship between the tsar and his people was built on mutual trust and 'a sincere reciprocal desire for the common good'.[56] But whereas Ivan Kireevsky, a first generation Slavophile, had objected to Western juridical culture on the grounds that it reduced the individual, as a legal entity, to a mere expression to the right to property, conservative nationalists, mainly comprising men close to the tsar and holding government posts, sought to inculcate national ideals capable of harnessing the state, the educated elite, and the people in a single unified whole. Together, their combined forces would withstand the menace brought on society in the form of radicalism, nihilism, and socialism.[57] Both Slavophiles and conservative nationalists, however (granted, in differing measures of subtlety), perpetuated the myth that, as a peace-loving and essentially apolitical people, the Russian nation had no need for law.

Within government circles, one of the most influential and articulate spokesmen for conservatism in Russia was Konstantin Pobedonostsev, chief procurator of the Holy Synod and adviser to the tsars from the 1880s until his death in 1907. Pobedonostsev had been highly critical of Pahlen's decision to turn the trials of revolutionaries in the 1870s into showcase pieces. If Pahlen believed (as it turned out mistakenly) that court prosecution – albeit a performance of legal transparency – would stigmatize the revolutionaries in the public eye, Pobedonostsev rightly predicted that such trials dangerously impinged on the autocrat's power of punishment. Thus, in the face of mounting radicalism and acts of terrorism carried out by the People's Will, Pobedonostsev did all he could to instil in his royal pupils the divinely sanctioned principles of autocratic rule:

> When we consider the infinite multitude of laws and regulations, and the bewilderment of legislators and judges, the fiction that ignorance of the law is in no way justification assumes an appalling significance. The simple man cannot know the law, or vindicate his rights, or defend himself against

> attacks and accusations; he falls then into the hands of attorneys, the sworn mechanics of the machine of justice, whom he pays for every step which advances his case in the courts.[58]

The attitudes sketched here, whatever the political or world view motivating them, from Marxist to national conservative, betrayed an instrumentalist concept of justice bolstered by a paternalistic view of authority. But they also imposed the highly restrictive cultural conditions under which reformers were obliged to work.

The 'liberal project' to ensure respect for the rights of the individual qua citizen in a monarchical rule of law state clearly outpaced the more watchful, measured gestures towards modernization guided by a concern to safeguard the status quo, namely the autocratic right to rule through law, albeit in the best interests of the *narod*, as professed by Pobedonostsev in its extreme form and succinctly captured in his counsel to the tsar quoted in the previous paragraph. In practice, however, as the changes introduced into the legislation attest, this dividing 'attitudinal wedge' between bureaucrats and progressive reformers eventually turned into a bridge for compromise on both sides as Russia proceeded along its path of controlled modernization. Liberal reformers, the intellectual progeny of the pioneers of reform, Kavelin and Chicherin, found themselves compelled to work within the ever-tightening restrictions reintroduced into the domain of criminal procedure as the promise of reform gradually dissolved. They quickly understood that modernizing the system required more than merely tinkering with statutory laws: painstaking efforts were needed to alter attitudes and prejudice. Hence, the emphasis they repeatedly placed on education and 'enlightenment' (*prosveshchenie*), a term one frequently comes across in the literature. And they just as quickly discovered that the reform process itself had opened up a Pandora's box of very basic, if nonetheless complex, questions concerning some of the most fundamental categories in juridical and, more broadly, 'political' science. If, by the late nineteenth century, notions such as citizenship and rule of law formed, nominally if not always practically, an integral part of Western juridical culture, in Russia, where the theoretical underpinnings of the law code were, as Konstantin Kavelin politely described them, 'casuistry', they had virtually no history at all. Moreover, simply turning one's mental gaze westwards and endorsing these concepts could not resolve the situation. While Russian scholars closely followed and responded to the latest developments in legal theory, they were all too aware that, despite the reform process, Russia's current social and economic structures in no way matched those of their Western neighbours, Germany, France, and least of all, Britain. To rely solely on ready-made solutions imported from Western legal thought would jeopardize their campaign even further, producing flagrant (and somewhat laughable) incongruities between 'the ideal' and the real, while fuelling the arguments of diehard conservative nationalists and advocates of Russia's special path into the bargain! The difficulties reformers faced are often illustrated with reference to the outcome of the emancipation of the serfs, who, until Stolypin's agrarian programme (1906), continued to be tied to the commune and thus could not enjoy legal rights equal with those of other social groups. But, other groups were also the targets of 'legal injustice': ethnic and religious minorities, and women too, continued to experience 'inequality before the law', thereby rendering 'inalienability' of the person qua citizen meaningless.[59] As for the nobility, clergy, and merchants who enjoyed such rights in the reform period, these proved incompatible with police powers and particularly the emergency laws, which suspended guarantees given to the individual under normal circumstances.

Rephrasing Wortman's comment, in a minor key, we might say that rather than reflect social change, the reforms vainly anticipated them. In some respects, first-generation reformist theories of crime and recommendations for a more humane penal system count as instances bringing the juridical community into headlong collision with a government unable, or unwilling, to accommodate such far-reaching proposals, even as, paradoxically, as I have suggested, many of their proposals took their cue from the admittedly hollow wording of the codes themselves. And, typically, once their work in this regard did eventually yield some positive results, it was success on paper, and did not filter down into practice integrally. The 1903 draft code is a case in point. Certainly, the important revisions to existing legislation that it embodied attest the achievements of the reformers to provide laws with strong theoretical underpinnings. For example, the inclusion of a stock of categories – premeditated murder, mitigating circumstances, negligence, and non-liability – suggests that the notion of a crime had, indeed, become more nuanced. Even if the code was held on ice, this did not prevent the juridical community from deepening its work on the subjective side of crime, in the light of which they would make practical recommendations (suspended sentences and early release, for example) for a more lenient and humane system of criminal justice after the promulgation of the Fundamental Laws in 1906. In a sense, though, the problem of implementing reform lay with liberal thinking itself, and, thus, successes and failures in the reform process should perhaps also be assessed in light of the attitudes and values that juridical thinkers, as liberal *intelligenty*, upheld. Given that reformers were rarely able to depart from the letter of existing, inherited, legislation as such, they endeavoured to refashion the spirit of some of its terms in the face of what Laura Engelstein has called the quintessential character of the autocracy – arbitrariness and self-contradiction.[60] The challenge they took up was to impart new meaning to a body of laws, elaborated in the 1830s, which was, in a sense, already inchoately 'modern', even as, of course, the legislation had been, and still was, designed to legitimate the state's claim to authority. The upshot was that proposals began operating with a 'two forked tongue', simultaneously reflecting the logic of an estate hierarchy, while endeavouring to answer (some of) the terms and conditions of the liberal intelligentsia. The real difficulty, however, that they were at pains to overcome was simply that Russia was still sorely wanting in those very structures constituting a modern state and society that their arguments, at the same time, assumed. This was most evident when it came to the 'criminal factor' and punishment, discussed in the next chapter, because it was here that the liberal assumptions of the kind 'Russia belonged to the family of modern states' and her *narod* were now *grazhdane* were unfortunate overstatements, often contradicted by reality.

Notwithstanding, the fate of the reform process, particularly during the reigns of Alexander III and Nicholas II when it experienced serious setbacks at the level of implementation 'from above', does point to a developing juridical consciousness and the social widening of its base. If the constant stalling that the commission faced is certainly evidence of a strong conservative resistance to change, the drawn-out process of rewriting the laws and the critique to which drafts were subjected (published in various journals such as the journal of the Ministry of Justice and in the *European Messenger*) may be interpreted as a sign of public involvement and consensus of opinion. As Arsen'ev put it: 'The more "legality" evaporates into theory and is ignored in practice, the more urgent becomes the role of the press to support it.'[61] Thus, while the letter of the reform seemed lost, the spirit was not. In particular, as contemporaries argued, this second phase of hesitant reform attests a change in social expectations relative to the greater emphasis placed on the idea of individual self-worth and education. Even within rural communities, which were beginning to benefit from elementary schooling, contemporaries spoke optimistically of a growing thirst for knowledge and an inchoate sense of legality to the point where villagers were beginning to perceive the enforcement of corporal punishment by the *volost'* courts, in any case now increasingly rare, as a primitive anachronism.[62] At the grass-roots level, architects of reform were noticing a sense of 'equal' rights (*ideya ravnopravnosti*) among the population, gradually emerging from the labours of collaborative representation at zemstvo meetings or in jury work, and cooperation across estates. More symbolically, but equally powerfully, commitment to the original pledges of reform was kept alive, thanks to the crafting of an entire corpus of commemorative literature – speeches, jubilee celebrations, and obituaries dedicated to the lives of the early champions of liberal values.[63] And somewhere halfway between these endeavours to sustain hope of lasting reform, its message was filtered into the schoolroom and lecture hall, where a nascent science of criminal justice was beginning to develop.

3 Theorizing crime and punishment

> We should remember that criminal justice (...) is tied to an entire web of social and state institutions; its proper implementation is a measure of social development and order.
>
> (V. Przheval'sky, 'Criminal legislation reform', 1888)

> Without guarantees of the person and her rights, (...) there can be neither social progress nor state order.
>
> (Tagantsev, *Russian Criminal Law*)[1]

The call to 'trust in the law' that campaigners for reform took as their motto was channelled through a variety of contexts. If the work of commissions to draft new laws or refine existing legislation was the most obvious route for conveying the new message, it was also, as I have argued, the least successful. Indeed, given the rapid erosion of the reform process almost as soon as it was born, failure was virtually inevitable. But to measure advances and setbacks solely in terms of the more visible political pendulum swings between cautious progress and reaction would, of course, be inadequate. Granted, these swings back and forth between reform and counter-reform, so typical of attempts to instigate change 'from above', are crucial for understanding Russia's awkward modernization process, but they arguably lead us to focus unduly on state measures – the 'above' precisely – and to ignore the real momentum of social change 'below', namely the growing complexity of the 'public sphere', which, since the second quarter of the century, had been witnessing, albeit reservedly, the spread of education, urbanization, and professionalization. Indeed, paradoxically, for all the bad press surrounding the reigns of Alexander III and Nicholas II as 'the triumph of aggressive Russian nationalism and conservatism', the dark, inauspicious days of their rule saw some of the most intensive, theoretically based work in the field of criminal law.[2]

Before juridical thinkers could even begin to delve into the meaning of crime and punishment, however, they needed to carve out a niche for criminal law as a discipline distinct from (if related to) other branches of law taught at the university. Given the pre-reform practice of a curriculum heavily oriented towards historicism and dogmatic analyses of current legislation (taught as 'encyclopaedia of law'), it is evident that the task confronting post-reform intellectuals involved a lot of rather basic groundwork. Textbooks setting out the basic concepts of crime and punishment started to appear in the early days of reform. Though little more than a first step towards theorizing crime (some of the outlines make for quite tedious reading), these textbooks symbolized a radical departure from a long tradition of historical studies, usually about early Russian law, which generally paid lip service to existing legal and socio-political institutions.[3] By contrast, reform authors began focusing their attention on current, predominantly Western, science of law, which, in the second half of the century, was witnessing a shift from 'absolutist' theories of law predicated on the notions of free will and responsibility towards legal positivism, an umbrella term for a whole host of approaches drawing variously on sociological and psychological explanations of crime and which incorporated a mass of statistical data in analyses of criminal trends and the effectiveness of the contemporary penal system. Over the next few decades, textbooks and original research more open to, if not uncritical of, the positivistic 'law for life's sake' approach began to dominate the field.[4] Monographs and scholarly articles dating from the 1880s and 1890s, especially, attest a steady progression and refinement in juridical thought with debate revisiting the classic questions of 'inalienable rights', inner and outer freedom, free will and determinism, but also engaging critically with some of the more recent trends in the human and social sciences, in particular the anthropological and sociological analyses of crime and punishment.[5]

This body of scholarly juridical literature was pivotal to the development of a legal consciousness in two distinct, yet complementary ways. First, of course, it helped forge a juridical vocabulary, providing those needed components on which to build a 'community of discourse'. In his *Course of Criminal Procedure* (1884), widely regarded as the first systematic outline in Russian of the history and theory of punishment, Ivan Foinitsky painstakingly spelled out the abc's of criminal law, offering useful equivalents in French and German of legal terminology for a novice readership having to navigate through a host of clumsy compound nouns such as *ugolovno-protsessual'noe zakonodatel'stvo*, ill-sounding loan words (*individualizatsiya* – Individualiserung), and neologisms (*prestupnost'* – criminality, *lichnye sostoyaniya prestupnosti* – individual states of criminality). By the turn of the century, however, these terms formed part of the warp and weft of Russian 'legalese'. Second, as a vehicle for disseminating veiled, covert criticism of current legal practice, legal scholarship had a wider 'ideological' resonance. Analysis of justice, social order, civic rights and duties with reference to Western models served to sharpen the reader's awareness of the flaws in the Imperial justice system, which was not just conceptually impoverished, but tended to hold most ideas and theories in suspicion as potential sources of insubordination. With public opinion more or less stifled by the new wave of censorship measures during the reigns of Alexander III and Nicholas II, it was the book review and scholarly article, whether written for specialist or 'thick journals', which became a frequently used medium for oblique criticism. In an otherwise not terribly complimentary review article of two textbooks on state law by N.M. Korkunov, *Edict and Law* (1894) and his two-volume *Russian State Law* (1892–1894), L. Slominsky, a regular contributor in the 1890s to the *European Messenger* on juridical matters, offered the reader a portrait of juridical culture in Western countries, with England, the model *par excellence*: 'The English have an innate juridical culture. It is ingrained.' Public rights of English citizens, Slominsky noted, stemmed from a strong awareness of the rights of the individual (*lichnost'*) as well as from the generally accepted principle that social and national interests coincide with the interests of each and everyone. Anything that is not explicitly prohibited is presumed legal, and every inhabitant who has not committed a crime or infraction is considered upright and honest until the contrary is proven. No law, or resolution as such, legitimates freedom of association (attending public meetings etc). It was, Slominsky concluded wistfully, simply the acknowledged right of an individual in England to go where he chooses whenever he likes.[6]

If accusing fingers were most readily found in periodical literature, couched in seemingly anodyne surveys of contemporary European juridical theory and legislative practice, subtle, but sharp, criticism of the current state of affairs in Russia also made its way into textbooks elaborated ostensibly for the classroom and lecture halls. As the author of the first landmark – and, politically, highly controversial – *Textbook of Criminal Law* in 1863, Spasovich pioneered a new approach to the study of law, providing the template format for Russian textbook literature thereafter. Explicit scientific premises, critical engagement with Western law, an interpretative slant became necessary tools of juridical research: Koni wrote, 'For its innovation and the boldness with which he expressed his convictions, (Spasovich's) textbook caused waves among the juridical community, purveyors of routine views of criminal law, but provoked criticism in the press not all of which was strictly scientific.' Outside the academic community, as Koni implies, Spasovich's book was perceived as thinly veiled criticism of government policy. Accused of harbouring subversive 'democratic' opinions, he was brought before a commission of the tsar's third department, which cited numerous examples of the author's 'hostile views' (*vrazhdebnye mysli*) such as his open hostility towards the retributive function of punishment (*vozmezdie*). Spasovich was subsequently pressured into resigning from his teaching post, while his book was withdrawn from the curriculum – a measure which did not, however, diminish its authority among scholars.[7]

On the surface, the historical comparative approach – possibly the most widely used methodology in the Reform era – closely followed in a tradition of Russian juridical literature, which, prior to the reforms, had privileged historical studies of early Russian law. But, whereas, in the pre-Reform decades, much juridical scholarship tended to serve as manifestos supporting autocratic rule, by the late 1860s, that too had turned into a potent channel for sharp critique of indigenous legal practices. Alexander Kistyakovsky's signature piece, *On Capital Punishment* (1867), for example, was a major reference in the Reform and Counter-Reform periods, both for its subject matter and in terms of the approach adopted. Operating with a concept of modern, industrialized society, Kistyakovsky stressed the importance of material and cultural development for rethinking criminal justice. As a society moves up the ladder of civilization, he argued, recourse to the death penalty and any form of torture to satisfy a need for revenge becomes abhorrent. For Kistyakovsky's readers, the suggestion of a direct correlation between a country's level of material and cultural development and the elimination of harsh measures from its penal system – the case in most West European countries – was an indictment of the backward nature of Russian legal culture and the broader social fabric which it both reflected and shaped.[8] Ivan Foinitsky also linked social progress to the humanization of criminal justice:

> The construction of criminal procedure stands in close relation to the status of the individual (*lichnost'*) in the state. In absolutist states, in which the individual has no rights, the accused is presented to the court as 'matter for business'. Sanctioned legal brutality reaches its peak: detention and torture are normal practice. By contrast, the freer a person is in a state, the greater the rights of the accused in a court of law. Nowadays (…), the Anglo-American principle of assumed innocence before proven guilty is becoming more widespread. Obviously, the manner in which criminal procedure is conducted is an indication of the political health of the country in question.[9]

Written just after the introduction of police surveillance (*politseiskii nadzor*), Foinitsky's projected ideal society, cited here, functioned as a sore reminder of what had been flagrantly denied by the Russian government's constant amendments to the Code of Criminal Procedure, namely its encroachment on personal inviolability for the sake of protecting, as it saw it, the security of society and (primarily) that of the state.

Common to the foregoing illustrations is a sense of mission, certainly – an ambition to secure *zakonnost'* through enlightenment. But a shared overriding goal did not necessarily translate into a neat, uniform body of thought. In his study of civil law in the Reform era, William Wagner speaks of a generational shift, with emphasis moving away from 'absolutist' theories to relativist ones, thus mirroring Western trends in the 1870s and 1880s.[10] Key to the former 'absolutist' theories was, of course, the notion of free will and responsibility elaborated with reference to philosophical idealism culminating in the thought of Kant and Hegel and indebted, juridically, to the foundational work of Anselm Feuerbach (1775–1833). As the high priest of the classical school in the early nineteenth century, Feuerbach formulated some of the lasting principles of modern criminal justice: nulla poena sine lege (no penalty without a law); differentiation between the objective side of a criminal act prohibited by law, and the subjective components of criminal responsibility including psychological factors – an innovation within the classical canon narrowly defined.[11] In stark contrast, legal positivism proposed innovative solutions to the key questions –

What is a crime? How are we to understand the criminal? What is the function of punishment? Instead of abstract theorizing, it drew heavily on quantifiable, statistical data, introducing extraneous factors such as social conditioning so as to rebalance the equation between criminal act and punitive response. If it was dismissive of the idea of free will, which, to the mind of classicists, was tantamount to dehumanizing the person and belittling the human spirit, this new relativism was welcomed by those – an increasing majority – pledged (paradoxically) to 'humanizing' the penal system by replacing retributive with restorative justice. However, despite declared intellectual affinities and differences, most 'first generation' reformist thinkers, active from roughly the 1870s to the turn of the century, tended to oscillate between schools of thought, on the one hand attracted by the opportunities afforded by new theories (if wary, certainly, of some of their extremes) but, on the other, conscious of the need to provide the building blocks for the science of law, for which purpose the classical premises of guilt and juridical norms were better suited. As Professor of St Petersburg University, N.D. Sergeevsky, put it: while there could be no single set of universally applicable punishments, there was a 'perennial jurisprudence'. Its lasting and unchanging task consisted in 'generating a feeling of respect for the law, a feeling of legality (*legal'nost'*) in individuals, and ensuring 'discipline before the law' – namely orderly behaviour that is innate in society as a whole.[12] It was only in the 1890s, as a moderate and more nuanced form of legal positivism was beginning to emerge, that we witness a sharper generational divide – including the typecasting of rivals as partisans of old or new schools. Critical of the one-sided approach of the anthropological and criminological schools, yet equally hostile towards the abstract formulism of the 'absolute' theories of law, this more integrated approach to criminal justice laid the foundations for the study of criminology and 'criminal politics' – new sister disciplines within the social sciences that developed rapidly over the next two decades up to the Revolution of 1917.

Russian readers of Western trends

From the 1870s onwards, among the Western schools most frequently discussed in the Russian press were Lombroso's criminal anthropology and the sociological approach associated with Gabriel Tarde in France. Both schools focused on the criminal, whether in terms of his individual psyche or as a symptom of the sickness of society at large. And both eschewed the classical concepts of free will and moral responsibility for various strains of determinism. Cesar Lombroso (1835–1909) was professor of clinical psychiatry in Turin. In his major work, *Uomo delinquente* (1876), he developed a theory of the 'criminal type' based on what, nowadays, would be regarded as one of the crudest examples of psycho-physiological parallelism: heavy, strong build, small cranium, low forehead, prominent eyebrows and cheekbones, asymmetrical features, deep-set eyes, and either a crooked or snub nose, often longsighted, left-handed, hirsute, but rarely growing a beard.[13] Lombroso believed it was possible to determine criminal proclivities by measuring the size of the cranium, the curve of the upper lip, or by checking whether the eyebrows meet in the middle at the bridge of the nose. The distinct physiological traits he uncovered formed the basis of his classification of criminal types, from murderers, thieves, and even political criminals to one-offs and recidivists. Typically, the murderer had a prominent jaw and cheekbones, an aquiline nose, long teeth, thin lips; a thief would usually have shifty eyes and a thin beard; a sexual deviant was recognizable for his thick lips and long hair. The hallmark of Lombroso's theory, however, was his account of the 'innate criminal'. Described as 'morally insane', this category of miscreants was sound in reason but incapable of distinguishing between good and evil. Highly reminiscent of Dostoevsky's underground characters in *Notes from the House of the Dead*, the innate criminal, according to Lombroso's observations, was prone to epileptic attacks.

For Lombroso and his school, the idea of free will was unsubstantiated. Left out of account was the realm of the unconscious mind, that hidden closet where motives and passions are born, and which our self-monitoring powers cannot access. Since there is no such thing as free will, it followed that there can be no moral accountability or, if taken to the arena of law, no determinable degree of guilt, which may be weighed up on the scales of justice and exchanged for a prison sentence or a term of penal servitude. Against the traditional retributive function of punishment, the criminal anthropologists conceived justice as a means of society's self-defence against transgressors of laws, whose crimes, induced by mental states such as dementia, melancholy, monomania, had their origins in purely physical or biological factors. They argued that courts be replaced by specialized administrative bodies with requisite skills in diagnosing mental derangement. Sentencing – including the death penalty for innate criminals, sterilization and castration – would involve an assessment by trained specialists of the offender's type and degree of criminality and of the potential danger he represented to society.

Among Lombroso's immediate successors, Enrico Ferri (1856–1929) was a specialist in criminal law whose influence reached into government chambers, in Italy, and into academic circles, internationally. The anthropological congress held in Rome in 1885 endorsed his classification of criminals that he had modelled on Lombroso's original typology, and in 1889, as the new Italian Criminal Code was reaching the final stages of ratification, Ferri's critique of the flaws in the current system of criminal justice and his bid for greater flexibility in sentencing were given due consideration. Ultimately, however, the theoretical premises on which his proposals were based were deemed 'not yet ripe for application', and Italian legislation remained steadfast in its 'classical Beccarian' principles. That said, as Spasovich notes, the 'humanizing ethos' of positivism with regard to punishment did leave its mark on the Code.[14]

Ferri refined Lombroso's distinctions between habitual, inveterate, accidental, and mentally unbalanced acts of lawlessness to produce five main categories comprising the insane criminal, the incorrigible or innate criminal, the recidivist or inveterate criminal, the passion-induced criminal, and the incidental criminal drawn into crime by force of circumstance. Central to Ferri's theory of criminal behaviour was, again, a critique of the idea of free will. Any mental or volitional process occurs as a consequence of a nervous reflex. This is rendered more complex because between the trigger to an action and the action itself, there is an intermediary mental phase consisting in an illusionary sense of arbitrary will. In essence, however, it is merely the case that the individual in question, having responded to an external stimulus, becomes, albeit involuntarily, the author of those transformations caused by him in the outside world, which, in turn, becomes the basis of his (or her) liability for these transformations. Building on this 'reflex' theory, Ferri challenged the more conventional notion of 'criminal' with an account of what he called the 'factors of criminality', which he broke down into the anthropological (inherent) factor, the physical, comprising a complex of circumstances within the criminal's immediate environment, and the social, a broad category covering morals, religion, industrial and economic structures, administration, courts and legislation. Since physical and anthropological factors stand outside the reach of legislation, in the sense they cannot be rectified by a prison sentence, this led Ferri to argue that, on its own, punishment has little impact on the growth or diminution of the crime rate. If there is no free will, then neither can there be guilt nor can there be responsibility. In other words, punishment as a proportionate response to culpability is a redundant gesture. Rather, society is empowered, through punishment, to protect itself from infractions of the laws it has established. Just as the criminal act is reducible to a nervous reflex, so too, Ferri argued, punishment is an instinctual response of self-defence by an individual or community in the struggle for existence. Such self-defence takes a variety of forms: it may be immediate or postponed for a more opportune moment (the case of revenge, for example). It may be military, judicial, or carried out through the institutions of state. Historically, punishment had evolved, he argued: originally it required no explanation or justification before a higher authority, but once it passed, as a right, into the hands of the priesthood, punitive action acquired a mystical colouration as revenge of the gods demanding purification. Up to the late nineteenth century, even as justice had moved from the religious to the classical phase of legislation (under the auspices of 'truth' and 'justice'), it was still customary to weigh guilt against punishment on an imaginary set of scales.[15]

Like the Lombroso school, sociologists of crime rejected free will as a non-issue: such theories, they argued, generally betrayed a narrow and highly abstract vision of the person. They failed to account for the impact of social, economic, and demographic change on the person who is at once unique, yet also, and primarily, a social being conforming to accepted patterns of social behaviour. That certain behavioural patterns are considered illegal should in fact direct our attention towards the flaws in the social environment, rather than towards the perpetrator of a crime. It followed that punishment inflicted on an individual criminal should be regarded as an indictment of society, with the criminal as the lamb of sacrifice.

The eminent French criminologist, Gabriel Tarde (1843–1904), a regular contributor to one of France's establishment periodicals, the *Revue philosophique*, pioneered work into the nature of crime from a sociological perspective. Clearly inspired by the example of the Italians (he attended the 1885 congress in Rome), in his own research Tarde focused on the social rather than the biological environment. His analysis of the material and/or economic conditions governing criminal acts highlighted the need for preventive measures, both within the penitentiary to prevent further crime and also outside it. In this regard, the role of schools and the Church in encouraging social responsibility was crucial.[16] Though Tarde agreed with Lombroso that the criminal may exhibit a peculiar nervous disposition, he was not a latter-day savage, nor insane, nor even prone to epileptic attacks: a criminal is first and foremost a product of society, a malignant social cancer, and justice is society's sanitizing function as a survival mechanism. As primarily a social phenomenon, Tarde argued, criminality may be best explained in terms of 'imitation'. If not couched in the same terms, Tarde's account of 'imitative behaviour' was strikingly similar to the distinction that the philosopher of 'intuition', Henri Bergson, made between the *moi profond* and the *moi superficial* in his celebrated study, *Essai sur les données immediate de la conscience* (1889). For Bergson, while the deeper levels of the person nurture one's enduring identity, uniqueness, and creative potential, which may come to expression in works of art and in acts of courage or in distorted form in a crime of passion, the superficial I is that which we encounter and parade in our everyday lives. Conformist and prone to imitation, we social beings model our behaviour on others. We observe and copy. In his analysis of the criminal, Tarde oscillated between these two realms of personal existence. Rejecting the cardboard cut-out criminal types of the anthropological school with no will of their own, Tarde made a case for criminal responsibility, attested, he argued, by the ability in some convicted offenders to express remorse for their actions when exploring or confronted by their deeper selves. That said, criminality, from petty crime to murder, spreads in society chiefly because of man's innate tendency to copy others. Appalling living conditions in the ghetto, for example, generate criminal behaviour. Pickpocketing becomes a 'way of life'; a penny-farthing murder story might trigger our embedded Jack the Ripper instincts: 'All infractions of the law depend on the nature of the society within which they occur, namely its inability to provide its members with the means to make the need for crime redundant.'[17]

Sociologists of crime proposed a two-pronged solution for regulating – and diminishing – criminal tendencies: pre-emptive measures focused on upbringing and education (*vospitanie lichnosti*, as Foinitsky summarized it), while punishment was conceived as a sort of sanitary-cum-medical cure. The more sophisticated a society becomes, correspondingly, the more refined its means of punishment should be. As the population benefits from a national education, and generally an improved standard of living, it expects a more rationalized penal system based on corrective measures. Thus, unlike Ferri, for whom punishment served no useful purpose, for Tarde it functioned both as a cautionary and a preventative measure. Tarde argued that in view of social and cultural change over time (from religious to secular models, from crusader to industrialist), and the growing refinement in human sensibilities making the very idea of ritual torture intolerable, punishment in the modern world ought to involve a component of correction through education and compassion as dispensed by the good offices of appropriately trained personnel through a network of charitable organizations designed to facilitate the offender's eventual social reintegration. To his mind, prison represented the only tolerable form of punishment in a modern society – the more serious the crime, the longer the sentence. In line with his understanding of punishment as a cautionary measure, Tarde advocated suspended sentences (introduced in France in 1890), but also solitary confinement for the inveterate criminal, while insisting that the mentally deranged criminal should be treated in a psychiatric clinic. Although he did not oppose communal cells, or mixed cells, Tarde argued for a strict separation between convicts on grounds of social – urban or remote backwater – origins and urged that the various prison chores allocated to inmates respect their experience and background. Training a hapless country bumpkin in factory skills, he warned, would result in his total undoing once he was released into a hostile, unfamiliar urban environment where he lacked the requisite abilities to cope. As experience showed, many ended up in prostitution or fell back, once again, into petty crime.

In the 1870s and 1880s, criminal anthropology enjoyed only a small following in Russia, with Neklyudov and Dril' as its leading exponents at home. Indeed, even prior to the international success of the Lombroso school, Neklyudov had presented research based on extensive use of statistics for his master degree on the relationship between age and criminality. However, their studies of juvenile crime, and the role of medical science in the judicial process rank as isolated, and possibly precocious, endorsements of the anthropological school, which would only begin to attract a wider body of interest in the 1890s and after 1900, once it had modified some of its more extreme claims associated with Lombroso's original research.[18] As a rule, Russian specialists writing before the turn of the century resisted the extreme logic of these arguments preferring to stick with the more classical notions of guilt and responsibility. One of the most outspoken critics of the new trends was Spasovich. He regretted the way in which such 'post-Darwinist secular accounts of human development', as he classed them, undermined 'what was once considered the unassailable axioms (…) of humanity and the Christian spirit, namely responsibility and free will'. To his mind, the current vogue for statistics combined with positivistic anthropological studies of human behaviour actually 'effaced the human person'.[19] Tagantsev also reserved his sharpest criticism for the anthropological school, vigorously opposing its criteria as fanciful: 'Attempts to establish natural historical symptoms of the criminal – whether he be a murderer, thief, or guilty of the most minor infraction (…) are not only pointless, but also dangerous, both theoretically and in practice. (…) It would be remiss of me not to say that, to a large degree, the findings of this new school are marred by an absence of serious research, haste, and given to sheer fantasy.'[20] Negative reactions in Russia were, understandably, dictated by broader objectives of instituting a workable judicial practice that would gain public trust. The outcome of the trial for the murder of a certain Sarah Becker, for example, in which the defendant was acquitted, was a case in point demonstrating that dabbling in current juridical trends threatened to undermine the integrity of the profession. Representing the defendant, a certain Professor Balinsky won the acquittal for the woman's killer on the grounds that he was a psychopath and that, therefore, any form of incarceration, including asylum for the mentally ill, would be of no use. The accused was set free.[21]

Although the Sarah Becker trial prompted widespread condemnation across the juridical community, literature of the period, nevertheless, attests the degree to which the vocabulary of criminal anthropology – *klass prestupnikov, psikhofiziologicheskie tipy, prestupnost'* (class of criminals; psycho-physiological types: criminality) – was assimilated by Russian scholars as they navigated a safer course combining some of its terms with a more common sense awareness of the traditional function of justice. Ivan Foinitsky, for example, used the anthropological approach to crime in order to shift attention away from crime to criminality. Echoing Ferri, Foinitsky argued that criminal law is about the *lichnoe sostoyanie prestupnosti* – personal states of being leading to a breach of the legal order. That said, he was certainly less radically inclined than the aforementioned Professor Balinsky and, indeed, like most of his more classically oriented peers, felt uncomfortable with the more far-reaching theses being developed in the West to the effect that 'criminal' and 'psychopath' were interchangeable terms and that acts of crime could not be punished. Thus, unlike the anthropological school, Foinitsky insisted on individual responsibility and on crime as an act, which, alongside social and physical circumstances, includes a consciously volitional moment; he wrote:

> There is no doubt, that, among criminals, a fair percentage of them are mentally unstable (…). But this does not constitute grounds for declaring all criminals insane. The notion of mentally ill is not reducible to that of criminal. The former is of a physical nature, while the latter belongs to the social–moral order.[22]

If ventures into the dark recesses of the criminal mind yielded, for Russian tastes, outrageous or faintly comical results, sociological 'prescriptions' for crime prevention were welcomed as a useful tool for tackling deeper social issues. Like many of his peers, Tagantsev found socially driven theories of law better suited to the problems they were confronting on home soil. Indeed, he even claimed that Russian scholars had developed theories in parallel with, yet independently of, Western trends.[23] But, while he openly admitted that his understanding of criminal justice was germane to the sociological point of view, he warned against pursuing this route too far on the grounds that it might lure the theorist into the realm of banal generalities (*obshchie mesta*). Thus, if he applauded the practical implications of Tarde's work in building a case for a more humane penal system, he nevertheless expressed serious reservations with respect to some of his theoretical premises. Tarde's innovative and challenging arguments, which effectively transferred criminal guilt to society at large and downplayed the notion of guilt as an integral part of criminal justice obviously clashed with a view of punishment as a means to protect the interests of society/state by effectively annihilating the offender. If this more traditionalist understanding was being increasingly modified by the call to consider the well-being of the accused, his or her eventual reintegration into society, which Tagantsev actively endorsed, it was not, however, a question of substituting one code of practice for another; rather, for Tagantsev, at issue here was the more difficult task of reconciling the two.

Responses to Western trends allow us to gauge not only the variety of ideas within a nascent Russian juridical culture; they also attest an underlying concern shared by reformers to establish theoretical foundations for law and juridical institutions at home. If Russian juridical thinkers hoped to introduce some parts of Western legal practice (assumed innocence before proven guilty), endorsement of current Western theories was virtually impossible for the simple reason that Russia lacked the necessary juridical–cultural credentials to accommodate what was, broadly speaking, the 'human turn' in criminology. Precisely because of the arbitrariness of Russian legal practice, and because of a level of juridical thinking only just coming to grips with the basic distinction to be observed between law/right (*pravo*) and laws (*zakon*), most first-generation reformers felt it inappropriate to abandon classical tenets altogether for arguments relating to climatic conditions, poverty, or genes – even if they opened avenues for further original research. With questions of liability and free will high on the agenda as tools to address weaknesses within the existing Criminal Code, wholesale assimilation of anthropological and sociological theories was, arguably, to jeopardize rather than to advance their cause. That said, while reformers appeared reluctant to endorse the new relativism unconditionally, they recognized the merit of these new theories in drawing attention to the person (-ality) of the criminal and to social ills leading to crime. Urging that each case be treated separately, this more humane approach was sensitive to the disciplinary, as opposed to punitive, function of sentencing. The upshot was that few Russian juridical thinkers carried one theoretical badge. While, as I have argued here, most Russian thinkers, working before the turn of the century (1870s–1890s), were generally reluctant to enter the murky recesses of the criminal mind as counselled by certain criminal anthropologists, and gingerly inclined to 'socially driven theories of law', few were ultimately diehard classicists. Even Spasovich, who regretted the dismissive attitude towards metaphysical questions of free will and freedom that these juridical fashions entailed, cannot be labelled a classicist *pur et dur*, because logically consistent with this view would be an acceptance of capital punishment, which he, like many reformers, campaigned against. In other words, rather than speak of a gradual shift away from classical interpretations to legal positivism, it might be more accurate to characterize Russian juridical thought during the closing decades of the nineteenth century in terms of an oscillation between trends and ad hoc adaptations of existing foreign models, all for the sake of tackling more effectively Russia's enduring legacy of 'legal nihilism'. Clearly, if current west European juridical culture remained the model to aspire to, it is equally true that Russians were not seeking ready-made solutions to rectify problems at home.

Law for law's sake versus *zhizneprigodnost'* (relevance to life)

'A criminal act', wrote Tagantsev, 'is a juridical affair.' It is a 'breach of norms, laws and rules endorsed by society for the sake of ensuring social order and security'. In real terms, violation of a legal norm (*pravo*) is a violation of law-enforced interests and lawful well being. Accordingly, justice concerns a relation between the criminal and the state, with the latter empowered through the judiciary to exact corrective or disciplinary measures appropriate to the nature of the crime committed.[24] If Tagantsev upheld the principle nulla poena sine lege (no penalty without a law), his sense of the social role of justice as played out by the state prompted him to venture beyond definitions of crime and punishment as straightforward unembellished formulas couched in strictly juridical terms. Despite the noble dream they exemplified – equality of all before the law and punishment commensurate with the crime committed – this strictly juridical approach was a self-contained abstraction that could not reckon with change or contingency:

> The punitive function of the state is not a logical consequence, a self-sufficient manifestation of Nemesis, but an expedient measure in tune with the overall raison d'être of the state in promoting and securing personal and social development. (…) Both the legal theorist and the legislator (…) should bear in mind the law's 'relevance to life' (*zhizneprigodnost'*). Life for life's sake – that's the motto that should be inscribed on the badge of every legislator.[25]

Beckoned by two masters – by the classical tenets he cleaved to in order to build the discipline and by the importance he attached to crime and punishment as social phenomena – Tagantsev struggled to reconcile two opposing tendencies in his definitions of crime, the criminal, punishment, justice, and the state. Time and again, he seems to vacillate between the two schools of thought, endeavouring, where possible, to anchor the terms of a normative abstract definition of crime and punishment in the flux of historical social reality:

> As an action forbidden by the law and cautioned by the threat of punishment, a crime exhibits a number of distinctive features. It involves legal-normative terms generated among members within a community (…) and its individual citizens. (Society) modifies existing juridical terms, overthrows or destabilizes rights or interests protected by rights (*prava*); it creates new terms between perpetrators and victims, between perpetrators and the state. The essence of a criminal act, then, even as it has as its object a concrete good (*blago*), does not consist in the degree of harm or damage

> inflicted, but is rather to be understood in terms of the response elicited by the law governed state.[26]

As a staunch defender of the correctional function of punishment, Tagantsev counselled due consideration to be given to the accused:

> Crime is the expression of a person (*lichnost'*); in punishing her the state is inflicting suffering not on an abstraction, but a living organism, a person (*chelovek*) (…). Without full consideration of the criminal, all reasoned theories of criminality are worthless.

However, Tagantsev, the classicist, qualified his claim in light of the accepted juridical distinction between the inner moral freedom of the person and her right to dispose of material wealth, freedom of movement, and choice of activity: only the second aspect of freedom comes within the province of law:

> The individual (*lichnost'*) enters the field of criminal-juridical research only insofar as her qualities are manifest in the criminal deed (…). (T)hus the object of criminal law (…) must be the criminal act and not 'criminality', it must be a person's activity not 'the person herself'.[27]

One must, he believed, differentiate between: 'the personal qualities of the criminal, his moral and juridical depravity' and the act committed brought before a court of law. If Tagantsev admitted a fascination for the inner motivations leading to a crime (and so brilliantly captured in some of the most memorable literary chef d'oeuvres – Macbeth and Raskol'nikov – which he cited as examples), his main concern was ultimately the social impact of the criminal act. Thus, his interest in the personal qualities of the criminal was less a departure from classical tenets, as a temporary suspension of his governing interest in the sociology of crime: 'As the manifestation of a criminal personality, a crime describes the prologue to a battle between the state and undesirable elements of society.' The study of crime, therefore, should direct the punitive measures taken by the state.[28]

Precisely, the odd cocktail of theoretical positions he defended, his oscillation between classical 'absolutist' and relativist positions, left Tagantsev open to criticism of logical inconsistency. By his immediate Russian contemporaries he was considered a sociological determinist and an adherent of the psychological approach to criminal law as defined by Feuerbach, one of the first to offer a substantial analysis of liability.[29] For Feuerbach, theories (notably the Kantian) that ground the juridical idea of punishment on free will (evil as an act of free will) were mistaken: criminal acts are governed by a cause emotionally inducing a person into an act of crime. Feuerbach's work, which, from within the classical framework, opened possibilities for reflection on the subjective side of crime, was a useful gauge in late-nineteenth-century enquiries into the nature of guilt and punishment. It encouraged evaluations of both the inner motivations and the outer manifestations of the criminal act and set the stage for arguments in favour of the individualization of punishment. Certainly, Tagantsev acknowledged the importance of Feuerbach in his own work, but, in the eyes of his peers, this was not sufficient to retain a place at the feet of old masters: his insistence that the criminal figure squarely in the equation of justice was taken to be too generous a concession to the new humanistic and worryingly relativistic approaches that were becoming fashionable in Italy and France.

In stark contrast, the next generation of juridical thinkers, who openly worked with the tools of sociology and anthropology, labelled Tagantsev a diehard, old-school classicist and a defender of norms and peddlers in abstract formulations:

> In vain, certain criminologists such as Hugo Meier, Tagantsev, Sergeevsky have tried to reduce concepts of crime and punishment to purely logical constructions. The futility of their attempts to protect juridical science from the grip of sociologists and anthropologists is all the more obvious when we consider the glaring contradictions in their own work.[30]

The author of these comments, Belogritz-Kotlyarevsky, suggested that Tagantsev was constantly usurping his own principles:

> Having shown that the object of criminal law is a criminal act, and not criminality, the action of a person, and not the person herself, he immediately concedes that juridical analysis of a criminal act cannot be confined to the act itself, but must reckon with the perpetrator of crime.[31]

Likewise, the work of Tagantsev's immediate contemporary N. Sergeevsky exhibited the same bizarre mixture of classical and sociological arguments. Openly defending the classical definitions of crime as a punishable breach of norms, with punishment as judgement and censure, Sergeevsky willy-nilly reverted to sociological explanations as the most pertinent tools for tackling issues of free will and in establishing degrees of culpability and recidivism. Indeed, as the author of a historical study of punishment in eighteenth-century Russia, Sergeevsky was obviously aware of the impact of social and economic change on judicial practice. He wrote:

> The specific aims of punishment change over time, and indeed, should change in accordance with development of the state, its various demands, and changes in ethical practices. (...) It is not the crime we judge and punish, ... but the criminal vested with anti-social qualities. The crime committed may provide the lawful reason for judgement and punishment, but the kind (*rod*) and degree (*razmer*) of punishment must be determined by the sum and particularities of anti-social characteristics of the criminal himself.[32]

Notwithstanding such evident concessions to the sociology of crime, in the eyes of their younger critics, Sergeevsky and Tagantsev produced an unmanageable union of classical and positivist tenets, typical of first-generation endeavours to satisfy two masters: rigorous science and social reality. For Belogritz-Kotlyarevsky, 'rigorous' ultimately meant rigid, reductionist definitions closed off from the requirements of modern society:

> Is it really feasible to resolve such questions as liability, punitive measures, by sticking to logical constructions? In such an event the inevitable outcome would be a purely scholastic, fleshless construction. Only a thoroughgoing study of a person's psychic makeup will enable us to throw light on the nature of man's volitional potential, and, it follows, to establish a more solid foundation for the study of liability (...). A comprehensive revision of the penal system is not possible without research into the entire personality of the criminal (*vsya lichnost' prestupnika'*); a better understanding of the personality of the criminal (*lichnost' prestupnika*) would open the way towards a more humane punitive system based on corrective principles.[33]

Belogritz-Kotlyarevsky's own choice of terms and argument bore the hallmark of 'new positivism', an update on some of the original premises of anthropology and sociology associated with the German scholar Franz von Liszt, to whom he was openly indebted in his own work published after 1900.[34] But, of this early generation of reformist thinkers at home, Ivan Foinitsky (1847–1913) also played a formative role in this regard. Among his immediate peers, Foinitsky was probably the most logically consistent in pursuing a moderate sociological and anthropological approach, particularly in view of the practical implications of these theories for rethinking the penal system, a topic which he privileged in his work and endeavoured to promote through his various senate posts and as founder of the Russian Union of Criminologists. As a branch of the larger International Union of Criminologists, Foinitsky's group, which collaborated with the Ministry of Justice, debated key issues of the day, for example, early release from prison, reduced sentences for one-off infractions, defence of children, and the role of the *patronat*. Proposals were then put forward for inclusion in the new Criminal Code commissioned by Alexander III. Encouraged by the abolition of corporal punishment for most estates in 1863, Foinitsky called for an end to exile and deportation, arguing that, as punitive measures, they were outdated and clearly contradicted the contemporary idea of punishment as 'deprivation of freedom'. However, as I mentioned earlier, inadequate funding and bureaucratic ineptitude and inertia effectively thwarted the numerous concrete recommendations he made in favour of imprisonment.[35]

Unlike his closest contemporaries, Foinitsky more readily endorsed the terms of legal positivism, which he made the cornerstones of his theory of crime and punishment. The terms of crime and law, he believed, could never be fully understood without the inclusion of sociological and psychological factors. Shifting attention away from crime to criminality, Foinitsky argued that criminal law is about the *lichnoe sostoyanie prestupnosti* – states of being leading to breach of the legal order: 'The object of criminal law is not crime, but criminality, that is, a person's state of mind (*sostoyanie litsa*) which induces a breach of the laws protected by punitive measures which are adapted to individual circumstances.'[36] If not quite a carbon copy of Ferri's definition of crime as an interplay of (*ravnodeistvuyushchie*) biological and social factors, Foinitsky urged that the person, in all his/her complexity, be taken into account in assessing the nature of the crime. As an abnormal activity (*nenormal'naya deyatel'nost'*), explanations for crime as a deviation from the norm may, in part, be found in the nervous, emotional disposition of the perpetrator, his habits, or character, which, together, shape and influence his strength of will.[37]

Foinitsky argued that attention to subjective circumstances (mental, emotional, physiological states of being) resulting in a criminal act, if not strictly part of the *corpus delicti*, was nevertheless crucial to the work of gauging the most appropriate punitive measures in each individual case: 'The person in her entirety is brought before the judge; her character, motives, evidence that her criminal activity is habitual are all especially significant in the adjudication process.'[38] Correspondingly, punishment understood as a battle with the complex body of circumstances that make up 'criminality' needed to be highly differentiated. Foinitsky distinguished three main types of criminal, each requiring a specific juridical response. An offender shown to be mentally deranged could not be held responsible for his actions: he was in need of a cure rather than punishment; a criminal who falls into crime by chance, perhaps committing just one crime, should be deterred from further crime; and punishment for re-offenders, however, should be corrective. In general, punishment had to be flexible and reversible (*nakazanie dolzhno obladat' gibkost'yu, delimost'yu*); it had to be just, corresponding both to the objective weight of the infraction as well as to the established degree of subjective guilt.[39]

At his own admission, Foinitsky was inspired by the English penal system with its classification of prisons into vocational and correctional institutions, which he characterized as the 'individualization of prison discipline'. He singled out its system of 'intermittent imprisonment' and the *patronat* – charities set up to ensure the successful reintegration of prisoners into society once they had completed their sentence as practices to emulate.[40] Having spent the early 1870s studying in various European cities (Berlin, Leipzig, Bern, and Paris), it was Foinitsky's stay in London and Ireland, and his attendance at the International Penitentiary Congress held in London in 1872 where he became familiar with recent developments in theories of correction and sentencing, that proved formative for his work on the 'prison question' in Russia. A model for his arguments must certainly have been the British philanthropist, John Howard (1726–1790), whose vision of a unified penal system based on the corrective function of prison had gained posthumous recognition after the official abolishment of exile by an act of parliament in 1857 (though already the practice had been sharply reduced in the 1840s).[41] Howard had argued that prisons should provide the inmates the opportunity, through discipline, schooling, and labour, to become honest, decent fellows. In particular, he emphasized the moral and religious aspects of education as keystones in the construction of a more humane and effective 'penitential system'. As it was, 'cramped accommodation with little surveillance, no work to develop skills, no schooling, no pastoral care outside liturgy to have a beneficial effect on the internees', the prison was, in Howard's time, the proverbial breeding ground for further crime.

Discipline or punish?

The appalling prison conditions Howard described in eighteenth-century England found a haunting echo in Dostoevsky's famous memoir *Notes from the House of the Dead*:

> Prison and forced labour do not, of course, reform the criminal; they only punish him and secure society against his further attempts on its peace. In the criminal himself, prison and the most strenuous forms of hard labour develop only hatred, a thirst for forbidden pleasures, and terrible irresponsibility.... It sucks the living sap out of a man, wears down his spirit, weakens it, terrifies it, and then presents the morally shrivelled, half-demented mummy as a pattern of repentance and reform.[42]

In Russia, prison conditions had scarcely improved since the age of Catherine the Great. In a report to the tsar in 1840, the Chief of Police described them as 'overcrowded, damp. Water drips through the roof; the beams, floors and window frames are rotting; there's nowhere for prisoners to lie down ... and they are forced to pass the night standing.' With hygiene standards 'far short of primitive', spread of disease and overcrowded cells led to further crime. It was, therefore, crucial, the report concluded, to make practical recommendations for modernizing the existing (sparse) network of prisons across the empire. As such, little, however, was done until the prison question reappeared on the reform agenda more than 30 years later.[43]

In 1874, a state commission, presided by Count V.A. Sologub, was set up under the auspices of the Ministry of Internal Affairs to study the penal systems in Western Europe and in Russia. In addition to surveying prison life and administration, a subgroup, led by Senator Frisch, was assigned the task of examining the existing legislation on crime and punishment from a critical and theoretical perspective. Foinitsky published the results of the commission in the first volume of a series of collective essays designed to inform society as impartially as possible of ongoing questions of governance and administration. However, the outcome, as he described it, was frustratingly disappointing: an eclectic array of proposals with no cohesive core attesting a comprehensive vision of the penal system.[44] Both Sologub and Frisch were guilty of incorporating their instinctive prejudices into the decision-making process. Accepting, on principle, that the penitentiary system should be more streamlined, Sologub quite happily endorsed the idea of loss of freedom in perpetuity. Frisch's commission pronounced itself strongly against loss of rights as 'incommensurate with current rational practices', yet condoned civil death with attendant physical hardships such as chaining katorga convicts. For Foinitsky, these 'blunders' betrayed the poverty of 'our national juridical–political literature',[45] which, as yet, was insufficiently developed to provide legislators with an appropriate theoretical framework. Remnants of past practices continued to undermine the aims of contemporary juridical science, thwarting hopes to implement a penal system based on constructive disciplinary measures: 'The regime of physical harm, and physical deprivation of any kind destroys the strongest convicts, whereas the prison, both demonstrates the nefariousness of crime, and elevates the prisoner, making him fit for an honest life.'[46] Foinitsky needed to remind the commissioners that crime was no longer the object of blind fear and revulsion, inciting revenge; it was, rather, a symptom of social ills, which needed to be addressed by scholars: 'The criminal has ceased to be the object of hatred (...), he is a "rights-enabled" (*pravosposobnyi*) subject, in relation to whom social obligations have not only not ceased, but, on the contrary, have broadened.' Overlooking the person as a person (*lichnost' kak lichnost'*) was not only to destroy any feeling of justice among prisoners, but also to hinder the corrective and preventative function of the prison.[47] Foinitsky conceded that the chief obstacle to penal equality was the estate system, which differentiated between the social origins of the accused and the punished accordingly, but he remained hopeful that the principle of individualized punishment as an opportunity for the judge to examine all the evidence might function even within the existing 'caste system'.

A year later, at the First Congress of Russian Jurists, Foinitsky presented a set of proposals for updating another vestige of pre-reform practice – 'loss of rights' (*lichenie prav*). The permanent stigma attached to *lichenie prav*, whatever their degree or number, meant that an offender, on completion of his term, 'was doomed to live beyond the law (*bezpravie*), to be victim of unrelenting attacks and abuse'.[48] For Foinitsky, that current plans to modernize the prison system overlooked this outmoded, indiscriminate institution leaving it unchanged was a gross error of judgement:

> You find it necessary to rationalize the classification of prisoners, but as soon as you try to do so you discover that there's nothing to classify: the law has made them all equal by placing every one of them under the banner of 'without rights' (*bezpravie*). You are eager to improve things, push forward a programme of individualization in prisons, simplify the custodial system, but everywhere you turn, at every step of the way, your good intentions crumble to nothing before that state of full or partial – but at any rate lasting – absence of rights (*bezpravie*), established as law in the Criminal Code, causing ex-prisoners to live out the remaining years of their lives in total isolation from the rest of society.[49]

Foinitsky's proposals for a range of disenfranchisement measures were very much ahead of their time. To his mind, it was crucially important to establish the volume of rights susceptible to temporary loss, and, where relevant, for example, in the event of less serious infractions, regulate their restitution. With respect to the rights themselves, one had to differentiate between rights that, taken together, made up the juridical concept of a person from those that corresponded to an individual's political competence, meaning those rights we have as a member of society or estate, entitling us to participate in social (*obshchestvennye*) elections, to exercise the right of proxy (*polnomochie*), to hold down a responsible job, and so on. As Foinitsky saw it, the category of individual rights pertaining to property, family, inheritance, the right to honour and to life, and 'in general all personal well being guaranteed by the state as such' was sacrosanct, because disenfranchisement at this level would result in *'lish' fizicheskii chelovek* – merely a physical body, a state of affairs which, sadly, was all too common under the current system. He therefore insisted that these rights be protected and guaranteed by the state 'irrespective of estate divisions, and without regard to the personal qualities of one or another individual (*individ*)'.[50]

The principle of inalienability that Foinitsky defended here was eventually built into the 1903 Criminal Code, but the 1895 *Project*, however, offered more detail on the matter. For less severe sentences (five years' deportation, ten years in a correctional house or hard labour), the loss of rights were specified as the right to vote or to be elected to zemstvo, municipal or estate reunions; entry into state service, the army or the navy; registering with a guild; and the right to be a guardian, teacher, serve as a jury member or occupy any administrative post. On completion of a term of hard labour, convicts were entitled to urban or village status (*zapisyvayutsya v gorodskoe ili sel'skoe sostoyanie*), thus ruling out the restoration of rank to nobles and clergy.[51]

Work on modernizing the Russian penal system did finally make some headway at governmental level when, in 1879, a centralized prison administration was instituted to oversee the construction of new prisons. That said, in practice, little changed. As I mentioned earlier, lack of funding hindered construction of new prisons to accommodate a swelling prison population. And, if piecemeal introduction in 1878 of English-inspired 'charities' providing moral and material support for ex-convicts, together with legislation (1884) facilitating liaisons between voluntary aid societies and governmental committees in aiding discharged prisoners represented a major step forward in containing recidivism, all of which were welcomed by Foinitsky, by the 1890s they had become increasingly bureaucratized and subjected to tighter government control.[52] In any case, tiny in numbers, they could never effectively fulfil their task as trustees. The upshot was the familiar widening gap between theoretical discourse projecting change and practice that remained stubbornly the same.

In 1889, Foinitsky published his seminal *Theory of Punishment and Imprisonment* a work, which, as its title suggests, offered a comprehensive study of the right to punish and the system of punitive measures. Indeed, this monograph was not only a landmark contribution to criminal law theory, it also became a major work of reference, motivating projects for a more modern, standard form of incarceration. Individual chapters covered issues of juvenile criminality, measures for dealing with theft, and models of investigative and punitive detention.[53]

Like Ferri, Foinitsky's vision was simplicity itself: the more serious the crime, the longer the sentence. While Foinitsky accepted, along with most of his peers, that one purpose of punishment was to protect social order, he downplayed the role of the state as an arbiter of justice. If he recognized, and, indeed, endorsed, the punitive prerogative of the state as expressed through its judiciary empowered to interpret and apply the law, he nuanced this generally accepted view by suggesting a relation of mutual interdependence between society and the criminal. Punishment was not only a form of deprivation for the person sentenced, but also an economic loss for society. Punishment should therefore be carried out with the least amount of effort and means.[54] Moreover, if the correctional aspect of punishment is strengthened, punishment may be of greater benefit to society. In short, punishment has to be just, individualized, serve a purpose, and encourage the possibility of correction: 'This is why, nowadays, life sentences, punishments involving an assault on one's honour (*porazhenie chesti*), overcrowding of prison cells with no categorization of offenders are no longer tolerated.'[55] Critical of some of the more extreme views put forward by anthropologists, which turned punishment into a sort of spa cure, Foinitsky echoed Ferri whose list of social sanctions – preventative measures, reward, social exclusion (for dealing with recidivists) – included repressive measures, which Ferri had ascribed to the role of the prison. Likewise, Foinitsky insisted on the punitive, indeed repressive, function of the prison:

> It should avoid that false philanthropy which does everything it can to improve the lot of the prisoner, forgetting that, by doing so, prison risks becoming a form of reward as opposed to punishment (*kara*). Therefore, prison should not be turned into a sort of finishing school, where the prisoner is held until he takes his exam, nor a hospital where the prisoner remains until he regains his health.

As a correctional measure, the prison term may consist in the religious and moral education of the convicted criminal, but it should primarily be centred on providing him with work skills vital for preventing him from falling into the same cycle of poverty-induced petty crime, and hence the trap of recidivism.[56]

Foinitsky had a group of younger followers (Belogritz-Kotlyarevsky among them) who, in the 1890s and 1900s, developed his modified anthropological and sociological approach;[57] but his immediate colleagues remained sceptical of his breach with purely juridical norms. Tagantsev, for example, raised the obvious objection: How is one to ascertain the degree of responsibility when it is no longer a matter of punishing a criminal act, through which the perpetrator does, of course, express his personality, but the person himself/herself with all his/her inherent qualities, and patterns of behaviour? For Tagantsev, if the notion of a 'state of criminality' (*sostoyanie prestupnosti*) was meaningless, the idea that punitive measures might be taken against the personality of an individual rather than the crime committed was, from the strictly juridical point of view, extremely worrying. In response, Foinitsky merely reiterated the 'person in flux' argument: punishment is always directed at the person and not at the crime (in his eyes, a nonsense), but it should never annihilate the person altogether, because states of criminality are, by definition, susceptible to change.[58]

Despite the major theoretical differences dividing colleagues into various camps, these never obstructed the common goal of modernizing judicial practice. Without exception, whether they cleaved to classical or positivist interpretations of law, reformers argued in favour of the correctional function of justice, with punishment as a necessary tool to preserve and protect the interest of the state. Kistyakovsky spoke of 'self-preservation' (*samosokhranenie*); for Spasovich, punishment should be '*obezpechitel'no'*, a guarantee of material wellbeing for society and correctional for the criminal'.[59] Tagantsev and Sergeevsky argued for short sentences on the grounds that overly long sentences had detrimental effects on the prisoner much in the Dostoevskian vein described earlier. As staunch opponents of exile in perpetuity, reformers argued for the individualization (*individualitsiya*) of sentencing so as to ensure that punishment would operate according to both the objective weight, severity (*tyazhest'*) of the act, and subjective criteria. The behaviour, physical strength, age, and sex of the accused 'must be taken into account when determining responsibility. It follows that punitive measures which are totally at odds with these principles of individualization, should be excluded from the system of punishments.'[60] This was especially relevant when it came to crimes against the state where establishing the degree of participation, the type of breach was crucial. Common sense perhaps, but in the Military Criminal Code, which, with the implementation of emergency legislation in 1881, became the basis for dealing with politically motivated crimes, intention, conspiracy, and perpetration of the act itself were condemned in equal share. Listing more than 20 offences punishable by death, the code effectively placed less serious subversive acts, such as attacks on the police or rioting on a par with revolt against the supreme power.[61]

Law and morality

> Jurists unequivocally agree that the punitive powers of the state concern only the civil and in no way the moral, so to say, human person of the criminal. Accordingly, the state, may remove her civic honour, but in no way her moral, personal honour. The limits and substance of the former are determined by the state and are legally sanctioned as civil rights and wellbeing. These are what the state deals with in a court of law, and in no way should it impinge on higher justice.
>
> (N. Murav'ev, 'The Ritual of Public Shaming', 1874)[62]

The debate concerning the relation between law and morality was a highly contentious one and, in the Reform era, is best known for the extreme positions that crystallized outside the profession. Lev Tolstoi, for example, was renowned for his hostility towards law, which he dismissed as institutionalized violence and unwarranted privilege of the few over the many. Law, he believed, could be dispensed with in the name of Christian love (a position he shared with the Slavophiles before him), because social relations based on trust and respect for one's elders were inherently better than those that required written rules and signed affidavits.[63] The effect of such prejudice against the law in the name of a 'higher morality' was to reinforce the image of the Russian as innately and incorrigibly anti-juridical, an image that was exploited in government circles as a means to block the process of reform. For Pobedonostsev, probably the most outspoken and influential critic of reform in the tsar's immediate entourage, the prototype of all laws was to be found in the Ten Commandments, 'based on (their) moral acceptation'. He subordinated law to morality as a means to reaffirm autocratic principles and to remind Alexander III of his role as an autocrat:

> The commandments have the power of affecting the consciences of men by establishing, with the authority of supreme power, the distinction between light and darkness, between equity and inequity. And not in the material punishment for its violation is the fundamental, invincible sanction of the law, but in the conscience of man, rebuking his inequity. Material punishment he may flee, the imperfection of human justice may cast it on the innocent, but from this internal chastisement he can in no way be delivered (...). The moral influence of the law is sapped by a multitude of provisions and definitions, accumulated in the incessant activity of the legislative machine.[64]

If some treated law and morality as incompatible opposites, and required that a choice be made between the two, the statutes scarcely seem to differentiate between them. Since the *Ulozhenie* of 1649, criminal legal procedures had heavily exploited the religious tones of 'moral retribution' for offences committed. The moral, or rather, 'moralizing' component of 'passing judgement' still figured heavily in literature on the eve of reform. Barshev's authoritative textbooks written in the 1840s expressed the standard view: punishment as 'retribution by the state, which is grounded in the moral law of justice emanating from the supreme powers'. For Barshev, crime is immoral, the criminal morally corrupt, and the role of punishment an act of moral justice in the name of preserving the legally ordered (*pravomernyi*) state.[65] The same attitude was expressed in no uncertain terms by Tsar Nicholas I, absolute monarch and lawmaker par excellence: 'The best theory of law', he said, 'is good morality, which should be in the heart regardless of these abstractions, and have religion as its foundation.'[66] Reformers were therefore challenged by a legal culture that traditionally either blurred the distinction between law and morality (or, more accurately 'moralizing') or appealed to morality as a way of somehow usurping the function of law. Even if such terms and enactments of moral condemnation through public shaming had traditionally been used in a highly ritualistic and formalistic way and so, in a sense, were empty of meaning, the fact they occupied a central place in traditional juridical discourse represented a major obstacle for reformers arguing for a strictly juridical understanding of justice.

Whether they cleaved to classical definitions of crime or identified its source in social and/or psychological factors, most reformers agreed on one fundamental point, namely to observe a distinction between the civil and the moral dimensions of the person and correspondingly (also in Kantian vein) his/her inner and outer freedom in establishing the territory of criminal justice. Even if some theorists argued that an assessment of the defendant's 'moral qualities' (meaning 'conduct') was integral to the task of handing down the appropriate sentence, they still objected to the intrusion of moral judgement into juridical affairs. Not only did it hinder the purpose of justice, it was simply an unwanted reminder of the verbal moralization of law that both pre-reform legislation and present custom shared. Foinitsky wrote:

> Spiritual freedom cannot be the object of punishment on two counts: first, man's inner world is hardly accessible to state measures; second, coercive measures against the human spirit would be the most severe encroachment on his person, and in stark contradiction with contemporary culture: humanity has long since rejected direct coercion in the realm of the spirit; instead it has adopted indirect action on the spirit and personal beliefs through the influence of upbringing and education.[67]

Indeed, by way of reply to Tolstoi's famous dictum of non-resistance to evil, Foinitsky stated categorically that the Christian principle 'return good for evil' should never serve as the basis for any code.[68] For Foinitsky, while punishment may involve the moral rebirth of the offender, this noble dream cannot be its main goal; rather, the social gains of punishment should be measured in terms of the comprehensive re-education of the offender. Tagantsev and Sergeevsky made the same point: a criminal offence may not, indeed must not, be regarded as immoral, nor treated as a sin. Falling within the realm of the juridical is the 'outward manifestation of the person' (*proyavlenie lichnosti vo vne*), his/her freedom of movement and activities in various spheres. Confusing crime with immorality or, worse, with sin, may, 'as the bitter lessons of history have shown', empower the state to persecute and outlaw 'ideas, convictions, passions and vices'. Human justice thereby acquires 'unlawfully' the attributes of the Kingdom of God (*nebesnyi*).[69] 'Of course, there is a link between law and morality, a continuous mutual reinforcement between them' (*postoyannoe vzaimodeistvie*), as Sergeevsky put it,

> but the point to stress is that the immoral does not coincide with a breach of law (*pravonarushenie*) nor with a criminal act. From this it follows that the moment of immorality inherent in a criminal act is of little real significance.[70]

In spelling out the abc's on the relation between law and morality, namely their differences in terms of origin, purpose, and application, Sergeevsky nonetheless acknowledged a degree of overlap between them. Juridical norms are public in their reach and concern merely the external relations among citizens; morality is both a private and a personal matter of self-regulation or self-perfection, but it may also affect external relations: 'It is often said', he added, probably with Ihering's command theory of law in mind,

> that morality concerns internal relations only, and law external. While this is true of law, it is not of morality: the norms 'do not kill', 'do not steal' concern external relations certainly, but they are both moral and legal injunctions.

However, what Sergeevsky offered with one hand, he immediately took back with the other:

> Partly coinciding in the sphere of external relations, morality and law nevertheless go their separate ways (*raskhodyatsya*) even here. Morality is broader than law. Law retains only those moral positions which come into the province of state protection, and state guarantees (its concern with the moral injunction 'don't lie', for example, is restricted to the regulation of public affairs such as court trials) … But law is also broader than morality in the sense that laws of state contain many positions which have absolutely nothing to do with morality.[71]

As I discuss in the next chapter, the mutual tie between law and morality that Sergeevsky described here as 'juridical common sense' was picked up by Solov'ev and used as the foundation stone in his bid to ground law more fully in morality (though his cue to do so came from Schopenhauer and Kant rather than Sergeevsky whom he never referred to). However, whereas Sergeevsky – and contemporaries shared the same opinion – saw no reason to take this point of coincidence between law and morality in the domain of external relations any further, Solov'ev, by contrast, would use it to construct a fairly comprehensive, if controversial, theory of criminal justice.

Enlightened stewards or innovators?

> In dealing with crime, the legislator should never forget that he is serving the general principles of the state, namely to raise the level of social living conditions nationally, and by the same token promote progress among mankind.
>
> (Tagantsev)[72]

Writing just after the turn of the century, Arsen'ev offered a thumbnail sketch of Russian legal thought as it had developed over the past 30 years. Most first-generation legal thinkers, he argued, recognized that 'a criminal act is a complex one, that it may be studied as a social phenomenon, but that criminal law is first and foremost a juridical science, and, as such, should concentrate on the juridical.'[73] As I have suggested, it was largely because of their inheritance of 'codified custom' that these pioneers of 'legality' tended to latch onto the classical definitions of crime and (just) punishment. They required a classical concept of justice, which admitted of responsibility, thereby recognizing the agency of the criminal, respected the social order, and was free of any pseudo-moralizing. Early reform monographs and articles, in particular, attest a concern to resolve the double inheritance of codified and customary law, both of which obscured the distinction between law and morality and barely differentiated between *pravo* and *zakon*. If, in the former case, this was due to juridical formalism, and in the latter out of ignorance, the upshot was in both instances the same: punitive measures were couched in terms of moral redemption.

Despite Arsen'ev's neat definition, however, first-generation reformers were clearly open to the sociology of crime. As I have argued, the impact in Russia of 'socially driven theories of law' is attested by the body of original literature in which the declared, or readily identifiable, intellectual affiliations of a given author to classical tenets of juridical thought were frequently offset by an undeniable interest in sociological explanations of crime and punishment. That said, once faced by a whole series of new juridical fashions originating in the social sciences – anthropology, sociology, evolutionism, Darwinism, and Spencerism – all being claimed by a younger generation of juridical thinkers as some sort of intellectual birthright, they became protective of their original 'law for law's sake' principles and began polarizing the differences between the 'new' and 'old' schools of thought. Writing in 1893, Sergeevsky accused the 'self-styled new positivists' of producing little more than 'a colourful kaleidoscope of effect making phrases, and shaky hypotheses, the only distinction of which is their risibility'. But he also recognized that in the eyes of those confident enough to challenge the most fundamental principle of law – nulla poena sine lege – his own generation had clearly outlived its time.[74]

Perceived differences expressing a generation gap, trading in labels 'old versus new', 'humanism versus clinical indifference', and the insistence on entrenched oppositions between positivists and classicists that we come across in speeches intended for polemical impact, no matter how persuasive, actually concealed as many shared practical goals as they exposed theoretical rivalries. By the turn of the century, a new generation of legal positivists was already well into the process of revising some of its cruder premises and was laying the foundations for further, more nuanced research in criminology and 'criminal politics' that would colour the contemporary landscape over the next two decades. Responding to developments in Western science as led by Jellinek, Liszt, and the Belgian scholar, Prins, young Russian apologists of the anthropological and sociological schools – a noticeable number of whom were affiliated with the provincial universities Kazan, Kharkov and Kiev – were beginning to challenge the evident reductionism and one-sidedness of these approaches, especially when taken in isolation.[75] Instead of the simplistic explanation of crime as a social phenomenon or as the pre-determined action of a criminal type, the 'new school' of legal positivists offered a more comprehensive picture of crime and punishment. Research papers then analysed 'the psycho-physical particularities of the criminal-degenerate' or 'the contemporary significance of psychopathology for the jurist'. Crime, they argued, was a social and psychological phenomenon, but it was also juridical and moral.[76] Like their 'classical' masters, they rejected as primitive, 'inhuman' even, denials of free will, but against the old style, and in their eyes, restrictive law for law's sake approach; 'new positivists' urged that even greater emphasis be placed on social responsibility both as a means to prevent and heal criminal tendencies:

> The question of human criminality is a very complicated and difficult one. It is not just a juridical or an anthropological issue, but is to a greater extent a social question. As a phenomenon, human criminality should be of equal interest to the criminalist, the sociologist, the moralist and the psychiatrist.[77]

Presented as a natural outgrowth of the legal positivism of the 1870s, representatives of this new current insisted on the lasting importance of some of their early findings but were just as eager to distance themselves from some of its more outlandish claims that had worked to their discredit:

> Social conditions, as factors of criminality, are hugely significant, but their impact is indirect rather than direct. Without any doubt – and this is borne out by statistics – the environment, the physical conditions in which one grows up are reflected in one's personality, both in terms of one's physical and psychological attributes, and morally as well.[78]

On the issue of punishment, new positivists endeavoured to correct the inadequacies of both abstract and positivistic theories of social self-defence pioneered by the Lombroso school. The complexities of crime and criminality, they argued, required far more than the existing logic underpinning judicial practice, which, if it answered the social requirement of well-being and security by restricting the offender's freedom, failed to engage the fundamental criteria of restorative justice, namely measures of isolation, labour, and education 'in the widest sense of the term'.[79] Drawing on the criminal typology developed by the anthropological school, from recidivists to one-off incidents, new positivists thus updated the corresponding penalties with proposals covering farming colonies, reimbursement through labour or fines, suspended sentences, and early release.

With the exception of references to the moral component, which, as I argue in Chapter 5, was gradually brought back into studies of crime in the 1890s and 1900s, it is not hard to see that the underlying thrust of the new positivist credo quoted here bears the hallmark of Foinitsky's teaching. Indeed, as Arsen'ev noted, the school around Foinitsky 'had not said its final word'. Not only did it attract classicists into its ranks, it also found interlocutors across Europe.[80] In other words, Russian legal theory at the end of the nineteenth century was in fact, as Arsen'ev tacitly conceded, a hybrid of trends that had succeeded fairly well in generating a uniform terminology encapsulating a set of goals and principles that were shared by all reformers. It was against this background that Solov'ev, as an amateur juridical thinker, would develop his own theory concerning the moral foundations of law and their application to criminal justice. First, he witnessed a polemical divide between a slighter older generation of established figures, who, even if they had advocated a law for life's sake principle, were written off by their juniors as old cart horses in the age of steam. Second, he followed and commented on the growing quantity of exploratory research carried out within the ever-expanding parameters of social science with its declared goal of instituting a more humane penal system. Solov'ev absorbed all these influences, bringing them to bear on his own original project to 'justify the good'.

4 Solov'ev as a philosopher of law

> Real justice and mercy to criminals without injury to the innocent – here is the most explicit and complete proof of the true connection between law and morality, or the true concept of law as the balance of two moral interests: the public good and individual freedom. Without this connection or this balance, a humane corrective establishment for criminals (…) is just nonsense.
>
> (*Law and Morality*, 1897)[1]

Shortly after Solov'ev's death in July 1900, tributes from close friends and colleagues on the editorial board of the *European Messenger* were printed in the journal's chronicle section.[2] As 'obituary notices', these personal reminiscences concentrated on the loss of a remarkable, unique spirit – a creative genius, brilliant polemicist, and a rare example of moral integrity. In private correspondence, they openly mourned the loss of a dear friend: 'I cannot come to terms with the thought that he is no more', wrote Koni, 'that we will never again hear his pure, child-like, infectious laughter, never again see that prophet-like head of his, nor hear his original and sublime (*vozvyshennye*) thoughts.'[3] Solov'ev was among the few who had the courage to announce their religious convictions in a society that was losing sight of human decency and moral rectitude and which was falling prey to increasing brutality (evidenced, it was noted, by practices in courts of law). As Koni saw things, should Solov'ev's message, unfashionable as it was, go unheard in the desert, it would be an irreparable loss:

> One might be quite critical of Solov'ev, or Tolstoi for that matter, but life today is sullied to such an extent by all kinds of rascals, by self-satisfied nobodies and predators on the nation's honour and wellbeing, that the loss of men such as Solov'ev, or indeed, Tolstoi, cannot be passed over in silence.[4]

That Koni paired Solov'ev with Tolstoi might strike the reader today as rather odd, and, indeed, an insult to both men, particularly since Solov'ev, as a staunch advocate of institutional structures, was appalled by Tolstoi's pacifist–anarchic credo and went to great lengths to discredit it. But it was a perception shared by many contemporaries, and intended as a tribute in recognition of their roles as public spokesmen in a number of key episodes that had marked their lives as eyewitnesses. Two events, in particular, brought them together on a shared platform of protest: the execution of Alexander II's assassins in 1881 and the famine that ravaged the countryside causing many unnecessary deaths a decade later. As a *philosophe engagé*, Solov'ev was deeply committed to social reform and campaigned on a variety of issues: he defended the Jewish community at a time of renewed pogroms, attacked nationalist chauvinism, and took up the cause of various minority group interests, including the question of women's rights. But it was his first-hand experience of the famine in 1891 that proved a watershed in his intellectual trajectory.[5] Like Tolstoi, Solov'ev helped organize relief aid for the victims of the famine in Southern Russia, and it was here, in this very real and appalling context of human misery, that the leit-motif of his social thought – all human beings have the right to a dignified existence – first muted in the 1880s acquired its particular force:

> The raison d'être of society in relation to its members is to assure for each not solely a material livelihood, but moreover a *dignified* livelihood. (…) Poverty beyond a certain threshold (…) is contrary to human dignity and therefore incompatible with true public morality.[6]

The shock of this experience prompted him to review his theocratic projects in terms of the more practical concerns of social justice, and in the years that followed, he presented a theory of economic–social welfare and legal rights that would become key chapters, if disputed, in *Justification of the Good*.

Solov'ev's definition of a dignified existence went beyond the obligation to satisfy basic physical needs: 'Everybody should have the means of existence and sufficient physical rest secured to him, and he should also be able to enjoy *leisure* for the sake of his spiritual development.'[7] The state, he believed, must allow the person freedom with regard to civil rights and private conduct. In addition, he counselled a form of government activity that, in some respects, bore similarities to the post-war welfare state. As Judith Zimmerman notes, 'by adding to the list of fundamental civil rights a new one, the right to a dignified (*dostoinyi*) existence, Solov'ev actually solicited state involvement in the economic life of the community'.[8]

That Solov'ev was admired by his contemporaries for his compassionate defence of justice – social, moral, political, and legal – is indisputable. But, as a religious–philosophical thinker, he was a lone voice, alienated by opposing Westernizing-Liberal and Slavophile-National conservative factions. The fact that he consistently expressed what, in modern-day terms would be called a 'human rights stand' in the language of Christian and biblical ethics, confounded 'both the religious conservatives on the right, with whom he ostensibly shared a confessional faith, and the secular left, which held his religious convictions suspect'.[9] Solov'ev's deep commitment to the positive principles of the state, and specifically, to the Russian state, estranged him from his liberal interlocutors, just as his polemic against nationalism and his impassioned struggle for human freedom, freedom of conscience, and for moral principles in the life of society and the state had alienated him from his erstwhile Slavophile allies.[10] For Evgeny Trubetskoi, he was misunderstood because his views eluded neat affinities with either camp. The political economist, Petr Struve, put it more bluntly: 'He was a strange phenomenon in Russian society.'[11]

Correspondence and posthumous assessments of Solov'ev's career attest, then, the degree to which he both inspired and perplexed his juridical and liberal-minded colleagues. They acknowledged the seminal importance of his work as a *publitsist* but were baffled by the underlying religious impulse in his philosophical work. If they accepted that it was integral to Solov'ev's 'mystical' vision, it caused havoc and confusion once they engaged with it critically and theoretically. 'Let's talk straight with no offence meant: in our view, Solov'ev was not a great philosopher, and, alone, his philosophical writings would not merit the praise he does in fact deserve.'[12] For Struve, Solov'ev was neither sufficiently critical nor sufficiently metaphysical to join the pantheon of philosophical idealism alongside Berkeley, Kant, Schopenhauer, Lotze, Fichte, Schelling, and Hegel. On the contrary, he should be ranked as a classic for his brilliant polemics with the Slavophiles, his attacks on nationalism, and anti-Semitism. In short, here was an 'original Russian philosopher', whose passing would be sorely felt by those for whom the future of Russian social thought was paramount.[13]

Most 'in memoriam' appraisals of Solov'ev's career included a section on his last major work, *Justification of the Good*, some draft chapters of which had appeared as articles in the *European Messenger* from the mid-90s onwards.[14] Spasovich compared it to

> an enormous temple, constructed with astonishing consistency in a uniform style, rich in carvings and paintings, striking for its finesse down to the smallest detail. The temple is lit with skill, and bathed in the warmth of sincere religious feeling.[15]

If less floridly expressed, Koni's point was much the same: this work was undoubtedly Solov'ev's finest achievement, his most systematic, integral account of the fundamental principles and tasks of moral philosophy, the defining characteristics of which Koni summarized as the inextricable tie between the process of moral perfection in each individual and a concern to ground the social order in the principles of morality and justice, principles which would be safeguarded by the state.[16] However, that Solov'ev conceived the state as a sort of benevolent custodian, which, through its institutions would ensure protection against infractions of one's rights and duties (*prava*/*obyazannosti*) as a good Christian, appalled rather than appealed to his colleagues. For liberal thinkers, such as Koni, who cherished the idea of a limited monarchy, constitutionalism, and rule of law, Solov'ev's preoccupation with the Kingdom of God rather than the organization of temporal power was symptomatic of mutually exclusive priorities and interests separating Solov'ev from his colleagues. Thus, from their perspective, Solov'ev's concept of a Christian state could at best be regarded as utopian, at worst archaic, to be taken on board, or rejected as such. The liberal conservative, Boris Chicherin, with whom Solov'ev was drawn into a double round of polemics, deplored it as a potential throwback to the Inquisition.

If the Solov'evian 'worldview' could be taken with a grain of salt, unacceptable in their eyes was their friend's handling of specialist fields, such as the economy, state policy, and law. With its grounding in the Christian principle of compassion (*zhalost'*), Solov'ev's social ethical world view framed the specific solutions he proposed in these domains, only to produce, for his critics, flawed arguments that could be easily picked apart. Even in his revised version of an article on Solov'ev's concept of economic welfare, Struve, newly converted to metaphysical idealism, felt obliged to maintain the same levels of attack as before:

> Entering the economic sphere in a carefree, light-hearted manner is not advisable, and could turn to one's serious disadvantage. Such have been the fortunes of our metaphysician. He has shown himself to be reckless both philosophically, and in economic theory, and is even lacking in good taste on occasion (. . .) If there's anything original in these arguments it's either mistakes, or that naïve tone of his in which he reiterates the mistakes and banalities of others.[17]

While Solov'ev, the economist, was easy bait for criticism, Solov'ev the juridical theorist met with bewildered dismay, his loss of perspective explained as a side-effect of the neurosis and emotional unease that troubled him in the last years of his life.[18] If the language in which Solov'ev couched his definitions of crime and punishment generally suggested a familiarity with the terms of classic – and current – 'rationalistic' legalese, by infusing these terms with a Christian spirit, he produced a body of vocabulary with an eerie resonance of the 'logic' of customary law practised in the peasant community: crime is 'lawless' and a 'sin'; the criminal is an 'unfortunate'. As the vocabulary of a religious philosopher, notions of sin, conscience, evil, and repentance were, of course, integral to his justification of the good and his combat with evil. But for the taste of juridical reformers, Solov'ev's juridical lexicon was strangely anachronistic. However, it was the relation between morality and law, which he argued for and which formed the basis of his theory of criminal justice, which became the prime target of criticism for his liberal friends and colleagues. For Koni, the chapter devoted to this question was the Achilles heel in what otherwise he esteemed a masterpiece. Solov'ev's definition of law/right (*pravo*) as 'a minimal coercive morality' (*kak o minimal'noi prinuditel'noi nravstvennosti*) respected neither its 'historical provenance' nor its essence; he confused the concepts of law and morality to the detriment of both.[19] This view was shared by most reviewers of the book, as I discuss here. Only Spasovich seemed willing to accept Solov'ev on his own terms, without conditions or excuses, pointing out that, in conversation, Solov'ev had openly admitted that he was no specialist in either fields of law or the economy. Rather, his goal had always been to demonstrate the practical implications of his 'Christian politics'.[20] Otherwise Arsen'ev, though he did mock Solov'ev by saying he was occasionally given to writing 'abracadabra',[21] also, more charitably, advised suspension of disbelief on this point, reminding the reader that the terms of the law/morality relation as Solov'ev defined them stemmed from the overall thrust of his objective ethics ('the sole *moral foundation of society* is the principle of human dignity'[22]) and should be read as such. Arsen'ev suggested that interpretation of Solov'ev's remarks on punishment be confined to the closed context of his long-standing differences with Lev Tolstoi. Solov'ev contended that the moral principle 'requires a practical counteraction to crime', but his definition of this counteraction (that is, punishment) as 'the lawful and obligatory means of an active love of fellowmen which lawfully and coercively restricts extreme manifestations of malicious will' could easily be interpreted as a veiled inversion, and, by implication, as a dismissal of Tolstoi's 'law of love versus the force of law'.

Since Solov'ev privileged the field of law and, specifically, criminal justice as examples of applied ethics, the responses his theory elicited, discussed below, are very telling of the differences and affinities that both separated him from, yet, at once, drew him towards, his liberal Westernizing interlocutors, more generally. All the while paralleling contemporary debates, even borrowing some of its findings, and fending off some of its more preposterous claims with the wisdom of juridical classics, Solov'ev's purpose was not to enter the territorial waters of his professional peers. If his concept of the moral foundations of punishment and the criminal as a moral human being complemented current concerns to institute the 'individualization' of punishment, his emphasis on the moral personhood of the criminal set him apart from the anthropological and sociological schools for whom the hallmark of criminal agency was biological, neuro-physiological, and social. For Solov'ev, these overlooked that which constitutes 'the peculiarity of man as an individual agent: the capacity to perceive purely moral reasons experienced in practice as the voice of conscience and as a sense of repentance'.[23] Thus, in practice, if, like Foinitsky, Solov'ev believed in the importance of social reintegration once a convict had completed his term, unlike his peers he counselled that the process of reintegration itself involve recognition on the part of the transgressor that something more than the mere violation of a rule was at issue and that he had simply been unlucky in being caught. Rather, for Solov'ev, it was a question of coming to terms with a fundamental wrong: crime was a sin, for which expiation by the transgressor and forgiveness by the victim were the key.

Origins and development of Solov'ev's juridical thought

> Three things are absolutely inadmissible in a Christian state: first, wars inspired by national egoism, conquests that raise up one nation on the ruins of another, because the dominant interest for the Christian state is universal

> solidarity or Christian peace; next, civil and economic slavery which makes one class the passive instrument of another; and finally, vindictive penalties (especially the death penalty) which society applies to the guilty individual, using him as a means of public safety. By committing a crime the individual shows that he regards society merely as a means, and the neighbour as an instrument of his egoism. One must not respond to this injustice by committing another, by abasing human dignity in the criminal himself, reducing him to the level of a passive instrument by a penalty, which excludes his improvement and regeneration.[24]

Solov'ev's theory of crime and punishment as touched upon here in this piece banned by the Russian censors, and eventually published in France in 1889, formed an integral part of his 'free theocracy', understood as 'the connecting of all the functions and institutions of society to the love of God'.[25] Elaborated and refined in articles, lectures, and monographs over the course of two decades beginning in the early 1880s, core features of immediate relevance to his theory of law and criminal justice remained unchanged, namely the unconditional significance of the person that Solov'ev conceived as a right to be protected by morally grounded social and political institutions. This view of man shaped his understanding of the criminal and the function of punishment, furnishing his critique of the logic of retribution and deterrence and bolstering his arguments in favour of compassion both for the victim and for the perpetrator of a crime.

Legal systems, Solov'ev argued, reflect and are reflected in the nature of the state. In an early piece, *The Spiritual Foundations of Life: On the Christian State and Society* (1882–1884), he sketched an ideal criminal justice as a 'synthesis' (not unlike a Hegelian *Aufhebung*) emerging from the opposed principles on which the Western pagan and Eastern despotic states were built. The first was a model of a 'state of law', while the second relied for its power on the practice of subordination and submission. Solov'ev's free theocratic ideal would reconcile the demands of law – a fulcrum balancing the competing forces of rights and interests – with those of a transcendent authority, which, unlike the Eastern kingdoms, would engage voluntary submission for the realization of three main goals: the propagation of Christianity; a peaceful drawing together of nations, and 'an arrangement of societal relations in accordance with the Christian ideal within each nation', what elsewhere he called 'free communality' (*svobodnaya obshchinnost'*).[26] Solov'ev illustrated this last point with reference to criminal justice. Already here, if somewhat naïvely and clumsily formulated, he attempted to unmask the fallacious and inhumane thinking behind retribution and deterrence, suggesting that punishment be conceived as an occasion for moral recovery. While he recognized that the modern function of punishment was to protect state interests, and that criminal justice was a state privilege, he sought to balance these secular prerogatives with the Christian principles of forgiveness and compassion: 'The Church mainly looks not at the lawlessness of the criminal and his harm to others, but at his own wretchedness, at the aggregate of the internal and external, mental and physical conditions which led the person to sin.' In Solov'ev's projected Christian state, punishment would both protect state interests and minister to the moral needs of the condemned man: 'Protecting itself against the criminal, and in no case justifying the crime, a Christian state must not forget about the criminal's human soul, which is capable of rebirth.'[27]

If Solov'ev's early ideas of criminal justice stemmed from his original social ideal of free theocracy 'as organised morality', his actual handling of law as a normative concept (*pravo*) that he developed in his doctoral thesis *Critique of Abstract Principles* (1877–1880) contained, as Walicki notes, little that was original.[28] His definition of law as freedom conditioned by equality (*pravo est' svoboda, obuslovennaya ravenstvom*), even if Chicherin challenged its validity, was indebted to certain rational legalist premises firmly anchored in the Kantian tradition: human beings are to be treated as free, rational agents, equal before the law. Undoubtedly, Solov'ev's belief in the absolute significance of human dignity also found support in the categorical imperative ('treat people as an end, never as a means'). But it was his greater indebtedness, as Walicki and others have noted, to Schopenhauer's account of law as negative justice working through discipline and constraint that left him with no option other than to oppose it to morality: law merely expresses the negative aspect of the moral principle.[29] Adopting Schopenhauer's formula, *neminem laede* (harm no one), Solov'ev defined law in negative terms: justice merely ensures personal freedom and formal equality. It followed that in a lawful state, members could not be obliged to help each other; on the strength of its laws (*zakon*), such a state could only demand that 'no one does any harm to anyone' (*nikto nikogo ne obizhal*).[30] However, missing in these cold-blooded accounts governed by the principle of 'equality' was the Christian principle of love (*caritas*) corresponding to the second part of Schopenhauer's formula 'to the best of your ability, help' (*imo omnes, quantum potes, juva*). It is this second principle that affords a sense of community or unity among members and provides a normative end or goal. In contrast to law, the negative sphere, morality, as the positive sphere, encompasses a willing fulfilment of duties in the name of the Christian ideal of love.[31]

In this early work, Solov'ev did not develop the relation between law and morality any further, though he did, inchoately, recognize their shared grounding in the principle of justice (*spravedlivost'*), suggesting a relation of degree rather than difference.[32] It was only in *Justification of the Good* that the relation acquired greater significance as part of a more ambitious project to construct a theory of 'objective ethics'.

The story of how Solov'ev came to write his last major work is well documented. In 1894, when he began work on a new edition of the *Critique*, he soon realized that his ideas had evolved to such a degree that it was better to write a new book instead. He now rejected Schopenhauer's balancing act with the negative ethic of justice on one end of the scales and the positive ethic of charity on the other to argue, as Walicki puts it, that 'justice and charity have a common root in the altruistic principle of compassion'.[33] In the light of his revised theory of morality and law, Solov'ev would quite forcefully argue that, should a positive law (*zakon*) be at odds with moral awareness of the good, then, *a priori*, this law no longer meets the essential requirements of law (*pravo*) itself. And the examples he privileged in this regard, once again, came from the field of criminal justice.

In addition, he incorporated his reformulated relation between law and morality into a separate monograph, *Law and Morality* (1897), which dealt specifically with criminal justice both in its historical development and as a theoretical issue. While he retained some of the formulas he had originally devised in the *Critique* (for example, law as freedom conditioned by equality), he also incorporated some substantial revisions and additions, elaborated with reference to current criminal law theory, notably, the sociology of crime, and criminal anthropological premises defended by Dril'.

As in the *Critique*, Solov'ev introduced the moral component of law with reference to Schopenhauer's formula:

> The concern of the state, as it is acknowledged by all, is to ensure that each not violate the balance with the advantages of others, not eliminate another's interest within those boundaries in which interest is right. Thus, a requirement of authority from those subjected to it is a general requirement of justice: *neminem laede*. Therefore, law is not determined by the concept of utility, but contains in itself a formal moral principle also.

From here, he went on to explore the relation between natural/positive law and morality as a set of distinct, yet clearly, complementary domains. As he saw it, the relation could be broken down to three main points: (1) *law is the lowest boundary or a certain minimum of morality equally binding for all*; (2) the essential objective of (positive) law is *the guaranteed implementation in practice of a certain minimum of good* or an actual elimination of a certain amount of evil; and (3) the requirement of moral perfection as an intrinsic condition presupposes free or voluntary performance. Inversely, 'the outward implementation of a certain order in accordance with law (...) allows direct or oblique *coercion*'. He then combined these features to arrive at what was to become a highly contested definition of law in its relation to morality: *law is the coercive requirement of the realization of a certain minimum good or of an order that does not allow certain extreme manifestations of evil.* He supplemented this definition with a second formula for positive law or coercive justice as a historical and socially relevant phenomenon even though, as Solov'ev himself claimed, 'natural law is essentially at the same time also positive law': *Law is the historically dynamic determination of a coercive equilibrium between two moral interests – the formal–moral interest of individual freedom and the material moral interest of the common good.* In other words, as an interstice between morality and positive law, *pravo* conjoins with morality to test the validity of codified laws.[34]

On the strength of this argument, Solov'ev believed that the moral dimension of *pravo* should always be accounted for in the elaboration of laws, and, as he had done in his earlier writings, he illustrated this point with reference to criminal justice, arguing, rather intriguingly and paradoxically perhaps, that certain positive laws should be abolished, not so much out of a sense of human compassion, as one might expect – Solov'ev had, of course, gone down that route in his unsuccessful appeal to Alexander III in 1881 – but because such laws failed to meet the moral criteria 'inscribed' in the notion of *pravo*. Punishment by outright suppression of supposed criminals, such as capital punishment and life sentences – the rationale of retribution and deterrence – was, he argued, wrong from a juridical point of view, precisely because it upsets the balance of moral interests between personal freedom and the common good, which *pravo* is meant to uphold. In *Justification of the Good*, he put it in these terms:

> The common good must, in one way or another, be the good of this man. But, should he be deprived of the possibility of free action, that is, deprived of the possibility of the good, then the good ceases to be a good for him. By becoming a partial interest, the good loses the right to limit personal freedom (...). Here we see (...) how moral claims coincide fully with the essence of law. In general, although law, in exercising constraint so as to guarantee a minimum good, differs from morality in the strict sense, through its very practice of constraint it actually respects the demands of morality, and must in no way enter into conflict with the latter. This is why we can be sure that, should a positive law be at odds with the moral consciousness of the good, then, *a priori*, this law no longer meets the essential requirements of law (*pravo*) itself.[35]

In *Law and Morality*, as well as in a separate article on punishment ('The Principle of Punishment from a Moral Point of View'[36]), Solov'ev dismantled the logic of these doctrines from two sides at once, echoing some of the arguments available in contemporary juridical theory, but also drawing on the law/morality relation given here. He knocked down the theory of retribution in a single blow, pointing out that, in the instance of the death penalty, the true restitution of a violated right, at the heart of this theory, obviously does not occur: 'As the Holy Fathers observed, it is not even possible for God Himself to make it so that what has happened did not take place.' As a reinforcing motif, deterrence was equally ineffective, because, by definition, all criminals – whether professionals or those guilty of crimes of passion – are immune to the idea of deterrence as a punitive motif. If the former, as professionals, simply have no track with state measures of deterrence/prevention, the latter have relinquished the basic instinct of self-preservation and 'drowned out the voice of reason'. Solov'ev's more serious objection to deterrence, however, stemmed from the intrinsic worth he ascribed to every human being. In stark contrast, the 'means to an end' logic of deterrence represented a violation of this basic human right:

> In the theory of deterrence, the punished criminal is ultimately considered, to all intents and purposes, as only a means of instilling fear in others for the sake of the preservation of public security. In fact, if the criminal's own

> good entered into the purpose of criminal law – keeping him from committing a crime by the fear of the threat of punishment – then once it is already committed, this motive falls away on its own. And from this point of view, the criminal who is punished is left only as a means for the deterrence of others, that is, for a purpose extraneous to himself, which now directly contradicts an absolute moral requirement. From this aspect, deterrent punishment would be permissible only as a threat; but a threat never acted upon loses all meaning. Thus the principle of deterrent punishment could be morally permissible only under condition of its uselessness, and it can be materially useful only under condition of its immoral application.[37]

The example of criminal justice not only served Solov'ev in his theoretical arguments; in the last chapter of *Law and Morality* entitled 'A model for Criminal Justice', he presented his personal view of what, ideally, would constitute an impartial system of justice (*pravosudie*), proposing a number of concrete measures for a more humane and modern penal system. Governed by 'norms', criminal legal procedure should uphold two ideas: 'the real defence of the victim (*ugrozhaemoe litso*) and the possible correction of the criminal'. Punishment was to be based on 'the unconditional significance or worth of the human person'; its purpose was to restore to both victim and accused 'a violated truth' (*pravda*).[38] While he accepted that, in certain cases, the social reintegration of the offender might not be possible (the anthropologists, of course, condoned capital punishment in the case of certain innate criminal types immune to curative measures), Solov'ev believed that it was feasible to place everyone in conditions permitting the greatest possible opportunity for correction. Concretely, his model for criminal justice entailed individualization of punishment (a 'holy truth') with provision for conditional sentences; deprivation of freedom (including a period of solitary confinement prior to the court hearing, which Solov'ev believed would allow the accused to reflect upon his deed, and hopefully, repent); and compensation, assured by the income derived from forced labour paid to the victim, a measure which he esteemed beneficial to the convicted criminal as well. In addition, he urged – and none of his juridical peers would disagree – that the courts become a forum for expert examination by learned jurists, 'a kind of commission of criminal legal advisors', thereby breaking with current practice, which, despite the reforms, continued mechanically to hand down predetermined punitive sentences listed in the statute books.[39]

Through his recommendations, Solov'ev was clearly seeking to align, though never quite match, his theory of law and morality with select aspects of current legal theory. This is evident in his definitions of the criminal and crime. Albeit eschewing the extremes of criminal anthropology and the current fashion for rejecting the idea of free will, Solov'ev's moral perspective, particularly in terms of its construction, complemented the contemporary accent on the subjective side of crime: the impression is one of transposing positivist phrasing to a new, moral key. Accordingly, the criminal is a person who had 'consciously evaded' the minimal requirements of good conduct as instituted in the criminal law 'for the sake of the security of the human community'. Crime

> is the result of an inner process in which there is always at least one instant of actual decision, that is, of the conscious rejection of a moral norm, of the conscious repudiation of good inner influences, and of the conscious giving over of oneself to a malevolent deed.[40]

Solov'ev's list of recommendations concerning sentencing likewise attest a familiarity with positivist schools of thought that placed the criminal, as opposed to the crime, in the spotlight. Pre-empting objections among jurists to his suggestion that moral recovery means to intrude into the criminal's inner world, Solov'ev argued that, by the act of his crime, the criminal 'has laid bare his inner world, and has need of a reverse influence in order to be returned to his normal boundaries'. On this point, he even invited his potential critics to imagine what would happen were they to apply their principle of 'non-interference' on the schooling of children or the insane in public hospitals. Second, by moral recovery, he meant 'self-correction' prompted by favourable conditions and assistance.[41] Though he failed to specify further on this point, he, presumably, did not necessarily mean enforced attendance at prison Bible classes – the current practice in Imperial Russia, which, as contemporaries complained, seemed to do more harm than good.

Besides resonances at the theoretical level, Solov'ev's proposals closely paralleled those put forward by specialists – Russian and European – at international meetings of criminologists. The coincidences between congressional reports and recommendations, many of which were reviewed in the *European Messenger*, which Solov'ev obviously read, and his own guidelines suggest, again, that he was anxious to demonstrate the feasibility of his 'moral–legal principle', balancing the rights and duties of the convict with those of society. Inverting the simple equation – poor prison conditions breed crime – the chief message of these congresses was resoundingly clear: for criminality to diminish, a prison culture based on humane principles was needed; punishment alone (*kara*) could not guarantee society protection of its material and spiritual well-being.[42] The need for an appropriately trained prison staff (currently sorely wanting) was widely recognized as key to encouraging the convicts' moral recovery. Likewise, Solov'ev's model punishment

> is reduced to the conditional restriction of the criminal's individual and property rights as the natural result of crime. This is what society should *take* from the criminal; but in place of this it should *give* him active assistance in his correction and moral regeneration. It is precisely from this aspect that a radical reform of prison institutions to transform them into moral-psychiatric establishments is particularly essential.[43]

But for all the coincidences with contemporary penitentiary studies, Solov'ev's own prescription for justice clearly stemmed from his principles of the 'human right to perfection' and 'compassion': even the criminal, having committed a moral wrong, punishable only by God, should not be denied the possibility of moral recovery.

> Thus, according to its true sense, punishment is something multifaceted, but its various aspects are identically conditional upon the common moral principle of love of fellowmen, which embraces both the offender and the one offended. The one suffering from a crime *has the right* to defence and compensation as far as possible; society *has the right* to security; the criminal *has the right* to instruction and correction. A lawful counteraction to crime on the part of organized society or the State, in agreement with the moral principle, must realize or at least always have in view the equal implementation of these rights.[44]

Solov'ev before the law: assessments by contemporaries

Perhaps unfairly, given that so much of what Solov'ev wrote on the subject actually coincided with current penitential theory and concrete proposals for reform, his punitive model was cited as a naïve portrait 'of a peace-loving fraternity' among inmates sentenced for murder, theft, arson, and rape.[45] Clearly, the 'sober politics' of the jurist-critic, Mokrinsky, the author of these comments, stood in stark contrast with the 'principles' of the moral philosopher: 'To speak of correction as the universal aim of punishment (...) is like dreaming of castles in fairy stories.' Mokrinsky categorically ruled out the possibility that prisons might be transformed into institutions of moral correction. 'Prisons', he wrote, 'do not teach the rapist to respect women. They do not instil moral feelings in child molesters, and have absolutely no effect at all on those convicted of religious or political crimes.'[46]

If Solov'ev's closest and most sympathetic readers found his ideas far-fetched, or simply naïve, his greatest intellectual rival, the liberal-conservative, Boris Chicherin (1828–1904), set about dismantling the entire edifice of his social ethics, stone by stone, sparing him nothing. This was not the first time that Chicherin had responded to Solov'ev's views: in 1880, he gave a lengthy critique of Solov'ev's doctoral thesis, *A Critique of Abstract Principles*, a study which contained the seeds of Solov'ev's later monograph.[47] However, that Chicherin resumed his quarrel nearly 20 years later was in part due to a sentiment of lese-majesty. In the introduction to *Law and Morality*, Solov'ev had drawn an admittedly crude caricature of opposing attitudes to the role of law in society and its relation to morality. One, he claimed, rejects any intrusion of the juridical in order to safeguard 'the purity of the moral interest'; the other refuses any link between the two in the name of law 'as an absolute principle'. While Tolstoi's message of 'non resistance to evil' and 'the law of love' represented for Solov'ev the first attitude, the second, legalistic, but amoral stance, found its clearest expression in the work of Chicherin. For this insult, alone, Chicherin no doubt felt compelled to reply. Their quarrel, which was first published in the leading philosophical journal, *Questions of Philosophy and Psychology*, and subsequently as a separate brochure, was angry and embittered, involving below the belt personal insults as theoretical premises (Solov'ev's notably), shattered under a barrage of principled, but well-reasoned objections. In many respects, though, their disagreement was little more than hair-splitting, as, indeed, is implied by the title Solov'ev chose for his initial reply, 'False Criticism' (*Mnimaya Kritika*). For both men, the concepts of freedom of conscience and the autonomy of the secular spheres were of central importance, and they each contended an inner link between morality and law originating in man's nature as a rationally free being. But, for Chicherin, exemplar in Solov'ev's eyes of rational legalism, morality, and law, in practice, related to different spheres of human activity – one, to man's inner impulses and conscience, while the other regulates external freedoms among individuals: 'each of these spheres have their own requirements and regulations (*zakony*)'.[48] Thus, despite a shared starting point, the resulting definitions of law that each formulated – a fulcrum balancing two moral interests of individual freedom and the common good, and law (*pravo*) as 'freedom determined by codes (*zakon*)' – announced two sharply conflicting world views that could never be reconciled.

As an adherent of a Kantian- and Hegelian-inspired concept of law according to which guilt and responsibility for a crime are the only issues falling within the competence of the courts, Chicherin was understandably impatient with Solov'ev's theory. Solov'ev's outright dismissal of absolutist theories of punishment was as untenable as it was unsubtle. Granted, Chicherin's criticism here was as much a sign of his wistful regret at the usurpation of classical legal theory by sociological trends as it was intended to undermine his rival's view of punishment as the moral rehabilitation of the offender. For Chicherin, punishment was not about repentance; rather its purpose was to restore respect for the law and its binding powers that had been violated: 'An encroachment on another person's rights entails certain losses (*umalenie*) of one's own. Such is the law (*zakon*) of justice, the expression of which is punishment of the criminal.'[49] Necessarily, therefore, the function of the court was to ensure restitution:

> If, in recent times, this theory has been reneged, if many jurists refuse it, then, this is down to the rejection of metaphysics, indeed all philosophy, the consequence of which has been to shake the philosophical foundations of law itself. Justice has been dismissed as metaphysical invention, law is reduced to partiality, morality to utility; the function of the court has been turned into an instrument of social defence.[50]

If, at one level, Chicherin's criticism attests a fundamental clash of world views – the sober realist versus the mystic – his more punctual observations were hefty blows indeed, belittling both Solov'ev's originality and depth of juridical knowledge. For one, he made short shrift of Solov'ev's definition of law as a minimum of morality, asking, tongue firmly in cheek, how was one to quantify the unquantifiable: 'can it be that the unconditional can be carved up into small pieces and administered in small doses?'[51] Most of his criticism, however, consisted in an unsparing exposure of Solov'ev's poor grasp of juridical textbook basics, namely his confusion of moral and legal obligations and his failure to differentiate between the subjective and objective meaning of law (*pravo*):

> Helping others may be the consequence of social obligation, in which case, there can be no talk of right or due, since it may be the free action of my own will. Such an act is not one of justice, rather charity. Failing to distinguish between these two principles, Mr. Solov'ev seems to think that to every moral obligation corresponds an extraneous law (*chuzhoe pravo*). On this basis he reasons that our enemies have the right to our love, because Christ instructed us to love our enemies. In the same vein one could argue that a thief, having stolen my overcoat, has the right to my shirt, because Christ so commanded.

If taken too far, he cautioned, the outcome of Solov'ev's premises risked turning the premises themselves upside down: the obligation to be moral is immorality (*prinuzhdenie k nravstvennosti est' beznravstvennost'*).[52] The second flaw risked serious muddling of civil suits with criminal acts. Dotting the i's and crossing the t's, Chicherin explained that, in a subjective sense, law implies, for example, a person's right to a property, but *pravo* is at once a general norm according to which a person's rights are defined. It follows that 'a person may break a law, without however infringing upon the general principle. In the given instance the latter does not apply. As such, it entails a civil suit and is not a criminal infraction.'[53]

For Chicherin, Solov'ev's definition of law as 'freedom conditioned by equality' (a definition which he had retained from *Kritika*) was also faulty. Between a father and son, officer and foot soldier, the relation is, of course, not one of equality, but one of authority, submission, and obedience. If freedom is an essential component of law (*pravo*), as Chicherin, like Solov'ev, contended, then its field of operation must be delineated by the law (*zakon*):

> The freedom of which man disposes within the limits of the law (*zakon*) is right (*pravo*) in a subjective sense; laws that delimit this freedom imply right in an objective sense. In each case, the basic concept here is freedom. It follows that, in order to determine philosophically the relation of law (*pravo*) to morality, as Mr Solov'ev is seeking to do, it is necessary to return to the concept of freedom, uncover its source in the self-determination of the human will, and to study the various realms – inner and outer – of its application. Only in so doing is it possible to establish the relationship between the two realms. Dealing with the external manifestations of freedom, the jurist need not concern himself with the metaphysical question of free will … but for the philosopher to circumvent this is unthinkable, since this alone serves as the foundation for his claims. Incidentally, Mr Solov'ev expulses this question from his moral philosophy. Consequently, in his work, the concept of freedom loses its meaning.[54]

That Solov'ev endeavoured to construct ethics without recourse to metaphysics was, in Chicherin's opinion, the fatal mistake that ultimately foiled many of the otherwise thought-provoking arguments in this work of intellectual quirkiness. Solov'ev's attempt to ground all social institutions in the moral principle was symptomatic of his philosophical recklessness. The sticking point in his quarrel with Solov'ev was that, if in practice the latter endorsed pluralism, that is, he recognized the roles of state, law, economy etc., at the theoretical level he situated the secular spheres in an all-inclusive vision of the good and higher truth. By contrast, Chicherin maintained that the state develops according to its own rules as the historical, outer layer of human existence, while moral questions relate to the metaphysical sphere as the inner realm of human life.[55] Law, therefore, belongs to the first of these spheres: law

> constitutes the necessary conditions for human society to satisfy a person's natural striving for wellbeing. Within limits established by laws a man may dispose of his rights as he pleases – morally or immorally – since it has no bearing on legislation. In fact, juridical laws not only permit, but actually encourage immoral behaviour.

The example Chicherin gives is that of credit payment: a moneylender is lawfully empowered to demand his money regardless of the poverty or ill-health by which his borrower might be afflicted. By contrast, 'the moral law has no coercive power. It concerns one's conscience uniquely (*lichnaya sovest'*); only here might it exercise its demands.'[56]

Generally, Chicherin's hard-hitting critique, even if biased by his rigid adherence to Kantian and Hegelian theories of law and the state, did succeed in exposing Solov'ev's utopianism and other-worldly reverie. The philosopher's reply only reinforces this impression. Solov'ev seemed particularly vexed – given his tone, which oscillated between defensiveness and sarcasm – by the suggestion that, failing to separate the historical–social–legal and inner moral spheres, Solov'ev's moral principle as the foundation of all social institutions (political, economic, legal) contained a coercive dimension (*prinuzhdenie*): if taken to extremes, Chicherin had warned, Solov'ev's model of social organization could serve as a template for a latter-day Inquisition. Solov'ev's parry, namely coercive measures would be minimal in a society in which 'the good reigns' (*tsarstvuet dobro*), is one striking example of a lingering utopianism in his work and of his inability to counter the force of his opponent's argument:

> When I speak of coercive good, or its coercive organization, I can only have in mind that periphery of good (*okraina dobra*) which is an attribute of the juridical and the safeguarding function of the state, and which both allows, even requires coercion. In a word – I am referring to those minimal requirements of good behaviour, respect for others' rights and interests, where, failure to do so would make life in society and human existence generally impossible.[57]

Were one to take an uncharitable view of Solov'ev's counter argument, one could say that it betokens a naïve understanding of human nature and social organization. Driven by his goal to establish within the absolute and moral principle, 'the internal and full connection between true religion and sound politics', his defence largely failed to register the thrust of Chicherin's attacks, even when these were mere reminders of accepted wisdom, such as the need to observe a clear distinction between the inner sphere of free will – the basis of morality – and constraint as the fundamental role of the state. Indeed, Solov'ev strikes the reader as somehow being cornered, with little option other than to deflect Chicherin's remarks by recourse to sarcasm (for which he later apologized) or simply remain silent, a case in point being Chicherin's just observation that, in practice, law may or may not be 'moral'. Nor did he dispute Chicherin's own definition of law as delimited freedom. But, if he was the mystic and utopian, he was also humane. Where Chicherin spoke of material (and spiritual) well-being, Solov'ev urged human dignity to be defended at all costs. In the legal sphere, this meant condemnation of the death penalty and life sentences, both of which his rival condoned: 'The greater the value attached to human life', Chicherin wrote, 'the greater the punishment should be for taking life away.'[58]

If, ultimately, Solov'ev's social ethics seemed to be leading him into another cosmos, it should not be forgotten that it was triggered by more down-to-earth concerns. Undoubtedly, his engagement with legal theory was prompted by revulsion for the stubborn relics of pre-modern thinking in current legal practice. Despite progress in the penitentiary system, continued use of unnecessary violence and torture (*muchitel'stvo*) could, he said, only be explained as the 'survival of the principles of retribution and deterrence which have outlived their day'. These principles, as Solov'ev saw it, sustained the rationale of the death penalty, life sentences (*bezsrochnoe lichenie svobody*), hard labour, and the appalling living conditions in exile.[59] That said, the depth of Solov'ev's juridical knowledge as such exposed him as a novice and (unwelcome) amateur dabbler in the community of trained jurists. Much of Chicherin's justified criticism of Solov'ev's flawed grasp of fundamental juridical premises was picked up by other reviewers too. Solov'ev's moral philosophy was not fully researched, but merely a descriptive account (*on ne izsleduet a zhivopisuet*); his work was inspired but contained too many unsubstantiated claims; it was sorely lacking in analysis and synthesis.[60] Certainly, some of Solov'ev's statements read as if they had been lifted from secondary school primers: 'things do not have rights'; 'the subject of criminal law is (1) the definition of crimes, and (2) the definition of punishments. The grounds of such definitions are analysed and evaluated by the *science* of criminal law.' Or, they contain uncontested Kantian-inspired formulas, which, again, could be readily sourced from contemporary textbook literature, for example, 'my freedom as a right (not a force) depends on the acknowledgement of the equal right of all others'.[61]

In his dedicatory note to Spasovich, printed as a preface to *Law and Morality*, Solov'ev readily admitted that he was entering the enormous and dreaded camp of juridical science 'alone, as a poorly equipped volunteer'. This self-ascribed status might explain some of his rather more unguarded comments, such as the brash outspokenness with which he attacked absolutist theories, 'connected to the aberrations of such great minds as Kant and Hegel' for their 'ridiculous presuppositions' concerning absolute freedom of choice and capital punishment, which both philosophers condoned, or the way he seemed to champion the reformers' cause, as if reminding them of their check list of goals still to be achieved: 'All are equal before the law; lacking this it is not law.'[62] On another level, Solov'ev occasionally seemed to fall prey to his own bait. For example, by reducing legal thought to the doctrine of revenge (*otmshchenie*) according to which 'only the victim has rights which the criminal has forfeited by breaching the law', and simply opposing this to 'verbal censure' (*slovesnoe vrazumlenie*), the hallmark of Tolstoian anarchism, Solov'ev was, in fact, turning a blind eye to the ever-growing complexities of contemporary juridical science – which he was otherwise so obviously aware of – for the sake of scoring points in a private battle with the great novelist:

> Rejecting any coercion at all, the principle of a passive attitude to criminals excludes not only measures of vengeance and deterrence – in which it is correct – but all measures of crime *prevention*, the necessary *defence* of self and others, and a positive *educational* effect on the criminals themselves.[63]

Using Tolstoi as a handy scapegoat in this way, Solov'ev produced a simplistic argument, which arguably disguised rather than highlighted the innovative qualities of his own, original concept of punishment.

A question of influences

As a novice volunteer, the range of Russian authorities Solov'ev openly cited in building his case was both unsurprisingly restricted – he was no expert – and also rather puzzling: he repeatedly deferred to Spasovich and Tagantsev whose criticism of the Lombroso school for the unacceptable clinical reductionism that its outright rejection of free will involved Solov'ev followed to the letter. Western authorities cited again included undisputed classics, such as A. Feuerbach and Beccaria. But, in the case he built for the moral foundations of punishment, which, he claimed, was supported by current theories, he was strangely (and annoyingly) reticent in identifying intellectual kinsmen by name.[64] From a strategic point of view, one could say that citing intellectual affinities might have shielded him from some of the harsh criticism the monographs received. The juridical thinker, Gabriel Shershenevich was, to my knowledge, the only reviewer to point out that the formulation of law as a minimum of morality was, 'of course', not Solov'ev's invention, but had several adherents.[65] Unfortunately, Shershenevich did not divulge names in his review but invited the reader to consult a footnote in another text, which I have been unable to locate.[66] However, it is clear, from other texts, that Shershenevich regarded Georg Jellinek as the chief architect of the theory of law as a moral minimum.[67]

Walicki speaks of similarities, rather than unacknowledged influence with the work of Jellinek, who, like Solov'ev, sought to demonstrate the religious–moral sources of human rights and spoke of law as a minimum good, even though, ironically, Jellinek himself was in fact regarded as the 'greatest German representative of a broadly conceived legal positivism', perhaps a fact sufficient in itself to explain Solov'ev's reluctance to find his name paired with that of the German scholar.[68] Although a positivist himself, Shershenevich found the definition unsatisfactory, and he put up the standard common-sense counter argument to oppose it. Thus, while he did not challenge the claim that the moral and juridical spheres are inextricably linked (*vzaimnoe otnoshenie*), he rejected the terms of their relation that Solov'ev argued for. For one, it was not clear to Shershenevich, as a reader, what kind of morality Solov'ev had in mind. If it was 'objective', then Solov'ev's argument collapsed on several counts: similar to Chicherin, who took a firm stand against the moralization of law, Shershenevich trammelled the accepted wisdom that law need not be moral at all. It could be 'immoral' (for example, in certain civil suits), just as the juridical sphere could also stand at the helm of morality. To illustrate this last point, Shershenevich referred to the lengthy preparation and formulation process of the Emancipation Act in which legal thinkers actively participated, offering their expertise.[69] If Solov'ev's morality was 'subjective', then the minimum becomes a moveable goal post (one man's minimum is another's maximum). Shershenevich wrote:

> I personally think that the coincidence of juridical and moral norms may be explained by the identity (*tozhestvo*) of their goals, just as the difference between them stems from the distinct means by which their goals are upheld. It follows, that to depict morality and law as concentric circles is completely mistaken.[70]

Solov'ev responded to these comments, succeeding quite masterfully in deflecting most of them, ridiculing Shershenevich, who was ten years his junior, for attributing too much importance to peripheral topics of the book, such as pessimism and suicide, which Solov'ev had only mentioned in passing in the preface. Interestingly, though, Solov'ev was keen to distance himself from the definition of 'law as a minimum good', which most critics – Shershenevich included – had singled out as the weakest part of the book. On this point, Solov'ev insisted that, by ignoring his definitive definition of law as a balance of two moral interests, the thrust of Shershenevich's criticism was grossly misplaced.[71] But, while Solov'ev may have had good reason to object here, the fact of the matter is that none of his immediate critics and reviewers seemed to regard his 'definitive formulation' as the crowning part of his theory; rather, it was the shorter and more memorable formulation that they identified with his theory of applied ethics. As I discuss in the next chapter, in the vast body of literature published between 1905 and the First World War, the formulation, 'law as a minimum good', was usually attributed to Jellinek, with Solov'ev occasionally referenced as a second, 'home grown' proponent of the same idea.

In juridical theory dating from the 1890s, however, challenging positivism narrowly defined (in the style of Ihering's command theory of law, for example) involved a return to early nineteenth-century thinkers as possible models. Works by Solov'ev's contemporary, professor of law at Warsaw University, V.V. Esipov are instructive here. As the author of textbook surveys, bibliographical listings and, especially, popular essays in which he encouraged the pathos of moral sentiment (*zhalost'*) in criminal justice, Esipov's admittedly somewhat pedestrian accounts offer useful insights into the changing landscape of juridical science towards a 'person centred' system of justice that he himself vigorously defended. In addition, his writings allow us to identify possible sources of confirmation, if not influence, for Solov'ev's theory of law as a fulcrum balancing the moral interests of the individual on which in his reply to Shershenevich – although not to Chicherin, where he seems to have been bullied into silence – he placed so much importance.

In an early piece based on his doctoral thesis, *Sin and Crime* (1894), Esipov outlined competing theories on crime, which he broke down into four categories – as a breach of rights, obligations, legislation, or norms.[72] The first theory, associated with Feuerbach and Köstlin, two leading German authorities in the first half of the century, had been cautiously introduced by Spasovich in his 1863 textbook: 'crime is an unlawful infringement of someone's inalienable right, which the state protects'.[73] Esipov named Kistyakovsky as a proponent of the positivist view of crime as a breach of the law (*zakon*), while Tagantsev is cited for his adaptation of the theory of juridical norms developed by Liszt and Binding to his concept of crime as a violation of a juridical norm in its concrete reality (*real'noe bytie*).[74]

Esipov's definition of crime – 'a criminal act is the manifestation, through the violation of rights and obligations, of individual states of criminality' – linked theories of rights and obligations, associated with Köstlin and Rossi, with the 'states of criminality' theory, which Esipov attributed to his former mentor, Foinitsky.[75] Both Köstlin and Rossi explored the proximity of law and morality. For Köstlin, as Esipov paraphrased him, law is a form of morality 'that which in its subjective form is morality, in its objective form is law'. As with all forms of the moral, law constitutes a unity (*edinstvo*) of the general will with individual (*otdel'naya*) will. As an expression of *nepravda* (misconduct, foul), a criminal act consists in divorcing (*otreshenie*) one's individual will from the general in the arena of the world around us. Esipov combined Köstlin's view with Rossi's formulation – a criminal act is breach of a moral obligation. However, while he accepted that Rossi's definition was applicable to civil law and, indeed, found parallels in the work of the Russian jurist, Kalmykov in the 1860s, it was inoperable in the domain of crime, where, Esipov contended, both rights and obligations are obviously violated.[76]

Foinitsky, Köstlin, and Rossi also provided Esipov with the social and moral conceptual markers for his formulation of punishment, but the account he produced of the purpose of justice uncannily pre-empted what was to become the controversial hallmark of Solov'ev's theory of criminal justice three years later:

> the object (*predmet*) of punishment may only be the concrete human person, who has laid bare her inner state of being. Since personal states of criminality vary in different people, so measures of punitive response should, likewise, be individual; punishment as a measure of social coercion must satisfy all the personal conditions (*uslovie*) of the individual.

Punishment must be coercive; its aim should be to force the offender into recognition of his mistakes and to make him a worthy (*dostoinyi*) member of society and the state. More specifically, this entailed – as we have read so many times before and after – provision for conditional sentences and the *patronat* bridging the worlds of incarceration and social freedom. Esipov also placed emphasis on the role of society, which he explicitly grounded in Christian morality, as a provider of both moral and material support in the process of reintegration.[77] In short, 'Criminal law is the science of man; it examines the means whereby a fallen man may be morally reborn.'[78]

If Esipov figured as Solov'ev's fortuitous or incidental precursor, it was probably by virtue of a common pool of influences from which both men took their inspiration. However, after the publication of *Justification of the Good* and *Law and Morality*, in 1897, Esipov openly took his cue from Solov'ev, the acclaimed philosophical master, to substantiate further his own arguments in favour of the moral foundations of law, and justice grounded in compassion (*miloserdie*): 'Christian religion is the ideal model for personal and social ethics or morality.' Esipov's collection of essays, intended for a wider audience, which carried the title *Morality and Law* (1907) was, surely, an allusion that no one could fail to miss.[79] He also paired Solov'ev's name with that of Jellinek. He wrote, 'Nowadays, the link between morality and law is widely accepted: it is discussed in contemporary moral philosophy, and in the latest juridical doctrines, with the exception of anthropology.' Pairing 'the criminal' with 'the immoral' found support in a number of complementary theories, the most renowned of which included Köstlin's theory ('law/*pravo* as morality in the form of objective reality/*bytie*'), Trendelenburg's ('law is the consolidation and development of the moral order'), and Jellinek's ('law as an ethical minimum').[80]

> Law, as Jellinek rightly defined it, is a minimum of morality, necessary for the regulation of human society. On the scales of such a minimum morality, that which may be deemed criminal will only be that which flaunts the established principles of social life. If sin may be a crime, in thought as well as in deed, from a juridical point of view a crime can only be something in breach of law, defined as a minimum of morality, necessary for the preservation of legal order.[81]

Tortuous tautologies, perhaps, but Esipov's point is clear: if law is a minimum of morality, crime, as a violation of this minimum, must, therefore, be immoral. Criminal law, it followed, determines the limit of that which is ethically permissible and that which is immoral.

In a footnote to this definition, Esipov listed Solov'ev's works on the subject – *Justification of the Good, Law and Morality*, and his piece on punishment – as further examples of the same type of argument. On the related issue of a Christian-inspired system of justice, which Esipov addressed in a separate chapter of the 1907 work (originally an essay bafflingly entitled 'Aesthetics and Law'), he added to his list of authorities the names of two French scholars, Charles Gides and Georges Belot. The two qualities of altruism and compassion argued for in their works, 'are powerful motifs, pointing the way towards the construction of a sound theory of moral responsibility for crimes, and correspondingly, of softer punitive measures, and means of prevention'.[82] That said, it was Solov'ev's contribution that stood out for this admirer as the 'clearest and most brilliant' expression of this humanistic turn in criminology – high praise, indeed, but a eulogy that, regrettably for the historian, Esipov decided not to labour with lengthy explanations.[83]

Posthumous acclaim

Thanks to Esipov's more transparent referencing and acknowledgement of influences, one could say that Solov'ev's programme for criminal justice was not entirely original or unique but belonged to a particular – if still marginal – discourse within contemporary debate. Thus, not quite the Osymandias figure crying in the desert, as Chicherin portrayed him, during his lifetime, Solov'ev's ideas were, in fact, shared by a few, possibly incidental, allies and interlocutors that he did not name or may have been unaware of. After his death, however, as his posthumous reputation as philosopher-poet reached iconic status, Solov'ev's ideas gained modest purchase among criminal sociologists whose research into crime as a social phenomenon combined emphasis on criminal psychology with an enquiry into the moral responsibility of society towards its members. His name was referenced in juridical literature, particularly in the new branch of 'criminal politics', to reinforce proposals for prison reform or to bolster arguments against the rationale of punishment as deterrence. But it was primarily as a philosopher of law that he would hold an important place in the revival of idealism and renewed emphasis on natural law spearheaded by figures such as Pavel Novgorodtsev and Sergei Gessen. In particular, it was his attention to the 'moral integrity of the person' that inspired philosophers of law and political thinkers writing after 1900. Not only was it a key in endeavours to conceptualize relations between man and society as a means to frame a socio-legal order, more specifically it operated as a catalyst of change in liberalism and its philosophical foundations.[84]

As a religious–philosophical influence, Solov'ev was acclaimed by a handful of enthusiasts who appropriated his ideas uncritically. Otherwise, reception of his ideas among theoretically minded jurists was diffuse. If Solov'ev 'gave irrefutable proof of the moral character of law in its genuine essence (*podlinnoe sushchestvo*)', his successors, as Bogdan Kistyakovsky noted, nuanced and re-emphasized his 'axiomatic truth' in a whole manner of ways with the result that they often betrayed the finesse with which Solov'ev had developed his views:

> Some teach that law contains a minimum of moral requirements, compulsory for everyone; others go so far as to argue that anything in conflict with moral requirements in existing legal orders is not law; a third group teaches that law and morality will attain full harmony only through the process of cultural development, in the deepening of human self-awareness and in the creation of new social forms.[85]

One interesting illustration of the way Solov'ev's ideas were appropriated to a theory of law and morality (fitting quite neatly in Kistyakovsky's third category just mentioned) is provided by Professor of Philosophy of Law at Tomsk University, Iosif Mikhailovsky. His major work, *An Outline of a Philosophy of Law* was published in 1914. 'As a whole', he wrote, 'law serves the good (...) it forms a part of the general ethical order (...). But from this it does not follow that juridical norms, without exception, possess a moral content.'[86] Mikhailovsky inherited Chicherin's hostility towards positivism, sociology of crime, and 'the invention of criminality'.[87] He was also critical of fellow proponents of natural law, Evgeny Trubetskoi and Novgorodtsev, for endeavouring to invest the metaphysical foundations of law with a content susceptible to change. But if, in some respects, his approach appears to be heavily indebted to the classical thought of Chicherin (for example, he differentiated between inner and outer freedom, and, in the quotation just given, clearly believed that many laws have nothing to do with morality), Mikhailovsky's exploration of the religious–moral foundations of law, together with his arguments pertaining to the ultimate purpose of law, clearly attests a positive assimilation of the Solov'-evian impulse.

Mikhailovsky broke down morality (*nravstvennost'*) and law (*pravo*) into four analogous components, or 'moments', as he called them. Forming two symmetrical halves, they each contained absolute principles (immutable moral principles/natural law) and the refraction of these principles in man's soul as moral conscience and a sense of fairness (*sovest'/spravedlivost'*). Third, these attributes are, in turn, complemented by the subjective, moral outlook (*vozzrenie*) of the individual and his juridical awareness, while fourth, positive morality and positive law concern the practical implementation in some form 'of absolute principles in a given concrete situation'. As a subspecies (*podvid*) of ethics, understood as an all-encompassing theory of human and social behaviour, juridical norms corresponding to the first two 'moments' just mentioned constitute a progressive factor both with respect to social development and in relation to morality, the province of man's inner freedom and conscience:

> The absolute rule of law (*zakon prava*) may be summed up in the formula 'to each his own'. Here of course it is not a matter of universal brotherhood, love, or the unending process of perfection: rather, all that is required is to respect the freedom of others within the confines of a peacefully organized community. And yet this 'rule' is the necessary complement to the law of morality (*zakon nravstvennosti*) – as captured in the dictum be perfect like

your heavenly Father; they are interdependent. Only law (*pravo*) furnishes the person with the possibility to perfect herself freely, to create the conditions for the collective labours of mankind on the path towards the realisation of the Kingdom of God.[88]

Echoing Solov'ev, Mikhailovsky's idea of law, then, was intended as a 'synthesis' (his term) of individual freedom and the social order, in which neither side would be sacrificed as a tool in service to the other.

'In the depths of his soul man has carried a divine spark (*iskra bozhiya*).'[89] The image of man to emerge from Mikhailovsky's theory of law and morality clearly supports a religious world view, and it served him in his sharp criticism of positivist 'instrumentalist' and socially conditioned ethics. In this regard, he singled out Shershenevich for propounding what, in his eyes, amounted to a 'command theory of moral behaviour', grouping his name with those of German social democrats, A. Menger (in his *New Theory of Morality*) and, in particular, Kautsky (*Ethics and Historical Materialism*), for his claim that

morality does not consist in self-directed requirements by the individual, rather, in the demands set by society on man. It is not man that determines how he should relate towards others; rather society determines how one individual should relate to another.[90]

For his part, Mikhailovsky's inclusion of a religious moral component was not only intended as a response to the purely materialistic and reductionist accounts of law by contemporary positivist-socialists; more importantly, it marked an attempt to reckon with the peculiarities of Russian juridical culture. Indeed, with its hallmarks of Solov'ev's socio-political and religious outlook, both directly, and as mediated via his neo-liberal successors, Novgorodtsev and Struve, Mikhailovsky's theory of law and morality figures as a telling example of what Walicki has called the 'spirited intellectual movement in liberal philosophy' and an important aspect of Silver Age culture.[91]

The work of one of Novgorodtsev's pupils, Aleksandr Yashchenko (1877–1934), known to Solov'ev specialists for his detailed monograph of Solov'ev's philosophy of law (*Filosofiya prava Vladimira Solov'eva*, 1912), is, again, entirely symptomatic of liberal theories with a Christian hue elaborated during the age of Russia's religious renaissance.[92] More explicitly than Mikhailovsky, Yashchenko argued for the inseparability of law, morality, and religion, contending that their interrelation is determined by the objective nature of the absolute good or well-being (*dobro, blago*):

The good is grounded in an analysis of human nature and in the mystical act of religious faith. Law is justified by the justification of the good (*opravdyvaetsya opravdaniem dobra*) since it is merely the realisation of the good, one stage in its realisation, just as morality is the living embodiment of religion.[93]

Like Mikhailovsky – and Novgorodtsev – Yashchenko favoured the concept of 'synthesis' in his construction of a juridical theory to oppose the pluralistic approach used by positivists with its 'arbitrary and contrived compilations of sociological, psychological and normative components'.[94] But, classed as one of Solov'ev's successors, Yashchenko's work is perhaps the most flattering vindication of virtually every premise in *Justification of the Good.* In the conclusion to his study of Solov'ev as philosopher of law, Yashchenko listed his elected mentor's main achievements, which he transposed (with little alteration) to his theory of law, power, and the state (*Teoriya Federalizma*, 1912). There one finds carbon copy claims – law is minimum of morality; the basic idea of law consists in establishing the necessary balance between strivings towards personal freedom and social well-being. The indebtedness of Yashchenko's world view to Solov'ev speaks for itself in the following summary of the relation between law and morality:

> The supreme moral goal is the attainment of perfected humanity (the Kingdom of God on Earth). (...) The perfection of mankind is a historical process, the main organizing condition for which is law (*pravo*). (...) Law should not be severed or isolated from morality. The opposition between them that we witness in so much recent literature is merely the insertion of an unnecessary and dangerous split (...) a violent breach of an integral system, a harbinger of strife where instead there should be peaceful collaboration. Law is merely the most secure and guaranteed implementation of moral demands. Social morality acquires life and its force in and through the power of law. Law is that part of morality which is given external and compulsory protection.[95]

Yashchenko did not merely reproduce Solov'ev's vision of the good society: many pages of his study of federalism contain lengthy defence of Solov'ev's claims against the critics who had first challenged him. A case in point concerns law as a minimum of morality. Chicherin, Shershenevich, Novgorodtsev, and Evgeny Trubetskoi had all objected to Solov'ev's definition on the grounds that in many areas of justice, law (criminal justice excepted) need not have anything to do with morality; indeed, it may, as Chicherin argued, actually be 'immoral'. However, for Yashhenko, underlying this straightforward and seemingly reasonable objection was a failure to pair like with like: the fault, as he saw it, was that Solov'ev's understanding of morality as a coincidence of norms, which in practice determine our lives and conscience (Solov'ev offered a material explanation of law), is often confused with ethics in the sense of a philosophical theory of ideal morality.[96] Like most legal philosophers of the Silver Age era, however, in endorsing Solov'ev's philosophy of law, even defending it from criticism, Yashchenko was notably silent on the one domain of law – criminal justice – that Solov'ev had privileged in his work. Typically, they applied his ideas to general theories of the state. Even Mikhailovsky who had trained in criminal law only briefly took up the issue of criminal motives, but in this instance it was to reinforce his allegiance to the Kantian distinction between law and morality as upheld by Chicherin. Regretting the prevalent tendency in current literature to blur the two – as exemplified by arguments of the type 'just as morality is not just a matter of feelings or attitude but comes to expression in deeds, criminal law, likewise is not confined to the criminal act but explores the inner mood of the perpetrator' – Mikhailovsky diligently put back the fence posts dividing them. To his mind, of primary concern for law is a person's action, and if at all law is interested in the inner make-up of the perpetrator, it is only in so far as his 'mood' (*nastroenie*) has direct bearing on the act itself:

> a person may exhibit anti-social tendencies, may even meditate a crime (and procure the tools to carry it out). But, so long as he does not commit the deed, his behaviour does not fall into the province of law, even though, from a moral point of view it is totally reprehensible.[97]

In his bitter polemics with Chicherin, Solov'ev had grudgingly retorted by way of a last ditch attempt to defend his views 'Chicherin doesn't want to know about progress in science'.[98] Part of the problem of determining Solov'ev's place in the development of legal theory in Russia is that he was in between generations, a sort of Janus-like figure in juridical culture, anticipating the quest to provide theoretical support for ethico-legal norms that could secure the dignity and well-being of the individual by limiting state power, yet, at the same time, seemingly archaic in some of his Christian-based views. The juridical authorities Solov'ev admired dismissed his theories as farfetched or backward looking, while they, themselves, endeavoured (mostly in vein) to impart new – secular – meaning to existing legal practice. Indeed, for his 'classicist' mentors and colleagues on the *European Messenger*, who, like Chicherin, urged a distinction to be observed between law and morality, Solov'ev's recipe for moral-based legality appeared atavistic, dangerously retrograde, redolent of customary law mentality, and blocking the path to modern rule of law principles. For this reason, Koni, for example, refused an invitation by the St Petersburg Philosophical Society to speak about Solov'ev's legal theory, suggesting that the task be taken up by Vvedensky, Troitsky, Spasovich, or Lukyanov instead.[99] But, paradoxically, for all the anachronisms his peers found in Solov'ev's legal thought, it was in many ways more attuned to the social reality he lived in – an impoverished legal culture and customs rich in Orthodox piety. Moreover, after 1905, as Duma politics failed, his vision of man and society seems to answer the esoteric mood of a God-seeking, religious renaissance that affected many sections of the intellectual elite.

Not long after his 'oraison funebre' to honour Solov'ev's memory, Judge Koni addressed an audience of law students. With his powerful command of rhetoric, he argued that without moral integrity, justice was an empty term.[100] Stressing the moral aspect of justice and judicial procedure, Koni combined the Kantian categorical imperative 'expressing respect for human dignity' with the Christian principle 'love thy neighbour' to produce a prescription for true justice that captured perfectly the spirit of moral idealism in a Christian key professed by Solov'ev:

> By implementing justice through the prism of active (*deyatel'naya*) love, moral duty fuses with the guiding principle of Christianity, which commands 'love thy neighbour as thyself' (...). Moral duty requires that we never forget that before the judge or barrister in a court of law stands a person (*chelovek*) vested with the inalienable right to respect for her human dignity.

He further remarked that procedural law recognizes as lawful the encroachment of moral demands into its domain (*priznaet zakonnost' vtorzheniya v oblast' svoego primeneniya trebovanii nravstvennosti'*).[101]

As a moral–religious philosopher, Solov'ev's main achievement in the arena of legal theory was that he championed the idea of 'trust in the law'. And this was the message that Novgorodtsev, in the wake of the 1905 Revolution, clearly endorsed as he waged his own attack on the dangers of Tolstoian anarchy and the narrowness of positivism:

> The experience of the nineteenth century has shown that law (*pravo*) alone does not have the force to bring about the complete transformation of society. And while, for some, this experience has become the grounds to argue that we can dispense with law altogether, for others it is proof of the need to complement law with new principles, to broaden its content so that it meets the needs of contemporary European society, which today requires more than the rule of law state has so far provided. (...) The rule of law state is not the crown of history, nor the ultimate moral ideal of life. It is no more than a tributary factor, operating as one partial element, among others, within the broader web of moral forces. From this it follows that law, in relation to the plenitude of moral demands, is an extremely poor, insufficient means to give body to the purity of moral principles.[102]

For Novgorodtsev, the route out of the positivist impasse lay in the 'human turn': 'Circumstances today can no longer be regarded in terms of a simple requirement for coherence, but should be viewed in terms of the categorical imperative of morality which invests prime importance in the unconditional significance of man (*lichnost'*).'[103] This view was shared by the main collaborators in the landmark symposiums of the decade – *Problems of Idealism* (1902, which Novgorodtsev edited) and *Vekhi* (Signposts/Landmarks, 1909), a collection of essays that provoked some of the most heated polemics among the Russian intelligentsia in its entire history.[104] Experience had taught them that emphasis on 'civic rights and duties' alone, which had been the hallmark of old liberalism – and a central premise in theories of criminal justice – had been inappropriate and ineffectual in raising political and civic awareness. By contrast, 'liberal' social philosophy must, they believed, be founded on the internal, ethical notion of the human soul and of human dignity. Thus, in order to manage the tension between the quest for universal Christian unity and social pluralism – a vision of society that new liberalism had inherited from Solov'ev – it was necessary to define individual freedom in terms of Christian morality rather than the secular language of contracts and mutual suspicion. The literary historian, Mikhail Gershenzon, gave this standpoint additional pathos in his editorial to the *Vekhi* collection in 1909, and his indebtedness to Solov'ev in this regard was unambiguous:

> The men who have joined forces here differ greatly among themselves both on basic questions of 'faith' and in their practical preferences; but there are no disagreements on this joint enterprise. Their common platform is the recognition of the theoretical and practical primacy of spiritual life over the external community. They mean by this that the individual's inner life is the sole creative force in human existence, and that this inner life, and not the self-sufficient principles of the political realm, constitutes the only solid basis on which a society can be built.[105]

Hymns to personhood (*lichnost'*) formed a leitmotif in some of the keynote liberal publications after the turn of the century. Whether informed by the new wave of spiritualist and life philosophies, anchored in the revival of Kantian thought, or explicitly indebted to Solov'ev, they urged recognition of the importance of personal morality and personal self-perfection in the construction of social–legal order. Neglecting individual spiritual freedom for the sake of the social cause had, it was argued, been the undoing of the radical intelligentsia, whose campaign had been too narrowly focused on the attainment of material well-being. In a sense, then, Solov'ev had seen into the crystal ball.

5 Criminal justice in the age of revolution (1900–1917)

In the opening decade of the twentieth century, Russian scholarship in criminal law became more complex, witnessing simultaneously a polarization and overlap between schools of thought. The appearance of the new sub-discipline of criminal politics to combat crime was matched by developments in criminal law theory inspired by the revival of philosophical idealism and new liberalism. Study of crime and punishment through the lens of social economic concerns took its cue from a slightly older generation of Russian positivists, such as M.P. Chubinsky and S.K. Gogel', who had begun publishing in the 1890s and were established scholars by the 1900s, and was taken further by a younger generation of *privat-dotsenty* including M.N. Gernet and S. Poznyshev whose careers bridged the October Revolution. Possibly, the most important figure to have marked this development abroad was the German scholar, Franz von Liszt (1851–1919). His work on crime as a social–psychological phenomenon, together with his endeavours to map out the theoretical territory in criminal politics, attracted many followers in Russia from the 1890s onwards.[1] Thus, while research into criminal behaviour remained sensitive to social and environmental conditions, new legal positivists were careful not to exaggerate a direct causal link between climate or alcoholism and criminal proclivities. Rather, the link was mediated through factors such as 'inherited degeneracy'. With mass poverty and ignorance now explained as the root cause of inherited disease and mental or emotional derangement, and not as the immediate reason for a criminal act, legal positivists began retracing a path back to the criminal as a person, and not unlike moral idealists, started analysing criminal behaviour as both a psychological and moral phenomenon. The upshot was that while the criminal remained a classifiable social phenomenon, he was also regarded as a moral person whose personal beliefs and moral standards were key to understanding crime.

If positivism was the fastest developing current in criminal law theory after 1900, this did not, however, entail a neat progression away from the premises of the classical law for law's sake theory and its application to criminal justice. On the contrary, firmly entrenched positions of first-generation classicists, whose approach to crime and punishment resisted the incursion of the social sciences for the sake of upholding juridical principles, continued to mark the field. The early 1900s saw new editions of old classics, with works by Tagantsev,

Sergeevsky, and Sluchevsky, first published in the 1870s and 1880s, still ranking high on lists of recommended reading in university curricula.[2] Moreover, after 1905, Tagantsev exercised some influence as a prominent statesman involved in the drawn-out Duma politics over matters of sentencing (early release and conditional sentences), prison conditions, and, of course, the political debate on capital punishment. As an author, however, if he updated his bibliography and accounted for recent trends, he nevertheless continued to pound out the same message, only now on two fronts: against the young Turks of criminology but also against signs of religious–moral pathos which, paradoxically, were beginning to creep into certain strands of new positivist thinking. The upshot was a stereotyping of positions, with declarations of unbridgeable differences between opposed classical and positivist 'schools' ignoring the more subtle delineations that had actually made it almost impossible to classify any given author with a single epithet. Tagantsev, whose motto 'law for life's sake' had, in its time, symbolized a breach with dry abstract formulas of the classical approach, was now viewed as an authoritative past master, steadfast in his defence of law against intrusions by the social sciences. For the younger generation of positivists, the fact that both he and Sergeevsky accepted condemnation and censure (*osuzhdenie*/*poritsanie*) as integral parts of judicial procedure, that they distrusted statistical evidence, and that their juridical lexicon contained the word 'norm' was enough to bracket them with diehard classicists. Ironically though, in rejecting what they regarded as the restrictive, abstract view of the classical school, certain positivists, especially those driven by a new ethos of enlightenment in a socialist key, were, themselves, guilty of gross simplification on their own home territory, diluting positivistic arguments into a formulaic credo. This situation, in turn, prompted some to re-enter theoretical territory in order to reflect on the current state of criminal law as a science and to test the theoretical foundations of criminal politics and criminal sociology.

Early twentieth-century theoretical definitions of criminal politics largely took their cue from contemporary philosophy of law and the revival of natural law most often associated with the names Pavel Novgorodtsev, in Moscow, and the 'positivist' Leon Petrazhitsky, professor of law at St Petersburg University. Mokrinsky, Lyublinsky, Chubinsky, and Poznyshev, all specialists in criminal law, frequently deferred to the writings of these two men generally considered, as Walicki notes, 'the principal legal theorists of the Kadet party'.[3] However, as I suggested in the previous chapter, Solov'ev's ideas concerning the right to a dignified existence and the moral foundations of law were also enjoying a resonance in new liberal theories as these were taking shape after the turn of the century. If critical of Solov'ev's theory of law and morality in its formulaic rendering, or wary of the pitfalls of mixing law 'such as it is in reality with the moral goal it should pursue',[4] natural law theorists were, nevertheless, inspired both by the terms of Solov'ev's argument and by the Christian world outlook that informed it. For Novgorodtsev, for example, the moral and juridical ideal should combine the individual and social principles in a supreme synthesis and uncover the link between the person in all her plenitude with the concrete aims of the community. The following remarks by Sergei Bulgakov are typical of the importance ascribed to idealism with a Christian hue by Solov'ev's closest successors:

> The norms constituting so-called *natural law*, or the legal ideal, emerge naturally from Christianity's doctrine that all are sons of God, that individuals have absolute value and are equal before God, thereby denying innate rights of man over man. The Christian ideal is the soul of the liberation movement in the broadest sense of the word, pursuing the political emancipation of the person. In this sense, the modern political movement of democracy, which gradually realizes this idea, is fulfilment of the norms of the Christian natural law, the gradual Christianization of political life.[5]

Thus, rather than rely on 'external' definitions of civic rights and duties – the holy of holies for old liberals but also a beacon for their young rival democrats – the new 'liberals' prioritized the 'internal', ethical notion of the human soul and of human dignity.

In conjunction with advances in juridical scholarship and philosophy of law, the opening decade of the twentieth century witnessed an increase in popular juridical literature, the purpose of which was to encourage *obshchestvennost'*. The social democrat M.N. Gernet (1874–1953), perhaps best known in the Soviet Union for his four-volume study of the tsarist prison system published in the 1940s, was responsible for numerous publications in the pre-Revolutionary era – textbooks, collective essays, and bibliographical compilations – in which he emphasized the underlying social–political weaponry to be gained from juridical knowledge. The preface to his 1906 textbook *Basic Concepts of Russian State, Civil and Criminal Law*, co-authored with fellow *privat-dotsenty* V.M. Ustinov and I.V. Novotsky, was emphatic in its message: knowledge of law encourages awareness among the people in their role as 'active citizens' whose voices count in the governing process of the country – in short, it is necessary 'for every thinking Russian citizen in the current period of our history'.[6] In addition to his efforts to ensure the dissemination of juridical knowledge and to anchor it in the public sphere, Gernet played a key role in the public outcry against the death penalty and in condemning the government backlash against revolutionaries.[7] A committed socialist – he believed that criminal law reflects class interests – Gernet's publications are symptomatic of that 'ethos of enlightenment' which his generation inherited from early 'liberal' reformers, only now adapted to overtly different political ends.[8]

Although not representing a theoretically unified corpus, the body of literature written in the opening decades of the new century helped forge what one might call a criminal law canon. Equally significantly, many of the works discussed in this chapter contained a vision of the social and educative role of law in a state that continued to withhold, or restrict, basic rights. In addition, public awareness of the uses and abuses of justice was sharpened in response to aggressive government measures in the wake of the 1905 Revolution. As I argue below, the issue of the death penalty not only figured on the Duma agenda; as a topic of urgent debate among public figures, literati, as well as the judiciary, it reached a wider audience, generating an attitude that was hostile to the regime.

For and against morality: developments in legal positivism

In 1903, the year in which a new Criminal Code was presented to the tsar, the Professor of Criminal Law L.S. Belogritz-Kotlyarevsky published a two-volume textbook based on lectures read at Kiev University.[9] In the introduction, in which he mapped out his intellectual affiliation with the sociological school, Belogritz-Kotlyarevsky argued that the study of social and individual factors combined was the most propitious path forward to ensure a fairer system of justice. At the centre of juridical science should be not so much crime, as criminality, that is, the activity of a person considered both as an individual and social phenomenon:

> Only on the basis of a comprehensive study of the perpetrator of a crime, careful observation of his individual particularities which viciously (*durno*) drive his will, together with the study of the entire class of similar individuals will it be possible to direct the penal system on the right path.[10]

The raison d'être of punishment was, of course, its corrective and preventative function: punitive action should facilitate the social reintegration of the accused, protect the interests of society in general, and provide aid to the victim of crime in particular. Correspondingly, criminal legislation should be grounded in principles of equality before the law, individualization, and flexibility. In addition, reckoning with social and economic change was an essential part in the process of reshaping and updating punitive measures.[11]

With its clear indebtedness to Foinitsky and Liszt, Belogritz-Kotlyarevsky's account of crime, criminality, and criminal justice served as a model that was reproduced in textbooks throughout the decade: Gogel', Chubinsky, Poznyshev, Gernet, among others, all worked with these new 'hallmark motifs' of positivism.[12] An anonymous conspectus, dated 1911, is a telling example of the way in which endeavours to conceptualize crime both as an individual and social phenomenon became frozen into catechism style formulae of the new positivistic doctrine:

> Crime (*prestuplenie*) is the individual activity of a person; its manifestation and character depend on the psycho-physiological makeup of the individual. The psycho-physiological makeup of the individual is determined by heredity (…) and by one's social, physical and economic environment. Crime is the product of interplay of physical, social and individual factors, and the dominant role in the formation of crimes belongs to physical and social factors.[13]

More subtly, in what was profiled as a seminal study in the theory and practice of criminal politics, M.P. Chubinsky, professor of law at St Petersburg University, explained the growing interest in the criminal individual as the natural response to a juridical culture that had traditionally ignored 'the rights of the criminal as an individual' (*prav prestupnoi lichnosti*) for the sake of ensuring social protection. In their effort to guarantee the rights of the criminal individual, 'criminal politicians', he argued, had inveighed against the cruelty and arbitrariness (*proizvol*) of juridical procedure, insisting that the power of the judiciary be extended, and that punitive measures take into account both objective and subjective aspects, so as to guarantee maximum security for society without sacrificing the maximum protection of criminal rights.[14]

Belogritz-Kotlyarevsky shared the predominant Lisztian-inspired view concerning the idea of punishment as an occasion for 'the juridical and social rebirth of the criminal', explicitly rejecting any idea of his moral rebirth. Contemporary theories of punishment, he reiterated, emphasize social correction 'by which it does not mean the moral rebirth of the criminal, but his social re-adaptation through a process of accustoming him to behaviour (*motivy*) beneficial to society, and to honest work'.[15] However, despite injunctions to resist the inclusion of moral considerations as counselled by Liszt (in part to protect the modern idea of law) and upheld by Belogritz-Kotlyarevsky, offsetting the social and personal dimensions of crime and punishment provided a convenient platform for a reflection upon the moral implications of crime and punishment within the framework of positivism. Certainly, some Russian positivists – both of Belogritz-Kotlyarevsky's generation and among younger juridical thinkers – were receptive to the idea of a socially conditioned morality, which they incorporated into their reflection of criminality. S.K. Gogel', for example, who offered the standard view of man as a social being (*lichnost' sotsial'naya*), with its implications of 'living in an organized community', did not preclude social morality arguing that, from a sociological perspective, a person's moral state, as affected by adverse social conditions, may indeed be the strongest factor inducing him or her into committing a legal infraction.[16] V.V. Esipov singled out Chubinsky for attributing importance to morals on the issue of criminal motives, thus ignoring the counter-indications of authoritative thinkers within the positivist and classical schools he otherwise followed. Chubinsky noted that although, nowadays, few criminalists would expel the ethical moment from law, counted among the very few who did were some of the most respected leaders in the field: Ferri, for whom punishment as a raw reaction against an individual precludes moral consideration; Karl Binding, on grounds of the clash he perceived between the nature and goals of ethics relating to individual conscience and the broader application of obligatory norms (this is, incidentally, similar to the argument that Chicherin used in his polemic with Solov'ev); and Liszt, for the sake of safeguarding law.[17] For Chubinsky, however, criminal motives necessarily contained a moral component (in Russian *moral'* meaning moral code, mores): together with other factors, which comprise the ethical views of society, understanding moral behaviour, he believed, yielded a more comprehensive evaluation of a criminal act. While punishment should of course account for the needs of society, this should also include consideration of the ethical and cultural level of society itself. It was, he added, crucial to ensure that the criminal legislation in any given region promote rather than lower the latter.[18]

One of the reasons Belogritz-Kotlyarevsky rejected the moral component was the trap of moral pathos to which he felt some fellow positivists had fallen prey and the almost blind New Testament manner in which they seemed to be preaching recognition of moral principles – good behaviour and compassion towards others. A case in point is the work of a younger colleague Poznyshev, at that time (1903) a *privat-dotsent* at the University of Moscow. Belogritz-Kotlyarevsky paired him with Lev Tolstoi for taking the 'mistaken' extremist view that punishment is a moral evil (*nrastvennoe zlo*), contrary to Christian ethics. For Belogritz-Kotlyarevsky, this argument was weak quite simply because it failed to recognize that the legal order is not grounded in any one stand-alone principle. The legal order

> provides the necessary condition for physical and moral development, for the process of perfection (*sovershenstvovaniya*) both of the individual person and of society as a whole. If this is so, then 'punishment' as one facet of the legal order cannot be a moral evil. Rather, it is crime that is evil, while the fight against it constitutes a moral obligation for each and everyone of us, especially for the state. Whence it follows that the state in conducting its struggle with crime by means of punishment – a fully lawful institution derived from the idea of community and from the essence of law (*pravo*) itself – can in no way be said to be committing a moral evil.[19]

Belogritz-Kotlyarevsky's criticism is instructive of the changing parameters of legal thought after 1900. Albeit a self-styled positivist, Belogritz-Kotlyarevsky's word of caution against sacrificing the juridical principle arguably put him back in a law for law's sake camp – again, a point he shared with Liszt. By contrast, the work of Poznyshev, nominally a fellow positivist, is representative of the ways in which some criminal law scholars were gradually accommodating the moral component – both in the common or garden sense of decent behaviour as well as normatively – in order to refine their understanding of what constitutes the criminal as both an individual and a type or class. If Poznyshev rapidly revised his Tolstoian pacifism to the point where he argued that punishment is morally legal (*nravstvenno zakonno*),[20] his arguments still turned on the relation between law and morality, which he explored with reference to the leading philosophers of law of the day, Novgorodtsev and Petrazhitsky. Their writings on the subject were regarded by contemporaries as a catalyst in the revival of natural law.

Poznyshev wrote:

> We have to admit the dependency of the punitive system on ethics (…). Both the means and ends of punishment should be grounded in moral principles (…). Moral correction of the criminal would enable the state to fulfil its role as protector and guarantor of social well-being (…). Judicial

> coercion is morally lawful in so far as it is needed by the state in its task to preserve the spiritual and physical well-being of all its citizens.[21]

For Poznyshev, criminal justice was not just about social self-defence, let alone retribution, but should consist in expedient, individualized measures, commensurate with the guilt of the person in question and with his 'moral profile' (*oblik*) as a class of criminal, that is, whether morally deficient, degenerate, or driven by an outburst of uncontrolled passion.[22] Thus, as a breach of the law, a criminal act exhibited all the signs of moral underdevelopment: lack of respect for the human person, inability to express sympathy, dishonesty in performance of duties (in state service, for the immediate community) or in matters of ownership.[23]

Poznyshev presented his psychological study of the moral personhood of the criminal (*kharakter ego nravstvennoi lichnosti*) as a natural development of the Lombroso school.[24] Indeed, on the surface, he argued, this progression in legal positivism might be deceptive, since most attempts to classify criminals had, in fact, already been gauged in terms of moral criteria; the criminal exhibited a lack of moral feeling or moral responsibility. Lombroso's 'innate criminal' was morally and emotionally deficient, impervious to the threat of punishment, vainglorious (more so than artists and literati, Poznyshev added), vengeful, proud with an inordinate sexual appetite. Lombroso had used long runs of statistics to demonstrate that this 'pazzo morale' was quantifiable, traceable to the set of the criminal's eyes, the narrowness of his brow, his build, and gait. If, however, criminal anthropologists were able to pinpoint the emotional and psychological impulses (*nastroenie*) triggering a criminal act, or indeed, apply their findings to establish the degree of guilt, they were not able to explore the correlation between criminal impulses (*nastroenie*) and the moral person of the criminal as such. For Poznyshev, by contrast, analyses of human comportment from a psychological point of view yielded a more subtle classification of criminals that, in turn, could be worked into the legislation so as to encourage more appropriate responses to breaches of the law on a case by case basis.

A key term in Poznyshev's psychological (and strictly anti-metaphysical) vocabulary was that of 'feeling' (*chustvovanie*), a term inspired by his reading of Petrazhitsky and to which he attached the epithets 'concrete' (to infer sensation, perception, etc.) and 'abstract'. Abstract feeling is an enabling power; thanks to it, a moral evaluation is able to exert greater or less influence 'on the soul, compelling the person to retain moral decorum'. For Poznyshev, 'abstract feeling' was connected with ideas that act as driving forces in our lives, for example, love of truth, justice, honour, respect for human worth, love of freedom, though, equally, it may concern traits traditionally disparaged by society such as love of money, or misanthropy.[25] This latter, in particular, was pertinent for understanding the class of criminals he referred to as 'morally impaired' (*nravstvenno-razslablennyi*): the morally weak criminal lacked 'abstract feeling', making him incapable of moral judgement.[26] As a positivist, Poznyshev did not, of course, accept metaphysical truths as such; rather, he treated the positive connotations associated with, for example, love of truth, and inversely, the stigma attached to avarice, as civilizational traits, which, no matter how enduring they might be, are susceptible to change. In other words, by exchanging the terms of psycho-physiology for psychology, Poznyshev was rejecting many of the simplistic parallelisms between body and soul that earlier positivists, such as Lombroso, had operated with in support of some of their more outlandish claims of the kind that 40 per cent of all criminals were 'innate criminals'. To his mind, the psychological perspective afforded far greater complexity to a criminal act, because it recognized criminal agency as that which comes to expression in the moment of deliberation (*reshimost'*).

Methodologically, inclusion of the moral-cum-psychological profile of the criminal person as cued by Petrazhitsky's 'emotional impulses' neatly dovetailed with the 'factors of criminality' pioneered by Ferri in Italy and championed by Foinitsky at home. The combined approach successfully brought individually intrinsic circumstances into the foreground alongside social and/or physical factors traditionally privileged by positivism. More importantly, Poznyshev hoped that a more refined classification of criminals would see changes in assessments of the crimes committed:

> The criminal is a multi-faceted object of study. It is obvious that the classification of criminals (...) should undergo further sub-divisions in accordance with newly worked criteria of differentiation. From it we will gain an entire web of interconnecting sub-divisions, which together encompass all those facets of the person of the criminal, which are of crucial significance when it comes to determining 'punishability' (*nakazuemost'*). This holds for legislation, for the application of the law by judges, and for the completion of the sentence in a penal institution.[27]

While Poznyshev worked with a typology of criminals inherited, though revised, from criminal anthropology, what saved him from the reductionism of the Lombroso school, which had effectively drained criminals of their flesh and blood individuality, was his vision of man as supreme value. Even though the terms of social relations he mentions in his work had a definite socialist resonance to them, as such, the image of man Poznyshev forged was not dissimilar to the man-centred vision of society that contemporary liberal-idealists such as Sergei Bulgakov and Nikolai Berdyaev fostered in their work. 'Ideally', he wrote in a text dated 1908, 'life in society should consist of the sum total of all those forms of collaboration and communication among people, through which each individual may channel the greatest benefit for himself and yet be beneficial for others.'[28] And he reiterated much the same view a few years later, employing the term '*usovershenstvovanie*' – a word much favoured by Solov'ev, whose works on criminal justice Poznyshev cited.[29]

> The larger community has no interests or goals separate from the interests and goals of those that compose it. Its function is to ensure the greatest possible spiritual and physical well being of the individual person, to enable her growth towards happiness and greater perfection (*usovershenstvovanie*).

Perhaps the most startling feature of Poznyshev's work was the degree to which he conflated law and morality in his theoretical work. In an implicit, yet oddly formulated, echo of what one might call the 'sentiment' underlying contemporary moral philosophies of law, he wrote: 'Juridical ideals elaborated by the juridical sciences form a part of the overall moral ideal of human life. Human behaviour comprises a single whole regulated by a higher moral goal to which a web of rules is subordinated.' He then spelled out the relation in the following terms:

> The moral domain comprises all codes of behaviour that people freely appropriate under the watchful eye of individual conscience and public opinion. Rules of behaviour, social regulations requiring special sanctions from a higher authority for them to be instituted (for example the monarch, or several nations in the case of international law) belong to the juridical sphere. Positive law comprises all those specially sanctioned rules of conduct. In conjunction with positive law there exist rules of moral conduct that have penetrated so deep into our conscience as individuals, and are so embedded in public opinion that any breach of these is widely regarded as reprehensible (*durnoe*). We call this 'positive morality of society' in analogy with positive law. Since it differs from moral ideals, we might also label these rules of moral conduct as the 'moral' (morals, moeurs) of a given society.[30]

The writings of Professor Vladimirov, predating those of Poznyshev, are also illustrative of a shift in emphasis within positivist thinking loosely defined, and of its susceptibility, possibly, to the 'Silver Age' mood of introspection and quest for spiritual values that afflicted many *intelligenty* – both Marxists and Liberals – in the wake of 1905.[31] His work on criminal law spanning several decades before and after 1900 presents a rare and somewhat odd mixture of Solov'evian-derived pathos with the sobriety of the juridical thinker stressing the responsibility of the state to foster, by harnessing, the process of man's perfectibility.[32]

Vladimirov conceived crime and punishment in terms of moral vice (*porok*) and moral justice. In a piece often cited by contemporaries, 'The Criminal Legislator as the Nation's Educator' (1903), he claimed, contrary to current legal practice – and wisdom, possibly – that criminals should be categorized according to their most salient moral vice, and he listed three types of criminal: those with an inadequate sense of morality; those with an underdeveloped sense of pity or compassion towards others; and those lacking in respect (*pochitanie*) towards others.[33] The aim of punishment was to recover the criminal's moral trustworthiness (*nravstevnnaya blagonadezhnost'*). No threatening or harsh punishment could attain this goal; rather, the cure to moral deficiency was to be found in the remedial powers of enlightenment. As the supreme model of morality, the state's main task was to encourage moral feeling through the instances of criminal justice.[34] As moral educator, the state demands, in the first instance, that its people develop a sense of responsibility. Here, Vladimirov argued, 'criminal legislation is the most important tool of moral education'. While he acknowledged that the family and schooling had a crucial role to play, it was, he believed, the criminal court that encapsulated most powerfully the 'drama of responsibility' for those directly involved in a case and for the reading public at large following events.[35]

An unusual textbook by any standards, Vladimirov's introduction was an exegesis on 'the purpose of life', offering a recipe for the process of perfection and attainment of well-being ('summum bonum', as he called it), which reads like a poorly ingested Solov'evian justification of the good. The levels of moral deficiency, or depravity, just mentioned read like an inversion of the moral attitudes of pity, sympathy, and reverence that Solov'ev described in the opening chapters of *Justification of the Good*. But Vladimirov goes further by adapting leitmotifs of Solov'ev's social ethics to his view that legal institutions are the necessary tools for ensuring the moral perfectibility of mankind:

> The unrelenting striving of mankind towards the higher good (*vyschee blago*) requires the support of a series of secondary goods (*blaga*) serving as means in relation to the self-sufficient summum bonum as an end in itself. Social and legal institutions are the tools necessary in this path towards the higher good (…). We have an innate ability to create, on the imperfect foundations of reality, the ideals of perfection, (…) to elaborate our ideal of moral perfection. From this ideal, which in different eras may assume different forms (for example as a buttress supporting state authority in past eras), one must single out the intransient traits of the ideal of the moral perfection of the person, shared by all peoples across time. It is this latter ideal that defines our obligations to ourselves, and our duties towards others.[36]

In the light of these definitions, Vladimirov positioned his conception of crime and punishment. Albeit acknowledging that crime is anti-social, a breach of state rules, he emphasized its immoral aspect, especially when it violates the moral injunction 'love thy neighbour'. The supreme aim of punishment is to instil a sense of responsibility for one's action, both in the criminal himself, but also in the society of which he is a member. The sense of responsibility, which the state endeavours tirelessly to inculcate, is 'a source of great moral well-being'. It offers the most effective form of social protection and security and is the basis of legal consciousness 'without which there can be no citizens, merely savages, restrained by lashes'. A sense of responsibility is propitious for the development of 'many moral qualities, necessary in the life of mankind, the most important of which are careful thought, self-observation, self-critique, self-possession (*obdumannost', samonabluydenie, samokritiki, samoobladenie*)'. As Vladimirov saw it, judicial institutions represented, potentially, the most potent vehicle for instilling these values, and he urged that criminal justice be enlivened by this ethos,

> such that in all her component parts – code, courts, and in sentencing – the criminal justice system would not provoke wild hatred on the part of the

> condemned man, but rather prompt an awareness that he has behaved unlawfully, immorally, anti-sociably, and that he should therefore suffer the toils inflicted for the sake of transforming his inner world.[37]

Although Vladimirov did not use the word 'repentance', his discussion of crime and punishment reads as a thinly disguised portrait of fall and redemption: 'The susceptibility of an action to punishment', he wrote, 'is motivated by a retreat from the ideal of man.'[38] Chubinsky, for one, criticized Vladimirov for blurring the boundaries of law and morality: 'He even argues that one has to regard one's own "moral person" in and of itself as a juridical obligation.'[39] Yet, if somewhat ludicrous in its formulation, the underlying message of Vladimirov's appeal to moral righteousness struck a poignant chord with his colleagues: instilling a sense of responsibility was the best form of self-liberation through self-monitoring and, by extension, the best way to make citizenship an unshakeable buttress of society. Thus, while Chubinsky may have been critical of Vladimirov's handling of law and morality, it was not 'on principle' but as an intellectual ally, whose own concern to combat 'immoral behaviour' by criminalizing it necessitated reflection on the law/morality issue at a very practical level. In his *Course of Criminal Politics*, where he addressed the relation between criminal politics and morals, Chubinsky heeded voices within legal positivism (Jellinek) and philosophy of law (Petrazhitsky), which placed greater emphasis on the relation between law and morality to argue that expelling moral considerations hindered rather than helped criminal justice:

> In practice, the law/morality relation may be usefully applied to two groups of activity for the sake of protecting the interests of society: personal vice (*lichnyi porok*), immoral professions, and acts of sexual violence; actions which evidence the 'anti-social behaviour' of the accused. (...) It is high time to take a different route, and recognize a definite, albeit minimum, feeling of solidarity among people. Correspondingly, evaluating a person's behaviour in breach of this solidarity should not fall to the domain of the lawful (*pravomernoe*), but should, instead, be constructed in terms of what is criminal and what is punishable (*prestupnoe/nakazuemoe*). Were this the case, failure to help someone who has fallen unconscious on the street, for example, would be severely punished.[40]

Vladimirov, whose juridical lexicon comprised terms such as 'moral responsibility', conscience', and 'perfection', explicitly anchored the criminal *lichnost'* in moral waters. As for Poznyshev, even if, overall, he placed the accent on man as a social phenomenon, by virtue of his interest in the psychology of crime and the more nuanced classification of criminal types he provided, his arguments contained traces of an approach that one would not immediately associate with the staples of legal positivism. His shift in vocabulary from the generic '*prestupnost*' to the moral character of the *prestupnik* as an individual attests a progression in his thought towards a position that contemporaries referred to as 'moral individualism'. Originating in the legal philosophies of Novgorodtsev and Petrazhitsky, it had filtered into juridical theory along with other hallmarks of their work – official versus intuitive law, imperative versus attributive–imperative norms (of morality and law respectively), – to serve as 'fidelity' tags in studies by juridical theorists in their respective endeavours to map out new theoretical territory for the science of criminal law.

Philosophies of law and criminal law theories

A signature piece by Novgorodtsev referred to in contemporary juridical literature was his contribution to *Problems of Idealism* (1902), a collective volume of essays seeking to strike a last knock-down blow against positivism and to restore 'absolute commandments and absolute principles' as tools in a critique of positive law. A leitmotif in many of the contributions in this collection was the renewed belief in the absolute value of the person: 'The new forms of life do not now appear as the demands of simple expediency; they appear rather as the categorical commands of morality which attribute paramount importance to the principle of the unconditional significance of the person.'[41] Novgorodtsev himself worked this principle into his essay, 'Ethical Idealism in the Philosophy of Law', a programmatic statement in defence of the revival of natural law. As he put it, 'We need a revival of natural law with its a-prioristic method, its idealistic yearnings, its recognition of moral autonomy and its normative approach.'[42]

The influence of Novgorodtsev is clearly felt in a piece by the professor of Tomsk University S. Mokrinsky, in which he set out the ethical–political foundations of criminal law in order to claim an alternative theoretical territory for the discipline distinct from the premises of sociology and anthropology while avoiding the pitfalls of moral pathos. Law, he contended, should not only be studied as a social and historical phenomenon but also as an 'individual-psychological and normative ethical' phenomenon.[43] In a long two-page footnote, he singled out Gernet and Poznyshev for overzealous subordination of law to the social sciences. In his *Social Factors of Criminality* (1905), Gernet explicitly made sociological and anthropological elements an integral part of the juridical study of crime and punishment, while Poznyshev, in his 1904 study, went so far as to consider juridical phenomena as a special class of social phenomena. According to Mokrinsky, by citing Liszt as their authority in this regard, they were, in fact, doing their elected master a major disservice. Although Liszt drew on sociology and anthropology, he nevertheless differentiated between criminal law in the narrow sense and the respective objectives and methods of criminology, penology etc. By contrast, in their enthusiasm for the sociological approach, certain criminologists made the mistake of ignoring the juridical premises that Liszt rigorously safeguarded.[44] Examples of this kind prompted Mokrinsky to reflect on criminal law methodology. To date, he believed, Russian juridical theory was still poor in defining the tasks of criminal law, with Tagantsev ranking as one of the few to have done so. In Mokrinsky's eyes, however, Tagantsev's argument, namely that principles of law be tested by their practical applicability (*ustoichivost', zhizneprigodnost'*), also wore the positivistic badge and as such could not provide durable conceptual ballast to sustain the discipline.

Using Novgorodtsev's breakdown of law into a description of given laws, which he had placed under the sign of the Kantian concept of 'being' (*sein*), and the study and evaluation of legal norms, which Novgorodtsev paired with the Kantian 'ought' (*sollen*),[45] Mokrinsky identified three facets within the science of law, each with their corresponding mode of study: dogma (description of given laws); politics (political construction of laws); and ethics (moral evaluation of given laws – and most notably the question of whether punishment is morally justified). The science of criminal law therefore involved dogma, which engaged formal logic, a political–teleological evaluation of given laws, and a normative construction of what law should be (*postroenie dolzhnogo prava*). Coined as 'juridical politics and ethics', the second and third aspects worked in tandem, with ethical prescriptions providing the all-important foundation: 'Ethical imperatives play a decisive role in political postulates, but they cannot direct the politician when it comes to seeking the most appropriate means to achieve the required ends.' Ethical imperatives cede their place to the politics of law, a legal–technical science ('*pravno–technicheskii*') that engages with more practical issues, regulating and accommodating the specifics of the economy, finance, and mass psychology in a given region.[46]

In his bid to build the science of law on ethical–political foundations, Mokrinsky needed to distinguish his understanding of morality from two competing uses: the common-sense wisdom of positivists and the lofty, but unrealistic reverie of moralists. Interestingly, in this regard, Mokrinsky singled out Solov'ev for his well-intentioned but muddled conception of punishment, mocking his naïve belief that a prison could be morally beneficial to inmates if the administration of prisons was entrusted to moralists and men of deep religious convictions: 'Criminal law does not require that we love our neighbour (and that failure to do so should be reprimanded), it merely strives to maintain a socially healthy atmosphere, eliminate anything unsuitable for moral culture.'[47] For Mokrinsky, morality is not the ticket taking us towards the kingdom of God; rather it is rooted in society and, accordingly, has a social function. Always pursuing a course equidistant from the opposing banks of positivism and moralism, he carefully distanced his own goal of 'salus populi' (the 'welfare of the people'), as he termed it,[48] from the prosaic idea of 'security' sought by the former and the lofty ideal of 'general good' cherished by the latter. Instead, he attached it to the notion of *obshchestvennost'*, defined as a 'complex of external terms and conditions', including coercive measures, which constitute or guarantee the possibility of a moral life or, 'what amounts to the same thing', of moral progress. Given that morality is anchored in an imperfect society, moral progress – the salus populi – can only be safeguarded by punitive measures. Only in a perfect state might one eventually conceive of 'the withering away of law'. Until then, criminal justice was justified as a necessary condition of moral progress: Without coercive measures we would be with left with Hobbes' proverbial 'war of all against all'.[49]

If Mokrinsky was inspired by Novgorodtsev's restoration of the Kantian *sein/sollen* dualism, his account of criminal law ethics (*ygolovno-pravovaya etika*) undoubtedly owed far more to Petrazhitsky both in terms of the general casting of the problem and with respect to specific details. Mokrinsky's summary of Petrazhitsky's 'politics of law' attests his enormous intellectual indebtedness: politics of law consists in (1) rationally directing individual and mass conduct by means of corresponding legal incentives (*pravovaya motivatsiya*); (2) it aims to perfect human psyche, counteract evil, and antisocial tendencies, by reinforcing positive ones; (3) the ideal of the politics of law 'is the perfectioning of the social character, a perfected realm of true love for mankind'.[50] Read as a rebuttal of Liszt whose exclusion of ethics from his criminal politics in fact betrayed a utilitarian interpretation of moral problems rather than a normative understanding, Mokrinsky joined ranks with Petrazhitsky in the cause of restoring the categorical imperative, and in doing so restored criminal law to its proper terrain, no longer subordinated to the social sciences, though without, however, abandoning some of the gains that positivism as a 'humane' science had made.

Were one to compile a citation index for pre-Revolutionary thought, figuring high on the list of legal theorists active after 1900 would be the name of Leon Petrazhitsky (1867–1931), Professor of Encyclopaedia of Law at St Petersburg since 1897. But although his contemporaries acknowledged that he was one of the major figures in Russian social science, and frequently referenced his work in footnotes, the fact that his work had many strands to it meant that the responses it elicited were often ambiguous, if not critical. According to Walicki, intellectually, Petrazhitsky hovered somewhere between idealism and positivism, with the result that the 'multidirectional' character of his thought and influence made him both incontestably a major figure in Russian legal thought but also a controversial one:

> Nobody went further than he did in emphasizing that law was not a system of abstract norms but a part of social reality which had to be studied causally – and yet nobody was more insistent on the vindication of the deontological, ethical foundation of law, and nobody was more committed to the idea of a purposeful, conscious law-making.[51]

His research, which privileged a psychological approach to law, and, generally, the anti-speculative character of his thought, brought him into the orbit of positivism. Like Tarde or Georg Jellinek, Petrazhitsky situated the psychological approach to law ('law is a psychic phenomenon') in a sociological perspective. As the most viable alternative to metaphysical speculation, the psychological approach provided the tools for the study of law as a phenomenon of real life. His analysis of emotions and impulsions as 'facts', which informed his study of the emergence of norms and normative judgements, constituted an important challenge to the (neo-)Kantian view of the day. That said, if he inverted Kantian premises to argue that norms and values could be derived from facts, Petrazhitsky's interest in the problem of the normative function of law, ethics, subjective rights, in short the idea of 'just law', brought him closer in spirit to the Kantian–Hegelian idealism defended by the older generation of legal thinkers before the onset of positivism.

The distinction Petrazhitsky observed between law and morality as two species of ethics is analysed in depth by Walicki. Moral impulsions are purely imperative: they are impulsions of duty, unilaterally binding and non-exigent. Legal impulsions, by contrast, which he termed imperative–attributive impulsions, are 'bilaterally binding, exigent, and connect duties with rights, obligations with claims'. This distinction had a resonance in Petrazhitsky's account of the social function of law and in the accent he placed on man as a citizen. Because of its attributive function, 'law', as Walicki summarizes it,

> exerts a more powerful pressure on human conduct than does the purely moral consciousness. Active motivation, that is, motivation starting from an awareness of our right (or the duty of another) is stronger and socially more 'educative' than passive motivation, originating in the pure consciousness of duty. It is the consciousness of one's own rights which makes one a citizen, feeling one's own worth.[52]

Leitmotifs of Petrazhitsky's theory – motivation, imperative impulsion, imperative–attributive impulsions, his distinction between 'intuitive and positive law', his notion of 'official law' – quickly entered the juridical theoretical lexicon of the day, sometimes serving as sorts of brand label tags, when not framing the nature of the debate.[53] The work of P.I. Lyublinsky, a younger contemporary who later collaborated with Petrazhitsky on the series *New Ideas in Legal Theory* (1914), provides one telling example of the way 'moral individualism', 'ethical intuitive principles', and 'intuitive and official law' quickly filtered into juridical literature, appropriated as tools in addressing specific issues of criminal procedure. For Lyublinsky, whose research focused on citizenship and the protection of rights in the court of law, the 'intuitive ethical consciousness' was the most appropriate measure for testing the viability of laws and judicial procedures.[54] Poznyshev, for his part, took over the term 'imperative-attributive conscience' (*imperativnoe-atributivnoe soznanie*) in an attempt to reset the dynamics Petrazhitsky had established between law and morality, namely the importance the latter ascribed to the power of law over moral conscience in people's lives. Poznyshev contended that 'the large majority of moral norms may in fact be called 'attributive-imperative': 'Quite often we demand that others observe certain "rules", such as "respect", in their behaviour towards us.' He also argued, not terribly convincingly admittedly, that while people, in general, tend to respond to the threat of laws, this is not always the case: 'It all depends on the individual and the circumstances (...). We should not forget that, in most cases, the voice of conscience conjoins with the dictates of law.'[55] If

Poznyshev pushed the logic of Petrazhitsky to extremes that the latter probably would have resisted, and failed to grasp the meaning Petrazhitsky ascribed to *pravo* (more understandably, given the multiple nuances it contained in Petrazhitsky's lexicon), his assimilation, like Lyublinsky, of Petrazhitsky's conceptual framework so soon after it was devised by the master himself suggests, as indeed, Walicki authoritatively claims, that the Petersburg professor was the most popular and charismatic influence on the post-1900 juridical scene.

Whatever scholarly progress this second generation made, and irrespective of their gains in the public eye, namely the positive recognition of certain individual jurists and their role as public figures, it should not be forgotten that the contrast with judicial practice was probably never as stark as it became during the reign of Nicholas II. Given that the 1903 Criminal Law Code was never ratified in its entirety, judges were often compromised in their work: religious and political offences were assessed on the basis of the new Code, while most general crimes still fell to the jurisdiction of the 1845 Code. The effect on public legal consciousness (*narodnoe pravosoznanie*) of two equally viable codes bearing on quite different juridical principles merely reinforced a deeply ingrained distrust of law and existing legal institutions. Chubinsky summed up the dilemma:

> If we try to turn our state into a rule of law state, if we really consider the display of public legal awareness important, and accept as crucial that the influence a legislator may and should have on a citizen's motivations be exercised via the channel of the law, then the first condition to be fulfilled is a unified, well defined and premised criminal code – precisely that which we are still lacking in this country.[56]

Given the conditions under which the commission had drafted the 1903 Code, with its stops and starts over a 20-year period, the headway it finally made in terms of updating pre-reform legislation, if considerable, nevertheless was checked by its deference to the autocratic system, the repressive and reactionary nature of which reached its peak in the closing decades of the nineteenth century. This proved to be the biggest insurmountable obstacle in constructing a radically improved Criminal Code according to the European model. 'Our code is already beginning to age without having experienced the rosy hue of youth.'[57] In short, the Code compromised many of the theoretical positions its compilers otherwise shared. Deferent and casuistic, the Criminal Code continued to privilege circumstances bearing on the material side of crime, to the exclusion of the 'will of the perpetrator', and still failed to reflect sufficiently the ethos of individualization – a staple concept in textbook literature and juridical theory since at least the 1880s.[58]

In the opening decade of the twentieth century, then, judicial practice seemed to be slipping ever further away from both theory and written laws, exacerbated by the declaration of a state of emergency, which only led to yet more abuses of the principle of 'inalienability'. By 1905, the jurist's commitment to vest *lichnost'* with rights and freedom and institute the principle of 'innocent before proven guilty' had become a joke in poor taste. If the October Manifesto renewed the reform pledge to a true inalienability of the individual (*deistvitel'naya neprikosnovennost' lichnosti*), it failed to live up to its promise. Widely discussed in the first and second Dumas, the matter remained unresolved (*ostalis' bez razsmotreniya*), and a commission for the third state Duma so deformed its purpose that instead of a bill on inalienability of the person, it produced a bill on the 'inalienability of existing restrictions in the area of limiting the rights of the person (*stesnenie prav lichnosti*)'.[59] This situation led some juridical thinkers to stress the idea of 'social responsibility', and the need to improve the level of education and culture, instead of relying on the casuistic regulations of the official code. Lyublinsky summed up the dilemma in the following way suggesting a 'make ends do' temporary solution:

> The long struggle for individual freedom (*lichnaya svoboda*) has taught us that it cannot be attained simply through the promulgation of laws. If today [1906 – FN], the repression of criminals continues to be very severe, and continues to rely quite heavily on principles of deterrence, if public sanction is not sufficiently strong (…) and if the moral level of the criminal person is still pitifully low, all this gives sufficient grounds to support the view that criminal justice is not ready to be grounded in the principle of individual freedom, and must still have recourse to coercive measures. Only when (…) the cultural foundations become more stable, will these chains snap, and the time will come to house them in the museum of history together with all the other remaining vestiges of inquisitorial logic. We are convinced that coercive measures are rapidly outliving their day; the future belongs to curative (*popechitel'nyi*) and psychologically motivated measures. But, in anticipation, our immediate task is to work through and offer a critique of current punitive measures, to look for compromises best adapted to the level of justice currently available to us.[60]

Legal culture and the death penalty

> It is a fact that the most consistent and authentic forms of revenge and deterrence have vanished in contemporary criminal legislation. (…) This single fact sufficiently demonstrates that the principle of 'uncivilized' justice and its 'barbarian' transformation have been outlived by a moral–legal consciousness and that another more lofty point of view has now arisen and achieved significant success here in the attitude of society toward crime and the criminal. Nevertheless, even in those countries where this progress is being made – in Europe and America – there still remain in punitive law and in penitentiary systems much unnecessary violence and torture, which can be explained only as the dead legacy of the obsolete principles of vengeance and deterrence. Such are life sentences, hard labour, long-term

> exile with ruinous conditions of survival. (…) And though the death penalty has lost its undergirding foundation, it is still stubbornly defended in certain circles.
>
> (Vladimir Solov'ev, *Law and Morality*, 1897)[61]

'In Russia,' wrote Spasovich in 1891, 'capital punishment is and will remain for many years to come a normal punishment for major political crimes.'[62] One might be forgiven for wondering why the death penalty was an issue at all, given that, compared to other European countries it was rarely applied in cases of ordinary, non-political crimes, such as murder of an individual or rape. In the eighteenth century, Empress Elizabeth Petrovna pledged never to use it during her reign and suspended the death penalty altogether by decree.[63] However, despite Elizabeth's outright ban, the death penalty, as such, was never removed from the statute books, and following the Pugachev Rebellion (1773–1775), Catherine the Great reinstated it for crimes against the state (meaning the person of the Emperor or his/her government). Successive updates of the criminal and penal codes up to and including the partially authorized code of 1903 restricted its use to a very small number of crimes, all bar one, namely flagrant violation of quarantine regulations during outbreaks of cholera first incorporated in the 1832 Digest, classifiable as 'major and political': attacks on the imperial family, insurrection directed against the throne or state, and extreme cases of treason in wartime.[64]

On the surface, Russian practice would seem to support Spasovich's unusually complacent-sounding statement cited above, since the number of executions actually carried out was, indeed, very low. In the year Spasovich was working on his article, not a single death sentence was passed in the civilian courts.[65] However, what might appear to be a high degree of leniency exercised by a civilized nation in the concert of Europe paradoxically masked the country's social political backwardness. The fact that only the tsar and state required due protection was, as Jonathan Daly has argued, symptomatic of a pre-modern, paternalistic attitude to human life:

> This notion contrasted with the West European conception of citizens as possessing inherent rights to life, liberty, and property which lay at the foundation of the existing political systems; an attack on an individual's life or property challenged the fundamental principles of the whole system.[66]

As Daly also notes, excessive use of administrative exile and *katorga*, which we witness in the late Imperial period, is also suggestive of a non-modern approach to punishment.[67]

Well into the Reform period, the tsar's approval was required for the death sentence to be passed. Empowered to pardon or punish, the tsar's intervention in the juridical process meant that all infractions of the law ultimately deserved his personal vengeance or his forgiveness. For critics, this raison d'être of capital punishment exhibited an oddly 'pre-modern mentality'. If, until the closing decades of the century, physical executions themselves were unusual, and generally commuted to permanent exile, the logic of 'political death' (the status of *mort vivante*) and the spectacle of 'civil execution', promulgated by Elizabeth Petrovna in lieu of the death penalty (1754) seemed strange anachronisms indeed, vestiges of the retributive function of punishment, and almost impossible to reconcile with contemporary theories of punishment based on the idea of protecting society, restorative justice, and assumptions concerning 'rule of law'.[68] In addition, with the majority of death sentences carried out for acts of terror, or suspected terror (between 1891 and 1900, a total of 126 death sentences were handed down by military courts in the Russian borderlands), the principal argument in favour of the death penalty as a deterrent seemed to misfire: more often than not, executions – especially when staged publicly – immortalized the accused as martyrs for the cause. For successive generations of radical and liberal *intelligenty*, officially designated rebels such as Pugachev, the leading Decembrists, Alexander II's assassins, or Lenin's brother (in an attempted assassination of Alexander III) became iconic reminders of the struggle still to be won.[69]

Two famous appeals for a stay of execution (as opposed to outright condemnation of the death penalty) were made by Vladimir Solov'ev and Lev Tolstoi in what turned out to be an unsuccessful bid to save Alexander II's assassins from execution in April 1881. Solov'ev took advantage of a public lecture to broadcast his views, while Tolstoi confined his thoughts to paper in a private letter addressed to the tsar.[70] Known for their marked intellectual differences (Solov'ev defended institutional structures as a means to improve the moral lot of society; Tolstoi, the anarchist, advocated the law of love over the law of violence), it is curious to note that the arguments of both men were framed by essentially pre-modern concepts of justice. By appealing to the idea of forgiveness, they were paying tribute to the 'divine' rights of the tsar as an absolute monarch as well as stressing the fact that he is first and foremost a Christian. The law of God dictates 'Thou shalt not kill' – so Solov'ev reminded his audience.[71] Tolstoi also stressed the same point, recasting the notion of punishment in terms of good and evil:

> I know (…) that it is impertinent and mad of me (…) to require of you a spiritual strength which has no precedent; to require that you, the Russian Tsar, under pressure from all who surround you, and being a loving son, should after a murder forgive the murderers and return them good for evil; but I cannot help wishing this, nor can I help seeing that your every step in the direction of forgiveness is a step towards good.[72]

For members of the legal profession, the stand that Solov'ev and Tolstoi took, while certainly courageous, was not the most effective way of tackling the deeper and more intricate problems of the existing practice of criminal justice. By couching their appeals in this way, they were not only failing to challenge the penal code itself but were reinforcing the traditional way of thinking about crime and justice: good versus evil, justice understood as moral retribution, and the tsar empowered by God to pardon or punish. Clearly, it was not enough to rely on 'persuasion through pathos' tactics for its abolishment: arguments against capital punishment required a cogent demonstration of its redundancy as well. Spasovich wrote:

> The very question of the death penalty is not a logical one, to which a solution may be found in clear cut rational proofs. From a logical point of view, all arguments against the death penalty are extremely weak and unconvincing. Objectors argue against it on the grounds that it excludes any repeal (*nedelima*), that it encourages rather than dissuades others to engage in crime, that it unjustifiably dramatises an event which in fact would be best forgotten.[73]

Arguments departing from the juridical terrain, by appealing to moral outrage, or Christian charity were 'weak', because they were little more than emotionally driven responses to the idea of physical brutality. But, while reformers would nod their heads in approval, agreeing that it is crucial to expel the moralizing retributive connotations of punishment, the arguments they drew on against the death penalty nevertheless caused some reformers who otherwise cleaved to an ideal of the strictly juridical to muddy the waters with 'persuasion through moral pathos' tactics themselves.

One reason for their temporary suspension of 'scientific rigor' may have been the role played by Mittermaier whose influence in the early Reform era was, as I have mentioned, quite considerable. Mittermaier was one of the first to have shifted the terms of the debate away from the philosophical and metaphysical plane, within which Beccaria had set out his argument, to the domain of criminal justice from where he challenged its efficacy as a form of deterrence. His work on the question ranked as one of the first to be translated into Russian.[74] Similarly, in the early 1860s, the *Journal of the Ministry of Justice* published translations of Victor Hugo's famous open letters to the French government condemning the death penalty and reported debates in England on the question. On home territory, however, contemporaries often cited Prince Orlov's '*zapiska*' of March 1861 as the initial spark triggering debate on capital punishment as a consciousness-raising issue soliciting public participation. Orlov's famous denunciation of the existing practices of criminal justice found a sympathetic echo among high-ranking statesmen and ultimately led to the promulgation of the Ordinance banning corporal punishment in April 1863. 'Shattering the penal staircase' of the 1845 code, it prompted a first wave of publications calling for the abolition of capital punishment.[75] The 1860s saw a slew of writings by academics and essayists on the question, culminating with the landmark publication by Kistyakovsky in 1867. For his student audience, this historical research into capital punishment in West European culture was a thinly veiled criticism of current practice in Russia. Among the factors strongly weighing against the death penalty, he listed Christian teaching and economic growth. With the emergence of the nation-state, Kistyakovsky argued, man has attained high levels of economic, social, intellectual, and moral development; greater material and spiritual well-being yield a softening of customs, mores (*nravy*).[76] Thus, as a society progresses up the ladder of civilization, use of the death penalty as a means to satisfy the need for revenge (even if couched in the language of divine retribution) loses ground to a more sophisticated understanding of the meaning and function of the penal system. The main arguments underlining the injustice, ineffectiveness, and harm of the death penalty were that it was not effective as a deterrent (*ne ustrashaet*); has a demoralizing effect on the public; and is irreversible. It is a form of barbarism that no longer corresponds to levels of sensitivity, nor expectations among peoples in today's civilization.[77] Thus, as physical torture becomes abhorrent, 'we witness the phasing out of capital punishment as a moral necessity – a generally accepted attitude reinforced by a philosophical awareness that the death penalty is an unjust, useless and unnecessary form of punishment'.[78]

With the tightening of censorship measures in the 1880s and 1890s and the introduction of emergency rule, the timid beginnings of public protest as encapsulated in Solov'ev and Tolstoi's appeals to the tsar were crushed, and, indeed, rendered ineffectual by the disappearance of executions from the public stage.[79] Thereafter confined to academic discussion, opinions expressed on the topic tended to be formulated within the safety net of 'science for the sake of science'. And it was the main thrust of Kistyakovsky's argument – in a modern society, the primary function of punishment should be corrective – that was echoed by virtually all the leading opponents of the death penalty. Sergeevsky, for example, used Western examples (France and Germany) to condemn the practice for its 'demoralizing, corrupt influences on national conscience'. In view of their history of inalienable rights, 'politically' the institution of capital punishment actually contradicted the place 'accorded to the human person as a citizen in a modern state', thus posing the rhetorical question: does the state in fact have the right to deprive one of its citizens of his life? Spasovich shared this view: in the present-day world, the death penalty is politically more harmful than useful as a measure, because it departs from the aims and meaning of punishment in a modern state.[80] The muted tones of the 'civilizational' argument, however, had several shortcomings, not the least of which was the fact that the societies that served as the basis for their criticism of the death penalty were models to emulate, not equivalent structures. Thus, in Russia, for punishment to mean 'loss of freedom' – as stated in the codes – and not a moral judgement as public shaming and the tsar's pardon in fact made it, it was vital to have a social framework incorporating notions of citizenship and inalienable rights. In late-nineteenth-century Russia, it was a regrettable point of fact that such notions were still not a part of mass – or even educated – consciousness. It was therefore perhaps inevitable that appeals to 'moral sensitivity' (*nravstvennoe nastroenie*), 'the human person' (*lichnost' cheloveka*), life as a gift of God – emotive arguments that fed public opinion and would be widely used after 1900 – crept into some of these earlier, ostensibly 'scientific' endeavours to outlaw the death penalty. A case in point is Sergeevsky, who spoke of the death penalty as an affront on the moral sensitivities shared by higher echelons of society, though he did go on to conclude that the fact that the death penalty is not individualized and irreversible (*nedelima i bezuslovno nevoznagradima*) was sufficient grounds for resolving the issue from a juridical perspective.[81] In his lectures, Tagantsev admitted the theoretical coherence of the absolutist viewpoint condoning capital punishment as normal but employed the common-sense tactics which Spasovich deplored to speak out against it: 'The death penalty cannot possibly serve as an appropriate tool of due justice', and he also included the transcendent perspective to drive home his point: 'Life is the gift of God. God alone can put an end to life or spare it (…). By taking life, the state is presumptuously and mistakenly assuming a right which it does not have.'[82]

Possibly, the single exception among first-generation reformers was Foinitsky whose scientifically couched protest against the death penalty and exile in perpetuity was wholly consistent with his understanding of the re-educational function of punishment and his overarching theory of criminality as a transient, curable, state of being. Accordingly, punishment could not involve the total annihilation of the person, nor cause her long-term suffering, since the state of being inducing the crime in the first place would have passed, substituted by new states: 'neither the death penalty nor life sentences are commensurate with individual states of criminality.' He also brought in the economic factor:

> Punishment is deprivation not only for the person sentenced, but also for society as a whole. Every criminal, albeit imprisoned for a determined period, is removed from society thereby depriving the latter of its work force; even more detrimental to the economy of society is the death penalty.[83]

However, if Foinitsky's arguments against the death penalty were woven seamlessly into his overall theory, like the historical–comparative approach used by most contemporaries, they seemed oddly suspended in an intellectual vacuum. Moreover, although they argued forcefully for softer measures to be taken in the event of non-political crimes, Spasovich, Foinitsky, and Sergeevsky all condoned the use of capital punishment for major political crimes, or during times of war, as a necessary means to protect state sovereignty.[84] If coherent as a principle, holding such a position during emergency rule was likely to undermine its otherwise acceptable premise. Indeed, according to Arsen'ev, that most specialists in military criminal law remained silent on the matter of court-martialling, with only a few venturing to say that it was theoretically justified in times of war, was eloquent proof of the degree to which the Criminal Code was currently being abused to cope with the infectious spread of suspected political crime. One noted exception was the jurist V.D. Kuz'min-Karavaev, a major general and professor at the St Petersburg Military-Judicial Academy. An outspoken critic of the death penalty, he denounced it even under martial law. After the 1905 Revolution, alongside Tagantsev, he actively campaigned for its abolition in the first two sessions of the Duma.[85]

A Neo-Kantian and religious–philosophical critique of the death penalty: Sergei Gessen and Vladimir Solov'ev

> Never and nowhere has punishment been the mechanical outcome of a criminal act with uniquely the external side taken into consideration.[86]

In a highly remarked essay, 'The Philosophy of Punishment', the neo-Kantian philosopher of law Sergei Gessen exposed the blind spots in classical juridical thought. But, while he accepted the grounds on which modern-day relativists sought to instate the criminal as a flesh and blood reality, he also believed that they squandered their practical gains on methodological sloppiness: drawing pell-mell on sociological and anthropological factors, their heteronomous concept of law meant sacrificing the 'autonomous concept of the legal person, as a bearer of rights', and therefore free.[87] For Gessen, each school scored points on the issue of punishment, certainly: the classical school of thought conceived punishment in terms of a formal loss of legal rights, resulting in reduced freedoms of the legal subject; the indisputable achievement of empirical schools was the emphasis they placed on the individualization or expedient character of punishment. Yet, despite their declared differences, both trends were seriously flawed in their understanding of the criminal person: both schools of thought failed to differentiate, be it by default or intent, between the 'psychophysical organism' and the 'legal subject'. If in condemning the legal subject, rationalists overlooked the fact that it was the physical subject that endures the punishment, criminologists simply rejected the 'legal subject' as a metaphysical construct, the consequence of which was 'the suicide of criminal law'.[88] Their tendency to substitute crime with factors of criminality was one telling example of their 'methodological bouillabaisse'.

The confusion of formal and material aspects of crime and punishment provided Gessen with a philosophical exercise in critical neo-Kantian vein at demarcating their respective fields of competence. Only after careful analysis of crime as a formal breach of law (*pravonarushenie*), distinct from crime as a deed involving a complex of material factors, and, likewise, after careful differentiation between punishment as 'condemnation' (*osuzhdenie*) as opposed to the enforcement of concrete measures (*materializatsiya*), would it be possible, he argued, to construct a genuinely 'critical synthesis of competing theories'.[89] For Gessen, *prestuplenie* is a formal definition of a breach of justice (*spravedlivost'*) and, as such, is an intrinsic part of law: 'Various forms of crime may disappear', he argued, 'but crime in general may only disappear together with law itself.' By contrast, 'factors of criminality' designate the material side of crime and therefore involve a complex of considerations extraneous to law, which, by nature, are subject to change.[90]

Taking an analogous approach to the concept of punishment, Gessen then used his differentiated definitions to construct a juridically sound case against capital punishment. Obviously, if punishment is to serve any purpose at all, it requires a legal subject vested with rights (the 'bearer of the idea of law').

Deprivation of rights through the process of materialization or the realization of a judgement

> is not in conflict with this fundamental requirement of punishment, so long as the criminal is not deprived of all of them. Were this the case, he would cease to exist as a legal subject since, in this instance, not only would certain concrete rights – the content of the legal subject (*pravosub'ektnost'*) – be affected, but the very idea of the legal person in general, too. Paradoxically, then, total deprivation of rights, in the form of life sentences and the death penalty, would effectively deprive punishment of its juridical raison d'être, turning it into a 'juridical nonsense' (*pravovaya bezsmyslitsa*).[91]

Gessen's rigorous critique of the death penalty as a juridical nonsense openly took its cue from Solov'ev: 'In many respects, we are following in his footsteps (*My vo mnogom sleduem zdes' ukazannomu im puti*).'[92] Solov'ev's attempt to reconcile rationalist and empirical trends had, Gessen acknowledged, influenced the broad framework of his own discussion, which he recast in the vocabulary of a critical philosophy of culture. Gessen was inspired by Solov'ev's quest for a purely juridical condemnation that might successfully answer Kant's formal and logically consistent justification of the death penalty. That Solov'ev did not entirely succeed did not make the task any less viable. In Gessen's eyes, Solov'ev failed to clarify the meaning of freedom with prerequisite philosophical rigour. By not differentiating between the formal concept of freedom, which defines the very essence of law as '*pravosub'ektnost*', and concrete forms of freedom (freedom of speech, movement etc.) of which a convicted criminal is deprived, Solov'ev's argument, 'here and there', confused the legal and psychophysical subject. Yet, if Gessen himself managed to tread an intellectual high wire in his differentiated concepts of crime and punishment, his discussion of the death penalty that brought the two aspects of the legal and psychophysiological subject into a pinnacle-like point of convergence was arguably too intellectualized to be of any immediate relevance for those actively engaged in campaigning against the institution. As he put it,

> No matter how important it is to separate the legal subject from the psychophysical organism, we should remember that the legal subject is only a form, unthinkable (*bezsmyslennaya*) without its matter which welds it together into an undifferentiated whole. (…) Here (i.e., in the death penalty) is the point where the differentiated legal and psychophysical subjects must be reunited, as two elements in need of each other.[93]

By contrast, Solov'ev's engagement with prescriptive solutions may have left him with chinks in his theoretical weaponry, but the thrust of his arguments against punishment as deterrence and his stature as a 'human rights' figure earned him posthumous recognition in the debate on the death penalty among educated public activists.

Solov'ev's definition of law as a balance of two moral interests – of personal freedom and the common good – allowed him to argue that the death penalty was not only in breach of moral sensibilities or Christian belief (a profane, inhumane, and shameful act, usurping divine justice) but was, in fact, a negation of the law in its very essence. The common good can only restrict the personal freedom of each, 'but in no case can it have the intention of its complete abolition, for then, obviously, any balance would be violated'. If Solov'ev called upon the Bible's prophetic norm of mercy, and attacked those who also drew on the Old Testament idea of vengeance to promote the death penalty, he was careful to stress that the 'inhumanity' of the death penalty was, in fact, a matter of principle rather than one of gut reaction. Like Alexander Kistyakovsky, Solov'ev maintained that it was 'materially useless for society (…) and spiritually harmful as an immoral action of society itself'. Granted, murder is an 'intrinsic renunciation of the basic moral norm', severing common human solidarity, but retribution in the form of the death penalty is 'absolute murder'.

> Society only has left an *animus interficiendi* in absolutely pure form with respect to the executed criminal, completely free from all those physiological and psychological conditions and motives which darkened and obscured the essence of the matter in the eyes of the criminal himself, whether he committed the murder from calculation of gain, or under the influence of a less shameful passion. There can be no such complexities of motivation in the death penalty (…). The death penalty is murder as such, absolute murder that is in principle the denial of a fundamental moral attitude toward man.[94]

In *Law and Morality*, Solov'ev explained that he had acquired his firm stand against the death penalty on Christian grounds from his father:

> Once while still in adolescence I expressed my revulsion to the cold-blooded murder of an unarmed man, and I heard from my father the following inspiring definition: 'the death penalty is a loathsome thing, it is a betrayal of Christianity!' Since that time, the denial of this 'loathsome thing' became in me a steadfast idea, which required later only a precise logical expression and factual corroboration.[95]

Unable to resolve the dilemma presented by the logic of retributive justice condoning capital punishment and the emotive power of Christian love and charity condemning it, in his *Critique* Solov'ev resorted to an appeal to gut reaction: 'We simply cannot concede that I could *actually* show Christian love to a neighbour whom I send to the gallows in my capacity as a judge.'[96] (It was, of course, in this spirit that he had couched his appeal to Alexander III.) In *Law and Morality*, however, thanks to his formulation of law as a balance of two moral interests, Solov'ev had at last succeeded in giving reasoned ballast to the 'revulsion to the cold-blooded murder of an unarmed man' he had experienced as a youth:

> If any positive law is found in contradiction of principle with a moral consciousness of the Good, then we can be certain in advance that it does not answer the essential requirements of rights either, and the interest of the law relative to such statutes can in no way consist in their preservation, but only in their *lawful* repeal.[97]

This critique became a landmark text for juridical thinkers and the wider intelligentsia in the public outcry against the massive wave of summary executions after 1905.

The death penalty and revolution

As the disciplinary codes for the army and navy were extended to the population at large, Russia, after 1905, seemed to be standing in the eerie shadow of Peter the Great, whose Military Statutes (1720) had prescribed the death penalty for a wide-ranging number of ordinary offences including murder, witchcraft, sodomy, attempted suicide, and various offences against property.[98] Granted, by the mid-nineteenth century, the number of sentences punishable by death in the Military Statutes had been reduced to five – for refusal to carry out orders, mutiny, murder of a sentry, desertion, or aiding the enemy – but under emergency rule, in the late nineteenth century, the number of designated capital offences went up again to approximately 30. In addition, convicts who committed crimes while serving their hard labour sentences could be tried by military courts and sentenced to death.

Articles 91 and 279 of the Military Code outlining special circumstances contained what were effectively legislative loopholes that would facilitate the application of harsher punishments for civilians during peacetime. Indeed, these had been applied during the reign of Alexander II, as he struggled to contain unrest in Poland after the 1863 uprising, quash peasant riots and combat revolutionary terrorism in Moscow and St Petersburg.[99] In response to mounting tides of terrorist activity, the government passed a succession of laws augmenting the powers of local authorities in the transfer of civilians to military courts and appointed governors-general in all the main provinces to expedite sentences according to the laws of wartime. With the introduction of reinforced and extraordinary protection under Alexander III, courts martial became ever more widespread. Thereafter, as Rawson has shown, the law of 14 August 1881 'became the judicial mainstay for the government's fight against political and social unrest', culminating in the dramatically high numbers of death sentences handed down as a response to revolutionary involvement. Between 1906 and 1912, just under 3,000 civilians were sentenced to death by district military courts, 2,400 of whom were convicted on the basis of the emergency law of 1881. The year 1908, when 1,340 executions were carried out, went down in the books as one of the most brutal in Russian history before 1917.[100] The gravity of the situation strikes home if one reckons that, for the entire 80-year period between 1826 and 1906, roughly 700 executions for political reasons were carried out. If half of these occurred in the final quarter of the century, the average annual number of executions was still a modest 17. In other words, the final decade of the tsarist regime should not be seen as the high point in a golden period of improvement; rather, as Stephen Wheatcroft argues, it marked the beginning of 'increased repression as the modern police state made its first incursions into a semi-modern and rapidly modernizing society'.[101] All this had repercussions on the terms of the debate against the death penalty and its re-entry into the public sphere.

As a collective body, jurists first formulated opposition to the death penalty in 1883 at a meeting of the Moscow Juridical Society convened to discuss the project for the new Criminal Code. Having discussed the proposals by the commission on the death penalty, the committee of the juridical society voted unanimously for its removal from the new Code of Punishments: 'The decision was made both in light of the history of the death penalty in Russia (reference was made to Elizabeth Petrovna – FN) and with view to current trends and attitudes to the question in Western Europe.' However, given the implications of disloyalty to the throne for suggesting that a penalty designed to protect the tsar should be removed, the commission set up to draft the Criminal Code was ultimately obliged to retain it, deferring the final decision to the powers of the state council.[102]

If, in 1883, the failed bid to abolish the death penalty had only minor repercussions on judicial practice given that relatively few executions were carried out, after 1900, the wide ambit for the application of the Military Code to the civilian population brought into sharp focus the uses and abuses by the state of the legal premises it instituted. The inclusion of the death penalty in the 1903 Code, which members of the legal profession regarded as a judicial anachronism, prompted the renewal of the campaign for abolition. In January 1905, at the Congress of the Russian Section of the International Union of Criminologists in Kiev, a resolution calling for an outright ban and carried unanimously by Congress members effectively became the first in a series of what might be termed 'contained' *obshchestvennost'* gestures, where a closed professional-cum-scientific forum served as a platform for discussion of urgent social ethical concerns.[103] Later, in October of the same year, a similar resolution was taken at the Second All Russian Congress of lawyers. In addition to exposing legislative loopholes and administrative *proizvol*, those present at the meeting decreed the institution of a 'special league for the fight against the death penalty', detailing a number of specific measures to be taken, from boycotts and blacklisting the names of people implicated in the trials and executions to public lectures and readings by members of the intelligentsia.[104]

The conceptual vocabulary of the debate also evolved. While early pioneers of reform had generally avoided addressing the issue of the death penalty in Russia head-on as a consciousness-raising issue, their research on the subjective side of crime that fostered a sense of the sovereignty of the individual did, however, foreshadow theoretical developments in both positivism and idealism at the turn of the century sensitive to the discovery of personhood. After 1905, conceptions of the modern state as an 'economic manager' as opposed to 'night watchman' required a corresponding change in the function of law (*pravo*) from that of a tool sanctioning coercive authority to that of underpinning the 'free ethical consciousness of its citizens'. According to Lyublinsky, key qualifiers in a modern state were respect for the individual and efforts to sustain social ethics at the required level by eliminating anything that threatened to destroy it. Failure to do so would be detrimental to its vital strength. Writing at the height of the state backlash against revolutionary activity, Lyublinsky's message was clear: use of the death penalty is a display of force by a weak state power.[105] As I discuss below, outside the juridical community, this defence of personal sovereignty – *tsennost' lichnosti*, as Zhizhilenko termed it – would dovetail with some of the more 'aesthetically' charged objections to the death penalty penned by leading literary and public figures.[106]

After 1905, with the easing of censorship, the natural home for juridical reformers to test out their theoretical ideas and reach a wider audience was the press and *publitsistika*. The liberal weekly newspaper *Pravo* with its respected editorial committee headed by Iosif V. Gessen in close collaboration with Petrazhitsky and Kuz'min-Karavaev played a key role in shaping Russian legal culture and, during the years of protest against the death penalty, it figured prominently as a conduit between legal specialists and the broader educated society. Arguments bearing the imprint of current juridical discourse, namely the accent on the moral worth of the person (Lyublinsky, Poznyshev) and the terms of criminal ethics (Mokrinsky) were applied to discussions of the death penalty. A piece by N.N. Rozin, professor at Tomsk University, for example, contained all the hallmarks of the latest juridical thinking on the death penalty: it was deemed an 'illegal' coercive measure (laws require consensus to be effective); unjustified as a means of practical necessity; ineffective as a way of containing revolutionary fervour; an anachronism. Most importantly, however, for this author, the death penalty was an affront on the religious and ethical sensitivities of contemporary society predicated on the notion of respect for the human person – 'for the human person is the centre and foundation of our culture'.[107] In making this last point, Rozin echoed almost verbatim some of the key objections Solov'ev had mounted against the death penalty in his analysis of punishment from a moral perspective. As Rozin put it, paraphrasing Solov'ev, 'the influence and success of the law is assured by its moral character'. Thus, in a society enriched by a moral–legal culture, the death penalty is simply 'dishonest, inhumane and shameful'. Applying the tools of 'criminal ethics', Mokrinsky phrased a similar objection in a rhetorical question:

> Do we have the right to regard the good (*blago*) in the moral life of an individual man as something incommensurably less valuable than, say, that of mankind? If preserving the moral life is the *ultima ratio* of criminal ethics, then are we right to encroach upon that which constitutes the truly necessary receptacle of that *ratio*?[108]

As 'legalized murder' – an expression widely used in the literature – the death penalty was simply in breach of the moral religious law: 'thou shalt not kill'.

Constant reminders of the inalienability, if not sanctity, of the person found their most powerful resonance in the public arena. The press, *publitsistika* and, in particular, published transcripts of Duma speeches effectively preyed on the moral sensibilities of a wider audience and also openly challenged the political privileges of the state.[109] If, previously, abolitionist arguments did not bear on the state's privilege to apply articles of the Military Code, Kuz'min-Karavaev now used his status as Duma deputy to attack state duplicity:

> As a general rule, our legislature is not fond of mentioning the death penalty, and instead of open recognition ('the accused is found guilty and is condemned to death'), it employs a referenced sanction (*ssylochnaya sanktsya*) of the sort 'in the name of preserving state order and social security....' Nowhere, in not one civilized state, will you find as vague a formulation for the use of the death penalty, at the present time, as in Russia.[110]

Explicitly designed to mobilize public opinion, speeches by newly elected jurist-deputies combined statistical evidence of the inefficacy of the death penalty as a deterrent with vivid illustrations drawn from case studies of its unwarranted brutality. In addition, they openly incorporated the psychological, moral, and religious perspective into their arguments, which they now backed with confessional style assertions of their principles as Christians. They cited the lay opinions of writers and intellectuals such as Aksakov, Turgenev, Dickens, and, of course, Tolstoi and Solov'ev, whose personal pleas for the tsar's pardon in 1881 now acquired a poignant resonance as a landmark moment in the struggle against 'legalized murder'. Solov'ev's emotional 'the death penalty is sickening for the spirit of the Russian people' was echoed by deputies in the Duma in their bid to abolish the institution through democratic procedure. Kuz'min-Karavaev, for example, spoke of the peace-loving nature of the Russian people.[111] In his address to the state council, just prior to the dissolution of the first Duma in June 1906, Tagantsev presented the, by now, well-rehearsed arguments based on statistical evidence, sociological and historical considerations. But the energy of his remarks came from the received ideas he traded in with respect to the Christian faith of the people:

> I believe that despite all the efforts at inciting the Russian people to bloody and evil deeds, they will not be lured by these wolves in sheep's clothing. I believe that the Russian people have not abandoned the moral grounding of love of one's neighbour, that it has not forgotten the commandment of He, Who, from the cross, prayed for his enemies (...). The Russian people will not yield to incitements of pogroms and mass destruction.[112]

Increasingly then, as the death penalty became a consciousness-raising issue, ethical religious considerations and the spirit of Christian teaching carried more weight than the arid juridical arguments found in textbooks. If logically sound, these latter proved to be inadequate to the task of resolving the issue once it had entered the social and political arena:

> At the present time, the question must be transposed to an ethical soil (...). Becoming aware of the ethical inadmissibility of the death penalty involves not so much logical reason as an appeal to moral feeling, to the conscience of cultured humanity (...). The task of contemporary abolitionists is to spread across society a sense of revulsion and horror at the barbarity (...), this stain on humanity, which inflicts so much shame.[113]

Thus, in a sense, by ceding a place to heartfelt conviction in their condemnation of the practice, jurists seemed to come full circle with Tolstoi and Solov'ev's original petitions to Alexander III. That Solov'ev later distanced himself from this approach in order to develop a juridically sound argument is not without a certain irony.

'I cannot be silent'

> No one had as many people put to death, and in such an outrageous manner as he, Stolypin. No one acted so arbitrarily, as he did; no one showed as little regard for the law (*opleval*) as he, Stolypin did (...), and all to the tune of the most liberal speeches and gestures (...). One might even be a supporter of the death penalty, but the Stolypin regime transformed it into sheer unadulterated murder, senseless, defying all comprehension.[114]

The immediate cause for mass condemnation of the death penalty was the apparent sleight of hand with which the government responded to the increase in terrorist acts and lawlessness across the country. Invoking Article 87 of the Fundamental Laws 1906, the Council of Ministers issued with imperial approval a new emergency law (19 August 1906) authorizing an accelerated judicial procedure for civilians transferred to military courts. Each case was to be decided within 48 hours and the sentence carried out within 24 hours of the verdict. By the time the law expired, eight months later, in April 1907, the number of deaths was, according to some estimates, well over 1,000, a staggering increase if compared with the previous year for which tables give a mere 25 with a count of 19 in 1904.[115] For the Duma, this 1906–1907 episode was merely the first in a series to undermine its political clout. Successive attempts to pass a bill abolishing capital punishment were thwarted, first by ministerial evasiveness, then by political hair-splitting. Having voted unanimously in June 1906 for the 'immediate suspension of the death penalty for both political and criminal offences', the Duma assembly was abruptly dissolved a month later and the bill consigned to a pile of unfinished business. If, during the following spring, it succeeded in abrogating the emergency law of 1906, efforts to renew debate of the original bill, in 1907, were postponed indefinitely.[116]

With the Duma effectively silenced, agitation against the emergency ruling filtered into the public sphere, where it took the form of strikes and petitions on the ground and *ad personam* denunciations penned by literary and philosophical intelligentsia in the *kabinet*. Parliamentary speeches and university conferences by the principal actors in drafting the original Duma bill – Nabokov, Kuz'min-Karavaev, and Tagantsev – were published in leading journals with a wide readership, and soon afterwards reprinted in single-authored and collective volumes.[117] In 1906, the first in a projected series of collective essays, *Against the Death Penalty*, at the initiative of M.N. Gernet, brought together the opinions of well-known spiritual authorities (Archimandrite Mikhail, Bishop Antonin), academics (Professor M.N. Chubinsky), essayists (Berdyaev, Bulgakov), and Duma representatives all calling for abolition.[118] Reproduced in an appendix were extracts from open letters written by a number of eminent West European and American academics and public figures, including Professor Jellinek, the philosopher Emile Boutroux, and Anatole France. As outside observers, their views from afar projected an image of Russia in turmoil, her population brutalized by an 'unending profanation of humanity'; they told of the hypocrisy of her rulers for presuming Russia's birthright as a member of the family of civilized states.[119]

Arguments against the death penalty in the public sphere mirrored the standard inventory of objections advanced by professional jurists: truth and justice as the keystones of legal order were invoked; observations concerning its ineffectiveness were backed with available statistics. For the anarchist Prince Kropotkin, the death penalty, far from being a deterrent, was the root cause of increasing brutality within society at large.

> If, in general, our penal system has failed to realize its goals of correction and deterrence, and, on the contrary, our prisons continue to aggravate forms of criminality, then, it follows, that the death penalty, like torture, is a meaningless act of cruelty.[120]

But, again, it was the incompatibility of the death penalty with moral – essentially Christian – consciousness, as couched in Solov'ev's sharpest indictment of the practice as 'a profane, inhumane, and shameful act', which fuelled the strongest, most emotive, denunciations of the death penalty. It was surely no coincidence that Gernet chose to open the volume with the section in Solov'ev's *Law and Morality* in which he had exposed the flimsy premises of theories defending the death penalty. This, as I suggested earlier, was one of the few parts of Solov'ev's work on criminal justice to earn positive approval among criminologists. But it was the brilliance with which Solov'ev expressed his loathing for the practice as a spiritually harmful and as an immoral action by society that made him ideal material for a wider audience as well. Solov'ev's horror and revulsion at the underlying hypocrisy of the death penalty was deepened by the spectacle of the execution as risk-free revenge in which the outcome is guaranteed well in advance:

> Here, a man who is unarmed and bound is ... wittingly killed by an armed man, risking absolutely nothing and acting exclusively out of lower self-interest. Hence the specifically shameful character of the death penalty and the limitless universal scorn for the executioner.[121]

For Bulgakov and Berdyaev, the widespread massacre authorized by the government could not be reckoned with or justified in the name of the law, since it went far beyond the terms of legality. It was a flagrant breach of the moral consciousness of mankind. Both portrayed the revolutionaries, now victims of state reprisal, as martyr heroes, whose sacrifice was in emulation of the crucifixion of Christ. And just as Solov'ev had called the death penalty 'absolute murder', that is, in principle the denial of a fundamental moral attitude towards man, Bulgakov described it as 'murder for murder's sake'. 'The death penalty is one of the most terrible forms of murder. It is cold, calculated, deliberate, bereft of feeling, without passion or purpose.'[122] The maverick intellectual and essayist, Vasily Rozanov, singled out the shameful character of the death penalty – murder of an unarmed, bound man – driving home his point with the uncomfortable reminder that for more than 2,000 years

> we have called ourselves 'Christians'. And look! On the instruction of a Christian Court, in compliance with the Christian law of 'holy Russia', the Christian-executioner, assisted by Christian-warriors (*voin*), tightens the noose around a man's neck and chokes him like an old horse at the knacker's yard.[123]

On the ground, the ruthlessness of the emergency law of 1906 provoked spontaneous strike action, especially in localities where field courts were conducting token trials. Shop assistants, factory workers, bank clerks, and waiters took to the streets in demonstrations of anger and outrage at the flagrant injustices being perpetrated almost every day. Some of the protests had a gruesome and graphic edge to them, such as an incident in September 1906 when protesters seized the bodies of five court-martialled men and placed them for public view in the village square.

> The revulsion Russian society and the Russian people at large feel for this punishment is beyond any doubt. Western states have never experienced as sharp a protest against the death penalty such as we have witnessed in Russia in the past few years: at meetings and reunions across the country, scholars, labourers, artists, politicians have felt it their duty to express their condemnation of the death penalty. Newspapers have been overflowing with protests.[124]

In 1906, the newspaper *Russian Bulletin* alone received 22,000 letters from readers appealing against the death penalty.[125] Petitions to cease the bloodshed were signed by public figures and intellectuals, but also in large numbers by peasants and workers in support of their elected deputies, who had represented their interests at the first, truncated session of the Duma. If amusingly naïve in expression, the logic of objections voiced by the peasantry found its place among protests reported in the press:

> We, peasants, have come to the conclusion that we must remove the death penalty. Killing a person is possible, but resurrect him – you'll never resurrect him, not with any magical waters. Many, many innocent people die. In vain will you try to bring them back.'[126]

Within educated society, collective protests were conducted from the platform of various academic, student, professional, and vocational associations. Women's equal rights movements in Moscow and Kazan were among the first to voice their opposition at meetings held in 1906 and, again, in 1909 at the first all-Russian Women's Congress. Zemstvo and municipal officials likewise condemned the emergency ruling at local meetings. University-linked juridical organizations in Kiev (1906) and St Petersburg (1909) also passed resolutions calling for the abolition of the death penalty. However, possibly the most telling episode in the short history of public protest against the death penalty was the fate of the Moscow 'League Against the Death Penalty'. Founded in the summer of 1908 as part of the celebrations to mark Tolstoi's eightieth birthday, it was closely modelled on similar organizations in Western Europe:

> We turn to all Russian citizens, men and women, regardless of their religious confession, social status, level of education, or political convictions. We are appealing to you to direct all your moral force and influence into the fight against the horror of our age – the death penalty.... Protest against the death penalty! At home with your families, with friends, at work, from the pulpit, cathedra, in the press. Use whatever means you have at your disposal to protest against the death penalty![127]

The League's programme of planned activity was modestly pitched: simply by disseminating data and pamphlets demonstrating the detrimental effect of the death penalty on social mores and its inefficacy as a means to prevent crime, the League hoped to encourage its removal 'from above' through legislative procedure. Its fate, however, describes a tragicomic catch-22 twist exploited by the government: application for registering as an official association according to the terms set out in the 1906 Temporary Regulations was eventually refused on the grounds that 'organizations aiming to fight, by whatever means, established laws can only been seen as a threat to society'.[128] Its banning in March 1909 coincided with the onset of more repressive measures involving closure of organizations and heavy fines imposed on the press for publishing what it regarded as subversive material.

According to contemporaries, the years 1908 and 1909, corresponding to the highest numbers of executions, were shrouded in silence. Voices that had once energetically protested against the death penalty – in the first two Dumas, in the press and in the streets – were now systematically repressed or cautioned. Instead, as Stolypin's conservative measures gained the upper hand, the voice of right-wing politicians, clergy, and supporters advocating the death penalty became more audible. Their arguments in favour of the practice, which usually relied on random citations from the Bible of the 'God is just' kind (and not without an anti-Semitic edge to them), were now given greater publicity:

> I have heard it said that punishment is a sin before God, before religion. I do not accept this. We were brought up to believe that God is just ... surely God could not pardon a murder and be indifferent to the suffering of the murderer's victim?

'Show me one intelligent Jew who would say that his religion forbids the death penalty.'[129] In the Duma, a new proposal in 1908 to change the legislation was carried by 103 signatories, but the heavy presence of Octobrists and monarchists guided by Stolypin's commanding hand made it relatively easy to stall procedures. In March 1909, when the bill finally came up before the State Council, it was rejected on the grounds that the Lower Chamber was not competent to assess military criminal laws, nor the application by these of capital punishment. The State Council also warned against 'general abstract arguments, which endeavour to undermine the purpose of punishment'.[130] In the meantime, laws passed in 1907 and 1909 concerning military legal procedure effectively reduced the defendant's chances for a fair trial even further. Military courts no longer required witnesses, and the use of written testimony was increasingly used in lieu of hearings based on oral evidence. The decision to reduce the number of judges from four to two officers recruited from local garrisons threatened even greater severity in the sentences passed as borne out by the figures in 1908 marking the climax in this episode of 'state terror' before subsiding to just over 700 the following year.[131]

With government and legal channels including the 'right' to form associations gradually blocked, protest in the form of an organized movement lost momentum, and members of educated society – professionals and *intelligenty* – retreated to their more familiar terrain of the scholarly essay and fictional narrative. In the more subdued atmosphere of Stolypin's strong-armed reform, Gernet published his second major collective volume, *The Death Penalty: Opinions of Russian Criminologists* (1909), as a reminder of 'how resolute and univocal Russian criminologists, men of science are in their condemnation of the death penalty'.[132] Similarly, the historian of literature, I. Malinovsky, professor at Tomsk University, published a two-volume anthology of fictionalized accounts of the death penalty, his aim, as he noted in his preface to the second volume, being to mirror Gernet's collection of scientifically informed criticism of the death penalty with examples taken from the world of literature.[133] If arguments by professional criminologists persuaded the reader of its ineffectiveness as a deterrent or as a guarantee of social security, literary masterpieces resonated with a gut feeling of revulsion and loathing that simply made the practice intolerable.

> When we read in a work of fiction that the death penalty elicits in the executioners, witnesses, and society at large reproaches of conscience, shame, pity, sympathy, revulsion, we understand that the author is protesting against the death penalty. But when we read that the death penalty is a matter of course, devoid of shame, that there is no indignation (…) then we understand that the author's protest is double edged: it means that the practice of capital punishment has led to the atrophy of moral feelings, and that it has stifled any expression of altruism in man.[134]

Traditionally, of course, literary criticism and the novel, rather than public addresses from the rostrum or even scientific discourse, had served the intelligentsia as props in their role as bearers of cultural values (*nositeli idealov narodov*), as Malinovsky put it, articulating and shaping the social vision and ideals of the people at large.[135] Thus, for example, as a juridical thinker, Nabokov might have argued that the criminal–political perspective should give way to the ethical. But as an *intelligent*, he willingly conceded that by far the most powerful denunciations of the death penalty did not belong to the professional jurist's pen at all; rather, they were to be found in literary accounts, where the focus and common denominator of concern was the person in the noose or before the firing squad, victim of a state in flagrant breach of its own legally and morally sanctioned authority. He wrote,

> They were by far more convincing and incontrovertible than the thousands of scholarly studies and columns of statistics. They do not *prove, they show* and in this resides their force. You cannot argue with them – you can only block your ears and shut your eyes.[136]

In making his point, Nabokov referred to some of the Russian classics by Turgenev, Tolstoi, and Dostoevsky, but he could easily have cited more recent fiction currently being serialized in thick journals.

The Stolypin years witnessed a slew of short stories and novellas exploring the inner world of the executioner and the condemned man. Well-known writers including Leonid Andreev, Fedor Sologub, M. Artsybashchev, I. Prishvin, and V. Korolenko, all wrote on the theme, couching their protest in deceptively muted accounts of the feelings experienced by members of the executioning body and bystanders – judges, procurator, officials, priests, physicians, and the hangman. They depicted the inner struggle experienced by the judge caught between a visceral loathing for the practice and his sense of duty or fear to do otherwise. Writers captured an underlying sense of diffused accountability between those who passed sentence and those who carried it out, the moral ambivalence that this 'passing the buck' mentality generated, and, above all, the apathy that ultimately served to perpetuate the practice. In stark contrast, whatever his crime, the condemned man confronted by his imminent death was portrayed as a victim of an unjust system. Exhibiting courage mixed with fear, as in Andreev's famous story, *The Seven Who Were Hanged*, the condemned men became martyrs. In the public eye, they were role models of defiance, an outcome, which, as criminologists had repeatedly warned, made the effectiveness of the death penalty as a deterrent highly questionable.[137]

By far, the famous voice to break the enforced silence of the Stolypin era was Tolstoi in his open letter 'I cannot be silent', possibly the best-known denunciation of capital punishment, both in Russia and abroad. Published in the summer of 1908 in all the main newspapers in St Petersburg and Moscow, as well as in the provinces and even outside Russia, the strength of the piece was that Tolstoi had abandoned the morally injunctive tone of his earlier comments on the topic for a poignant personal plea from the heart:

> You see, everything that's going on in Russia nowadays is done in the name of the general good (*obshchoe blago*), all for the sake of ensuring the safety and security of the 'population living in Russia'. For me, this 'population' also means the poorest of the poor deprived of their primordial natural right – the use of the land on which they were born; it means the expulsion of entire peoples, shunted from place to place, the hundreds and thousands of starving labourers, the hundreds and thousands suffering from typhoid and scurvy in overcrowded prisons. It means the suffering of mothers, wives, fathers of those who have been expelled, locked up, or hanged.... Being aware of all this, I can no longer tolerate it. I cannot. I must free myself from this agonizing situation. It is not possible to live this way. I, for one, cannot live this way. I cannot, nor shall I.[138]

In a piece of creative genius, Tolstoi brilliantly exposed the horror of execution, dismantling the actual procedure of an execution of 12 men in Kherson, recently reported in the press, into the minutiae of perfunctory, mechanistic gestures, routinely carried out by officials, attendants, and the hangman himself:

> Their arms were tied behind their backs so that they could not grab the noose from which they would soon be hanged, and they were brought to the gallows ... the hangmen – there were several of them since one alone could not carry out such a complicated task – having used the soap to grease the noose so that the cords would stretch more easily, now took their position behind the shackled men, placed a shroud over them, led them to the gallows platform, and placed the greased nooses around their necks ... and so, one after the other, living people are jolted against the low benches as these are pushed out from under their feet, their necks extended on the cords by the weight of their bodies, and in agony they choke. Just seconds earlier alive, the suspended bodies at first slowly rock from side to side, then become motionless.[139]

The essay contained some extremely harsh indictments of government policy, its hypocrisy, and moral ambivalence likened to that of the revolutionary opponents it sought to repress:

> You government people call the acts of the revolutionaries 'atrocities' and 'great crimes'; but the revolutionaries have done and are doing what you have done, and done to an incomparably greater extent. They only do what you do; you keep spies, practise deception, and spread printed lies, and so do they. You take people's property by all sorts of violent means and use it as you consider best, and they do the same. You execute those whom you think dangerous, and so do they (...); not to mention that you do much evil that they do not commit, such as squandering the wealth of the nation, preparing for war, making war, subduing and oppressing foreign nationalities, and much else.[140]

Even though only abridged versions were printed in Russia, the political repercussions of Tolstoi's essay were, as he predicted, quite devastating. Heavy fines were imposed on journals and newspapers for daring to publish the piece, followed by a wave of repressive measures targeting public assemblies in an attempt to deny freedom of expression. However, by resorting to ruthlessness, in order to assert its authority, the government inadvertently contributed to the development of *obshchestvennost'* as a countervailing force. Tolstoi understood this all too well: 'That is why I write this and will circulate it by all means in my power both in Russia and abroad.' He predicted

> that one of two things may happen; either that these inhuman deeds may be stopped, or that my connection with them may be snapped and I put in prison, where I may be clearly conscious that these horrors are not committed on my behalf.[141]

It was only in March 1917 that the death penalty was finally abolished by the Provisional Government, though it remained in force on the front for cases of desertion and mutiny. The Bolsheviks, likewise, outlawed it when they seized power in October, only to reinstate it the following summer at the onset of Red Terror. Thus, as a 'temporary measure', the death penalty turned out to be one of the most enduring features of the Soviet regime.

> In modern times, wrote Solov'ev, the principle of restoration of a violated right by means of equal recompense was defended in its pure form more by abstract philosophers than jurists. The latter in general adopt the equation of punishment with the crime only in the relatively quantitative sense (the *measure* of punishment); that is, they require that a crime more serious compared to another be subject also to a more serious punishment, so that there exists a scale (in Latin, '*scala*') of punishments corresponding to the scale of crime. But meanwhile the base, or the bottom end, and thus the top

> of the punitive scale as well, remains indeterminate from the point of view of this single requirement and, thus, the nature of the punishments themselves also can be whatever one likes – inhumanely horrible or, on the contrary, extremely mild.[142]

In his brilliant dismantling of the crude eye for an eye logic of retribution theory as part of the problematic Kantian legacy in juridical thought, Solov'ev also exposed the hard-to-manage truth that, in practice, criminal justice is, indeed, determined by extraneous factors such as political pressures and historical change. In the 1880s, when leading jurists – Nabokov, Tagantsev, and Foinitsky – decided to commit the issue of the death penalty to the scrutiny of political authority, they were, of course, tacitly acknowledging the limits of law as an institutional body, even though as jurists they condemned the practice. And Nabokov did much the same again, only at a more conceptual level, when he admitted that the most powerful argument against the death penalty belonged to the novelist's pen.

If Solov'ev argued that 'the cracking clay of "absolute" metaphysical criminalistics, which requires the preservation of the death penalty as a necessary payback for crime, cannot be repaired with useless, falsely religious putty',[143] for legal practitioners, the concrete proposals that followed from his 'juridical' solution for testing the validity of positive laws more generally against a barometer of the good were either too audacious or naïve to be workable. That said, the underlying spirit of Solov'ev's argument, situated as it was, on the cusp of law and moral consciousness, and persuasively brought together in his condemnation of the death penalty, did have purchase among the judiciary in its quest to secure a trustworthy corporate identity. In his 'afterward' to *Fathers and Sons of Judicial Reform*, Koni's portrait of the ideal judge was essentially drawn on a canvas of Christian teaching: in his dealings with people and activities in which he is solicited to invest his mind, labours and professional authority, the judge or barrister must always endeavour to act according to the moral law. Negligence, overlooking the fact that one is dealing with a living human being, 'a brother in Christ', reduces everything – the judge's mind, talent, and the supposed usefulness of his work – to nought.[144] Arguably, Koni's insistence on moral professional conduct and Solov'ev's justification of the good reflected more accurately the needs of a culture that had no history of rights, and where, as Tolstoi put it, 'people regard every criminal as a man to be pitied' than did the liberal dream that had driven the men of jurisprudence in their quest for reform.

If it was hard to produce a juridical argument against the death penalty, when viewed as a human rights issue, it is clear that a mature 'civic consciousness' was required in order to sustain the momentum of public protest against the practice. Undisputedly, we see glimmerings of this in late tsarist Russia. Collectively organized protests helped generate, no matter how inchoately, a sense of social identity, a social-cum-civic counterweight to the overweening presence of the state in people's day-to-day lives through its administrative bodies and police control. In the end, though, it failed to exert sufficient pressure on the government to revise its policy.

The late- and post-Soviet era witnessed a similar dynamic only with a radical repositioning of roles between public opinion on the one side and the government on the other. When, in 1989, the question of the death penalty was placed on the government agenda in a climate of newly unleashed public opinion after being stifled for much of the century, renewed debate exposed a public that was generally hostile to abolition: the criminal was no longer an object of pity, but worrying proof that public safety could no longer be guaranteed.[145] In stark contrast with the pre-Revolutionary era, then, it was the government supported by a liberal judiciary, which, for a variety of reasons, including political gains, was set on removing the death penalty from the statute books.

6 Rehabilitating law

Criminal justice after communism

In 1989, at the height of Gorbachev's programme of reform, two publications brought the issue of the death penalty back into the public arena, this time however, triggering a debate that would in some ways become more complex and ambivalent than its pre-Revolutionary precedent. The first publication, *The Death Penalty: For and Against*, was an anthology comprising many of the views of those pre-revolutionary campaigners for the abolition of the death penalty that we discussed in the previous chapter.[1] In addition, it incorporated the opinions of contemporary academics and specialists in law, such as Sergei Alekseev, a prominent figure of the Sverdlovsk Juridical Institute, and Vasily Kudryatsev, vice-president of the Academy of Sciences and Director of the Institute of State and Law in Moscow, both of whom enjoyed close contact with Gorbachev and played an important role in setting out the terms of the new political thinking.[2] Other well-known names included the former dissident Andrei Sakharov, recently released from exile. Presenting the death penalty as a human rights issue, this landmark piece, rubber stamped with Gorbachev's approval, was a high-profile attempt to link the perestroika principles of 'socialism with a human face' to the liberal credo of pre-Revolutionary predecessors.

One of the book's co-editors and contributors, S.G. Kelinga, a researcher at the Institute of State and Law, was also the driving force, as editor and translator, of the second landmark publication, an Amnesty International initiative entitled, *When the State Kills*, the televised launch of which at the Institute of State and Law ensured its place as a groundbreaking 'happening' (*sobytie*) in the public eye.[3] A factually rich compendium, the book detailed the application of the death penalty in various countries across the world, including the Soviet Union, up to the present day. The Russian edition carried a foreword by the prominent human rights campaigner and recently elected People's Deputy, F.M. Burlatsky. Written as a sort of declaration of belief, Burlatsky highlighted the notions of dignity, rights, and freedom, which, rather than the simplistic idea of majority vote, were, he said, the cornerstones of democracy:

> The dignity of man are the gains (*dostoyaniya*) of the state. Only by observing this rule can one count on turning each and every one of us into a good

> citizen. If a man is not defended, but annihilated then even the most powerful state is not worthy of respect.[4]

For Burlatsky, it was crucial to free the administration of justice from its current subservience to the party–state bureaucracy, and to upturn the hierarchy of power, which, at the time of writing, found the judiciary at the bottom:

> The pyramid should be inverted, and at its summit should be the judge to whom is entrusted the holiest of holies – man. He should be treated humanely when he has suffered an infringement of his rights; those who break the law should be punished in strict accordance with the law. It is the role of the judge to awaken a sense of dignity in the accused and in doing so begin the process of re-education.[5]

Burlatsky's open condemnation of the death penalty as a barbaric denial of human rights (*lichnye prava cheloveka*) was intended as a tribute to a tradition of liberal thought, which, he regretted, had never been fully established in Russia. This sentiment was shared by a number of prominent non-conformist thinkers and erstwhile *shestidesyatniki* – 'men of the sixties' – such as the historian Yuri Afanasyev and the reformist-economist Gavriil Popov. However, for certain diehard communist or neo-Stalinist critics, both within the party and among the public, this pledge to revive liberal values was merely a thinly veiled slavish cult of Western style democracy, namely individualism and blue jeans. This opinion was expressed with some virulence by the Leningrad Lecturer Nina Andreeva in her *cause célèbre* piece 'I cannot forego principles' (1988), which, momentarily, brought perestroika to a standstill: she wrote,

> The first and most ideological swollen current which has already manifested itself in the course of restructuring claims to offer a model of some sort of Left-wing liberal intellectual socialism which allegedly expresses the most genuine humanism, 'cleansed' of class secretions. Its champions counter proletarian collectivism with 'the intrinsic value of the individual' – modernistic quests in the cultural sphere, God-seeking tendencies, technocratic idols, homilies to the 'democratic' charms of contemporary capitalism and kowtowing to its real and supposed achievements.[6]

Undoubtedly, there was some truth in the fact that Russian liberals were turning their gaze westwards in the hope of importing the principles of rule of law and the market economy, but they also alluded nostalgically to an indigenous tradition cut short by the Bolshevik Revolution. In this context, the names of Tagantsev and Judge Koni, for example, were often cited as eminent 'past masters', celebrated as beacons in the renewed quest to encourage a juridical consciousness in a population that had, since the Stalin era, been victim of terrible injustices in the name of building socialism.

The politics of judicial reform

Between 1962 and 1990, a total of 24,000 offenders were executed. While figures yield a yearly average of 1,300 a year, it was during the thaw, with which – ironically in this instance – perestroika is often paralleled in the literature, that the death penalty was used quite widely for economic crimes. In 1962 alone, approximately 3,000 offenders faced the firing squad (roughly eight per day). Beginning in the early 1980s, steps were taken to reduce the number of capital offences (at that time, the statute books listed 30 offences) by, for example, downgrading the penalty for certain instances of rape and recidivism in *valuta* (hard currency) speculation.[7]

Comprehensive government-led measures to phase out the death penalty as part of broader efforts to revise the penal system can be dated to February 1987, when plans announcing a revision of capital offences saw further substantial reductions in the number of capital offences as well as a downward trend in the number of executions carried out.[8] As Gordon Smith suggests, the gesture towards decriminalizing a number of economic crimes and downgrading certain capital offences was prompted by press reports: *Moscow News* (Moskovskie Novosti) and *The Week* (Nedelya) had detailed instances of faulty verdicts resulting in the execution of innocent people, victims of fabricated evidence concocted by law-enforcement officials susceptible to bribes.[9] However, as the Amnesty report showed, despite successive amendments to the 1958 Criminal legislation, including Gorbachev's, to reduce the overall number of capital offences, the late-Soviet era system of justice continued to privilege state interests over those of its citizens. The number of capital offences against the state, such as hijacking, attempted murder of a militiaman, war crimes and espionage, and victimless crimes including embezzlement of large-scale socialist property, bribery, and money laundering, still outweighed by far those afflicting the 'life, health, freedom and dignity of man'.[10]

The next significant step in scaling back the number of capital offences by decriminalizing victimless crimes dates to December 1988, when a draft criminal code outlining new bases of criminal legislation was published in the press.[11] Compiled by researchers at the Institute of State and Law, its recommendations included shorter sentences, doing away with internal exile and a significant lowering of the number of capital offences from 18 to six (for treason, espionage, terrorism, sabotage, premeditated murder, and child rape) with exemptions for minors, and men and women over the age of 60. (At the time of publication, 71 executions were still pending.) As a direct outcome of Gorbachev's pledge to create a law-governed state, which he made a priority in his address to the 19th Party Conference (June–July 1988), the timing of this document was, according to Kelinga, crucial: the humanistic principles running through the draft Criminal Code supplemented the agenda of candidates standing for election to the Congress of People's Deputies the following spring. In particular, their views on the question of the death penalty counted as a decisive factor in the success of their campaign.[12] Indeed, despite the fact that adoption of the revised Criminal Code during Gorbachev's rule was delayed and ultimately thwarted by growing political instability, measures to abolish the death penalty as a human rights issue remained high on the government agenda of radical reform right up to the final moments of the communist regime. In November 1991, the Supreme Soviet ratified the declaration of the rights and freedom of man, Article 7 of which permitted the death penalty only as an exceptional measure for the very worst crimes, and in December of the same year, just prior to Gorbachev's resignation and dissolution of the Soviet Union, a law was passed prohibiting use of the death penalty for large-scale embezzlement, breach of the *valuta* code of operation, and bribery.

Gorbachev's pledge to socialism with a human face established the conceptual parameters for a radical reassessment of the penal system, which his successor, Boris Yeltsin, endeavoured to adapt to the new post-Soviet political and ideological setting. A new draft Criminal Code was published in January 1992. Updating the terms of the recently ditched proposal to meet the new reality of the Russian Federation, its main goals – formal adoption of presumed innocence, equality before the law – were prompted by a concern to protect civil liberties and to redress the status of individual citizens vis-à-vis the state, thereby bringing to an end the advantages the latter had traditionally enjoyed through the offices of an aggressive and overbearing Procuracy working in its interests. This humanistic turn was reflected in the terms of the new Constitution (1993), which, again, had originated in the euphoric atmosphere of perestroika, indeed, was largely the brainchild of Andrei Sakharov before his untimely death in December 1989. Henceforth, the death penalty, pending its removal from the statute books ('*vpred' do ee otmeny*'), would be restricted to the most serious crimes involving loss of life ('*protiv lichnosti*'):

> 1) Each person shall have the right to life. 2) The death penalty, until its abolition, may be prescribed by federal law as an exceptional penalty for particularly grave crimes against life with the granting to the accused of the right to have the case heard by a court with the participation of jurors.[13]

Correspondingly, the Criminal Code, which, after successive drafts and amendments, was ratified in 1996 and officially enacted in January 1997, ruled the death penalty as an exceptional measure in five categories of life-threatening offences ('*posyagayushche na zhizn*'): murder under 'aggravated circumstances' namely murder for profit, murder to cover up a previous crime, murder of a pregnant woman, or an especially brutal murder; attempt on the life of a statesman or public figure; attempt on the life of a member of the judiciary or a criminal investigator; attempt on the life of an employee of a law-enforcing body, genocide.[14] However, the number of exemptions (notably, minors, anyone over the age of 65, and women of any age), together with the inbuilt provision for clemency whereby the sentence could be commuted to life imprisonment or 25 years in a high-security colony (*strogii regime*), effectively provided abolitionists with a convenient loophole to exploit. And, indeed, Yeltsin exercised his presidential privilege of pardon – a gesture of his 'humanizing government' – with astonishing consistency. Through the channels of the Commission for questions of clemency set up in 1992, he spared virtually all prisoners on death row: in 1992, 55 out of 56 cases were commuted to life sentences; in 1993, 149 out of 153, and in 1994, Yeltsin pardoned 124 murderers out of a total of 137 cases reviewed.[15]

Undeniably, like the first perestroika enthusiasts, Yeltsin was driven by a genuine concern to restore humane values and by the belief that, like other European countries, Russia could eventually dispense with the death penalty altogether.[16] But his commitment to abolish capital punishment was also influenced by the potential political gains to be had in the international arena: one condition for securing Russia's coveted entry into the Council of Europe was the abolition of the death penalty. Thus, in May 1996, Yeltsin signed the famous Protocol Number 6 to the European Convention on the rights of man relative to the abolition of the death penalty in peacetime, and, in anticipation of the ratification of the Protocol by Russian federal law, he imposed a three-year moratorium on executions. His edict 'On the gradual phasing out of the death penalty in connection with Russia's entry to the Council of Europe' instructed the Russian government to prepare a project for a federal law to be put to the State Duma for discussion the following month. In addition, the ukase included recommendations to the chamber of the federal assembly, charged with the review of the Criminal Code project, for a further reduction in the number of capital offences. The outcome of this first round of initiatives was, however, doubly disappointing, and, if anything points to the hurdles obstructing the passage to democracy: the multiple non-cohesive factions within parliament, each with their own divisive interests, had the effect of throttling the process of legal reform. The upshot was that the project for such a law was never discussed in the State Duma, nor did the moratorium receive official authorization.[17] In January 1997, the Parliamentary Assembly of the Council of Europe, concerned by the nature of Russian operations on Chechen territory, issued a warning that failure to impose the moratorium as an interim measure would lead to suspension of the Russian delegation's powers. The following month, Yeltsin accordingly passed an instruction entitled 'On signing Protocol no. 6, 28 April 1983, to the human rights and freedom convention, 4 November, 1950, relative to the abolition of the death penalty' and called upon the Ministry of Justice to draft measures for a phased solution to the problems posed by the ratification of the Protocol. Once again, the Duma failed to ratify the Protocol, thereby rendering the document juridically void.[18]

Regardless of parliament's obdurate failure to authorize the three-year moratorium, since September 1996 the death sentence has not been carried out – all thanks to Yeltsin's systematic exercise of clemency as his presidential privilege.[19] Indeed, in January 1998, a Presidential initiative was passed to this effect resulting in a situation that was uncannily reminiscent of tsarist practice: henceforth for the death sentence to be carried out permission from the President was required.[20] Finally, in February 1999, after the three-year period granted for ratification had expired, the peculiar juridical and constitutional limbo was cleverly turned to work in favour of those who opposed the death penalty. In the absence of a federal law making trial by jury de rigueur in all regions as stipulated in the Constitution, the Constitutional Court of the Russian Federation took the decision to suspend application of the death penalty temporarily: until every citizen of the Russian Federation has the guarantee that his case will be discussed in the presence of an impartial jury, no court is empowered to pass the death sentence.[21] With Chechnya the last remaining stubborn exception to this ruling – a situation that is likely to remain unchanged in the foreseeable future – the government has effectively managed to contain use of the death penalty ever since.[22]

The requirement of fiat to bulldoze through new democratic principles, as the issue of the death penalty demonstrates so dramatically, raises questions about the foundation stones of Russian democracy. If the outcome was fortuitous for abolitionists whose place in the wider arena of public debate was otherwise massively overshadowed by sceptics and self-styled 'apologists' for maintaining the death penalty, the means Yeltsin used – Presidential prerogative, dexterous manoeuvring between constitutional and criminal law interests – offer a latter-day example of tsarist '*proizvol*' (arbitrariness susceptible in equal share to mercy and wrath) and rule through law. Clearly, the experience of October 1993, when Russian special military forces shelled the parliament building to dislodge opponents of Yeltsin hostile to the Constitution he was about to enact, had cast its shadow on post-Soviet politics. As Gordon Smith put it: 'Faced with parliamentary immobilism, the president and other executive authorities are forced to rule by decree, which inevitably results in a cascade of accusations of a return to authoritarian rule.'[23] Ultimately, however, abolitionists and apologists agree that, while the moratorium imposed in 1999 (and still in effect today, 2006) has safeguarded many capital offenders from the firing squad, it is an unsound compromise, leaving both core juridical issues and the broader cultural, social, and political implications of the debate unresolved. The 'on hold' logic of the moratorium has not only failed to settle the question through legislative channels, it has also fudged the debate intellectually. For those who oppose its removal, this paradoxical situation, whereby the death penalty is built into the Russian Constitution and the Criminal Code and yet cannot be applied, is an annoying impasse disrupting normal legal procedure. For critics, the 'political-declaratory' means by which the judges of the Constitutional Court achieved their 'noble humanitarian' ends overstepped the boundaries of judicial competence, and, as one commentator noted in exasperation in 2001,

> in Russia, for some time now we have a non-legal moratorium which has a deleterious effect on judges, prosecutors, and other law-enforcing bodies dealing with serious crimes. Not only does this situation not facilitate their work, it obstructs guarantees of legality and legal order.[24]

For their part, abolitionists have found themselves trapped between principle and compromise. Given the officially proclaimed post-Soviet ethos of 'human respect' broadcast everywhere, inclusion of the death penalty in the new Criminal Code was, as a point of principle, inconsistent with the premises of punishment as a correctional tool with a view to restoring social justice advocated by reformers and, in fact, endorsed in the legislation.[25] Yet, as many recognized, for the Code to gain public acceptance as a viable document, and to be able to contend with the influential lobbying powers of those critical of its removal, the compilers were duty-bound to accommodate certain social stereotypical views of punishment and 'contain' these by recourse to presidential privilege of clemency (*pomilovanie*): 'Were we to present the Code without the death penalty', Kelinga noted, 'it would have been a failed undertaking (*proval'noe meropriyatie*).'[26]

'Something old, something new, something borrowed…' Debating the death penalty after communism

While Gorbachev and Yeltsin actively encouraged the restoration of humanism in criminal justice, competing 'democratic' – or, more accurately 'populist' – tendencies relying on, if not exploiting, the damaged legal consciousness of the general public put forward persuasive arguments that effectively authorized the retributive logic of punishment. Already in 1989, Kelinga had alluded to an attitude of sober common sense shared by professional bodies and the wider public condoning capital punishment. If reducing the number of offences susceptible to the '*vysshaya mera*' (literally, the 'highest measure') enjoyed consensus of opinion, a high proportion of People's deputies, legislative bodies, and the general public was nevertheless reluctant to see its removal from the statute books altogether. A referendum, Kelinga noted, would merely confirm this.[27] Indeed, the findings of an opinion poll conducted in 1988 registered 80–85 per cent opposed to abolition.[28] For many professionals in the legal and political sphere, the death penalty provided the needed assurances of social and legal security in a state that lacked authority and which historically had flaunted internationally recognized standards of human rights. Even Professor Shishov, compiler of *The Death Penalty – For or Against*, mentioned at the beginning of this chapter and well known for his criticism of the death penalty, warned against its premature removal from the statute books on the grounds that the general public was not ready for this. (He proposed that the death penalty be applied for cases of high treason, acts of terrorism, sabotage, and premeditated murder with aggravated circumstances.)

Since the collapse of the Soviet Union, the escalating crime rate, events in Chechnya, and the threat of terrorism, real and/or orchestrated, have driven the dividing wedge between public opinion and government policy even deeper, resulting in a hardening of attitudes among a public anxious for its security and frustrated by its political leadership that has persisted in seemingly blinkered fashion on a course of humanization, broadcasting its achievements with unwarranted fanfare.[29] For example, in 1999, four months after the second moratorium came into effect, the Presidential Commission for clemency in collaboration with the Council of Europe organized a two-day conference on the problem of abolishing the death penalty. Speakers included high-profile representatives of various state and judicial institutions, academics, spokespersons for legal defence organizations, Amnesty International, and the Council of Europe – all with showcase contributions in favour of abolition.[30] And on the opening day of the conference, in a gesture designed to capture the significance of the event, Yeltsin signed documents commuting all remaining capital offenders to life sentences. For critics, the oddly belated effort to open debate when, de facto, the death penalty had been suspended was a suspect parade of humanistic values, thinly masking the political strategies of the Yeltsin government to gain respect internationally and to justify the imposition of a moratorium as a legally irregular *fait accompli* at home.

If the two-day conference formalized official positions with a view to closing the chapter on the death penalty, within the juridical community, the moratorium has triggered a slew of new publications on the subject – both as a question of actuality and as an object of scholarly surveys of its history – often, it should be noted, expressing a degree of carefully reasoned sympathy for the practice.[31] In the wider press, the issue of the death penalty has never been far away from the headlines. Indeed, an afternoon spent browsing in Metro bookstalls attests the degree to which lawlessness, murder (crime of passion and Mafiosi style intrigues) have become a popular genre of crime fiction and tabloid publications. Sensationalist articles relating the gruesome dealings of hired killers in gang vendettas, serial killers, maniacs, or narcotics traffickers are common in the periodical press. The journal *Man and Law* (Chelovek i Zakon), for example, which is printed in a handy pocket-sized, glossy format, serializes thrillers and detective stories with titles such as ‘To Die in Normandy’. In addition, and perhaps oddly for Western tastes, it combines photographic reportage of prison life with informed comment by invited legal specialists on some of the finer points of current legislation. In 1997, for example, it covered the inconclusive parliamentary debate on the death penalty tabled for discussion by two Deputies, Valery Borshchev and Yulii Rybakov, in response to Yeltsin’s instruction concerning the signing of Protocol no. 6.[32]

In December 1998 and January 1999, the newspapers *Moscow Komsomol* (Moskovskii Komsomol’ets) and *Russian Newspaper* (Rossiiskaya Gazeta) published the results of a questionnaire on the death penalty. The responses encapsulate very tellingly the gamut of opinions that today popularly inform ‘for and against’ positions. New elements impacting on the nature and terms of the debate on both sides include Russia’s commitment to international governing bodies, the official endorsement of human rights in the Constitution, and the underlying political thinking of the moratorium.[33] Otherwise, in the sample analysed, abolitionists drew on statistical evidence to argue that there is no causal link between the growth of crime and the removal of the death penalty. They spoke of the terrible tragedies caused by miscarriages of justice and combined moral and religious considerations with more pragmatic economic considerations: prison labour is, in fact, cost effective. Top on the list for maintaining the penalty was what one might call a mild scaremongering tactic masked as reasonableness – 'Russia is not yet ready: abolition would merely prompt a surge in crime.' Then came an instinctual 'eye for an eye' logic of retribution, justified in terms of the recognition due to the victim's relatives and the lasting pain and suffering they are forced to endure. Economic considerations also worked in favour of apologists: it is cheaper to execute than fork out for the long-term upkeep of a miscreant. But the trump card carried the emblem of wounded national pride: 'why should we accept the conditions imposed by the Council of Europe as an edict when the United States carries out the death penalty and "that's all right" (*nichego'*)?'

As a rule, then, abolitionists depart from points of principle – moral, sociological, and religious – established in the canon of abolitionist literature. The death penalty does not serve as a deterrent; rather, it hardens attitudes and social behaviour (*nravy*) and denies the offender the chance of repentance. Condemning the practice on the grounds that it is against 'God's law', abolitionists draw on the body of arguments forged by original campaigners such as Victor Hugo, Tolstoi, Solov'ev, Gernet, Tagantsev, or Kuz'min-Karavaev: 'thou shalt not kill'; 'life as a supreme value can only be taken by Him who gave it. There is no argument more convincing than this'; 'It is a profane, inhumane, and shameful act.'[34] Whether intentionally or by coincidence, this distant echo of the stock of original abolitionist arguments also functions as ironic reminders of the fact that at the beginning of the twentieth century, the Russian public actually led the way in condemning the practice.[35] In stark contrast, a cold, head-on look at the harsh realities of post-Soviet society scarred by corruption, lawlessness, petty crime, and under the threat of terrorism (so official political discourse goes) has prompted a growing number of specialists and high-ranking political advisers to advise retention of the penalty. For example, S. Mikhlin, a leading specialist on the prison system at the Scientific Research Institute of the Ministry of the Interior, has revived the logic of deterrence to this effect. Other apologists, however, have been more overt in politicizing the debate by exploiting a narrow chauvinism and crude social psychology. The paper by A.D. Boikov (a specialist in questions of law enforcement attached to the Procuracy General) read at the two-day Conference in 1999 received spotlight treatment when it was published separately in the journal *Legality* (Zakonnost'). A hard-hitting challenge to the decisions taken at state level, Boikov's piece seemed to reflect the public mood: despite the soaring crime rate, 'we persist in the name of irresponsible "democrats" and "experts" of the Council of Europe, to orientate polices towards some abstract "universal" values and principles'. To counter these internationally imposed conditions, Boikov made a case for a strongly nationalistic and particularist solution:

> Attitudes towards Russia are special – they are not always dictated by good will, as we have had the chance to witness on more than one occasion. In this instance, as in many others, we should be guided by our own

> experience, and by social economic conditions. In short, we should trust our own instincts.[36]

In building their case, apologists have also managed to undermine rival views by appropriating them for diametrically opposed purposes. Since the second moratorium, in particular, an inverted 'civilizational argument', powerfully demonstrating that Russia is still deeply scarred by her Soviet–Stalinist experience and therefore not yet ready to do away with the death penalty, has become quite widespread in apologist literature:

> When society learns to defend the lives of its law abiding citizens, instils respect for law (*pravo*) in the majority of the population, only then will we have objective grounds to abolish the death penalty, an act which will signify a true victory of humanism and human rights.

Since other restraining components of social regulation – cultural development, moral example, religious norms – 'have not yet demonstrated their effectiveness', the death penalty as a juridical restraint is therefore currently needed.[37] The same argument – a veritable apology for the death penalty – was used ten years earlier by the director of the All-Union scientific-research institute for problems of law enforcement and legal order of the USSR Office of the Public Procurator, I.I. Karpets:

> Today, the death penalty is not revenge vented against the offender but retribution for a terrible evil. At the given stage in the development of our society to rule out a just retribution is not possible, although it is necessary to look forward to the day when it will be.[38]

This type of reasoning, however, as Kistyakovsky, the Russian pioneer of the 'civilizational argument' in the 1860s already noted, is an attempt to mask an evident lack of principle with an appeal to common sense: 'Practically all advocates of the death penalty defend it not on principle, but as a temporary and useful measure so long as society is not yet ready for its removal.'[39] Indeed, as some scholars have pointed out, phrasing the problem in the terms that Karpets chose was eerily reminiscent of Soviet formulations, which invariably spoke of the temporary character of the death penalty: except for a short interval in the post-war period, it remained a permanent feature of the Code.[40]

Apologist arguments rely heavily on opinion polls, which, since the early 1990s, have repeatedly found a public in favour of keeping the death penalty on the statute books. Figures for 1999, for example, cited 70 per cent of Russians questioned in favour of maintaining the death penalty.[41] An article published in a May 1999 issue of *Moscow Truth* (Moskovskaya Pravda), carrying the subtitle 'Murder is Rectified in the Grave', noted that 91 per cent of Muscovites were against the ban on the death penalty.[42] The reliance on opinion polls, however, has been challenged by abolitionists, suspicious that the polls may be manipulated for political purposes. As black-and-white responses to a simplified set of questions affording little or no nuanced interpretation, they fail to do justice to the complexity of the issue. Pristavkin, president of the Commission for Clemency, wrote:

> The trouble is that all arguments in favour of abolition, even the Christian perspective, fall on deaf ears among a public gripped with fear and exposed to cruelty. The crowds cling to the belief that punishment frightens the offender, and therefore reduces the crime rate. This massive confusion is impossible to dispel with reasonable arguments. (…) It might seem as if everything has changed (ie with the break up of the Soviet Union), but a repressed awareness (*repressivnost' soznaniya*) has remained. This repressed awareness is the greatest scourge when we start bringing people's opinion into the picture. It is often said that, as a people, we are kind and compassionate. But this is a legend. We are cruel, vindictive, and prefer legends to the truth.[43]

Since Putin came to power, attitudes have polarized even further, mostly fuelled by the threat of terrorism. In the summer of 2000, shortly after a terrorist attack in the capital (9 August 2000, Pushkin Square), Putin issued a statement, the implications of which required only minimum skills of interpretation: 'We have still to devise an effective way of combating terrorism. Only one medicine is an adequate response.'[44] A number of Duma deputies have since proposed that the moratorium be lifted for acts of terrorism, a view, incidentally, shared by Alexander Solzhenitsyn, once one of the most outspoken critics of the practice, and, in private endorsed by the President himself.[45] However, possibly the most specious and complacent-sounding arguments have come from officials of the Russian Orthodox Church. Basing their refusal to condemn the death penalty on passages from the Old Testament, they also claimed to find no grounds for its removal either in the Gospels, or, historically, in the heritage of the Orthodox Church.[46] One can only imagine that Solov'ev, who, we recall, condemned reliance on the Bible as an authoritative voice in favour of the death penalty as a sign of 'hopeless incomprehension or boundless insolence', would be turning in his grave.

Both abolitionists and apologists are obliged to reckon with a damaged social psychology as part of the Soviet legacy. They agree that Russia's history of social and political paternalism has undermined notions of social responsibility or initiative, and that, generally, it has generated a condition of political–legal infantilism among its citizens. According to Vitaly Kvashis, the upshot is that, nowadays, far from observing any categorical imperative, members of the public seem to be demanding greater respect for themselves but are inhumane in their relation to others – a situation that feeds into both apologist and abolitionist arguments:

> The paradoxes of Russian mentality come to view in two parallel psychological processes: on the one hand, evil is banal, trivialized, the criminal

> situation has been de-dramatized. People become inured to the abuse of human rights, they tolerate violence and shrug their shoulders at flagrant breaches of the law. At the same time, mass consciousness is in the grip of panic, fear, seized with apocalyptic foreboding. Together, these contradictory tendencies exercise a powerful influence on the formation of social psychology and go a long way to explaining the repressed nature of mass consciousness. Granted, the population does not constitute a uniform social–cultural entity, but the marked decline in public opinion resulting in poor judgement and extremism is in many ways linked with atavistic trends and mystification.[47]

Unfortunately, coming to terms with this legacy has merely produced a classic 'catch twenty-two' situation: if apologists urge that issues of civic awareness must be dealt with first from the bottom up, 'liberal' abolitionists wave an albeit 'benevolent' paternalist baton calling for an example of civic mindedness from above. 'The state should lead the way, informing the public, explicating new principles, weigh up the social and political perspectives of retaining the death penalty' (Sakharov).

> The legislator has to exhibit a degree of boldness, rise above the level of ordinary consciousness, give society moral orientation. As a rule, experience in other countries shows that abolishing the death penalty results in a diminution in the number of supporters, a rethinking of conservative views and a general easing of harsh customs, and social behaviour.[48]

Compared, then, to the pre-Revolutionary situation, the dynamics between people and power in post-Soviet Russia have been inverted without, however, modifying the divisive 'us/them' relation of mutual suspicion that has traditionally characterized a 'dual Russia' of governors and governed. Whereas Nicholas II resisted the pressures of public opinion that liberal reformers succeeded in harnessing in their bid to abolish the death penalty, in post-Soviet Russia the government has proclaimed a moratorium in the face of resistance from high-ranking statesmen, public figures, and in flagrant disregard for the opinions of the public at large.

The Criminal Code 1996

> Juridical science has the obligation to explain how it was possible that criminal legislation deprived Soviet man of the most important individual rights. Understanding this is a safeguard against it happening again.
>
> (A.V. Naumov, 'Criminal law and Human Rights', 1990)

> The legislator finds himself in a difficult position. On the one hand it is not possible not to take public opinion into account; on the other, he should not be guided by philistine views calling for punitive measures that are as inef-

> fective as they are inhumane. Obviously, now and in the near future compromise cannot be avoided, but this should be surmounted gradually through sustained efforts to demystify stereotypes and by careful elucidation of the social and scientific bases for containing crime in Russia
>
> (A.L. Tsvetinovich, 'Current Tendencies in the Development of Criminal Legislation and Criminal Law Theory', 1994)[49]

If, as a topic of debate, the issue of the death penalty provides insights into social psychology, its inclusion in the new Criminal Code also brings to view the problems confronting the liberal juridical community in its endeavours to lay down the general principles of the post-Soviet judicial system. Much like the challenges facing their distant precursors in the 1860s, the generation of criminologists in the Gorbachov–Yeltsin eras needed to revise the existing legislation, the bases of which were elaborated during the Krushchev years, in order to meet current social and economic reality, but more importantly to provide anchorage for the ideals of a democratic rule of law state as enunciated in the 1993 Constitution.[50] The core principles of the Constitution – recognition of the rights and freedom of man as a supreme value (Art. 2) – with precedence given to norms of international law for the sake of global security, provided the general framework for the new Criminal Code.[51] Premised on new democratic-cum-humanistic principles, which it prioritized in the order of man – society – state, the new Code effectively upturned the hierarchy of social values inscribed in socialist doctrine: 'The criminal legislation of the Russian Federation secures human safety' (Pt I, Art. 7); 'Punishment and other measures of a criminal law character applied to a criminal offender are not intended to inflict physical suffering or denigrate human dignity' (Pt II, Art. 7); 'Punishment is applied with the aim of restoring social justice, correcting the offender, and with a view to preventing further crimes' (Pt II, Art. 43). Just how radically new these underlying premises of the 1996 Code are become evident once we remember that the 1922 Criminal Code set out its task as: 'the legal defence of the proletarian state (*gosudarstvo trudyashchikhsya*) against crimes and socially dangerous elements through punishment (...) applied to destructors of the revolutionary order.'[52] This call to order provided the foundations of a judicial system that would be built on repression, the crude practice of inculpation by analogy, together with a brutal penal system encapsulated by the 'savage tyranny' (*dikii proizvol*) of the Gulag.[53]

Advocating legality (*zakonnost'*), equality of citizens before the law, fair assessment of criminal responsibility, justice (*spravedlivost'*), and humanism (Arts 3–7), the Code formulated as its main tasks: protection against criminal violation; recognition of the rights and freedom of the individual and citizen, property, social order and security; and care for the environment. It pledged to uphold the constitutional system of the Russian Federation; ensure peace and security; and take preventative measures against crime (Arts 1 and 2).[54] At one level, this simple inversion of the ideological and class-based premises on which Soviet legislation had been built translated into the straightforward decriminalization of many crimes listed in the Soviet Code – in the first instance, expressions of spiritual freedom and religious confession and the right to exercise a choice of domicile and occupation. Other relatively uncomplicated measures included raising the age of criminal responsibility and introducing provisions for early release. At a deeper level, however, the process of modernization involved the conceptually more demanding task of imparting new meaning to a set of core concepts of crime, punishment, legality, citizenship, and rights, which, even if they had been sapped of any significance, were integral to Soviet–Stalinist legislation. To this end, numerous revisions were derived from West European models, but durable conceptual premises were also sourced in Russia's own history of criminal law science, including the pledges and goals of her political dissident movement of the 1960s and 1970s to secure unbiased criminal procedure and a fair trial. Unsurprisingly, perhaps, a strong bid was made to restore the spirit of classic principles. Classical concepts, it was argued, represented the most powerful antidote to the ideological bias of the Soviet Code premised on class struggle and which deemed incrimination of anyone branded as an 'enemy of the people' lawful and just.

A major concern was to enable recognition of, and differentiation between, the public and private spheres – traditionally a blind spot in Russian legal culture, and, again, the tragic consequences of which were told in the Stalinist era.[55] Thus, participants in one round-table discussion organized by the Institute of State and Law in 1994 argued for the restoration of the universal character of human rights (after the 1789 declaration of the rights of man and citizen and the 1948 universal declaration of the rights of man) and its natural law normative premises as the most relevant conceptual tools for demarcating, in contemporary post-Soviet society, the appropriate boundaries of juridical competence. But, reference was also made to the pre-Revolutionary reformers who had combined certain classical principles (formal equality before the law, nullen crimen sine lege – 'there is no crime without a law') with the accent on *lichnost'* as part of the revival of natural law in early twentieth-century criminal politics and legal thought. One or two discussants even suggested that inclusion of the moral dimension was crucial for coping with what was widely recognized as a spiritual malaise in Yeltsin's new Russia. Positive laws, it was argued, are grounded in religious consciousness. Inversely: 'The implementation of non-moral legislation (*beznravstvennost zakona*) is an additional crime-inducing factor (*kriminogennyi faktor*).'[56] However, while discussants may have sympathized with this view, they were at the same time aware that they were dealing with a legacy, which, like Imperial legislation, was cluttered with common or garden moralization: paradoxically, in Soviet criminal justice, it was common to stress the amoral (qua anti-Soviet) connotations of a crime. For reformers, therefore, it was crucial to distance themselves from these unfortunate associations, and the obvious way to do so was to revive the classical perspective, broadly conceived, of crime and punishment.

At the project phase, efforts to elaborate a concept of crime initially focused on the formal definition (an act prohibited by criminal law) commonly found in

European Codes but also reminiscent of the last Imperial Code of 1903 that was never fully enacted. This was later combined with a material component – crime is a danger to society – an addition inspired by the North American model, which defines crime as 'unjustifiable inexcusable behaviour causing essential harm to the interests of an individual and society or conduct which threatens to do such harm'.[57] According to Anatoly Naumov, initial attempts to preclude the material definition were clearly in reaction to the Soviet Code, which, of course, prioritized the material 'base' of social danger and generally abused the 'derivative' formal concept of criminal responsibility. But for Naumov, who welcomed this amendment to the original draft, the purely formalistic definition alone failed to explain why certain acts are prohibited on pain of punishment. On this point, interestingly, he noted that in pre-Revolutionary textbook literature, definitions of crime had generally been broader than the narrow formalism found in the Imperial Code. A case in point was Tagantsev's famous definition, which, as I discussed in Chapter 3, had exposed him to criticism oscillating between classical and positivist perspectives: A criminal act

> is an infringement on the juridical norm in its living reality (*v ee real'nom bytii*) prohibited by the law of the place where it was committed on pain of punishment or, put in more concrete terms, crime is an infringement on a normatively protected interest of life, which in a given country or given period is accepted as being so essential, that the state, in the absence of other suitable measures, imposes punishment.

For Naumov, Tagantsev's formulation was entirely operable in the post-Soviet context.[58]

The new Code defined the concept and the purpose of punishment as a coercive state measure consisting in loss or restriction of rights and freedoms, which is effected through the courts and applied to an individual found guilty of an offence. Punishment is inflicted for the purpose of re-establishing social justice, correcting the offender, and as a preventative measure (Pt III, Ch. 9, Art. 43). The emphasis that the new Code placed on respect for human life as part of its more general commitment to the terms of the Constitution required guarantees of protection that could only be secured by imposing appropriate sanctions. Thus, in cases of murder, embezzlement, fraud, organized crime, ecological damage threatening this fundamental right it suggested long-term prison sentences without parole. Inversely, though in the same spirit, the new concept of punishment ruled exemptions from incarceration for women with young children, minors, and the elderly. In connection with this, an important part of the Code – not least because of the commentary it generated in specialist and more popular legal publications – was Article 60, 'General principles for determining punishment'.[59] Determining criminal responsibility and implementing appropriate punishment – two aspects of Soviet law open to abuse – was, henceforth, to involve the principles flagged earlier: legality, equality of rights before the law, defining guilt, social justice, and humanism. In particular, *zakonnost'*, meaning that a criminal act is defined in accordance with breaches of laws itemized in the existing Code, together with stricter definitions of guilt were introduced in order to rectify the Soviet practice of inculpation by analogy which, even though officially abolished in 1960, still featured surreptitiously in 'directional explanations', whereby the Supreme Court was empowered at will to restrict or expand the limits to criminal responsibility.

In many ways, Article 60 typifies the spirit of the new Code and encapsulates its indebtedness to the endeavours of pre-Revolutionary legal reformers. Suffice it to mention the new emphasis on the 'individualization of punishment' requiring strict adherence to rulings yet with room for flexibility in sentencing in the light of mitigating circumstances, first-time offenders, or, inversely, harsher sentences for recidivists. Emphasis on the social danger of a crime is offset by attention to the person of the offender (*lichnost' vinovogo*), bearing in mind the possible impact on the offender of punishment as a curative tool, together with repercussions of punishment for his immediate family (Art. 60: 3). Personal data examined by the courts now include records of personal and professional conduct, health, and family relations. While, at one level, this marks a refinement of the Krushchev Code wherein individual mitigating factors influencing the severity of a sentence covered only the age of the offender, the number of young dependants, and, in the case of a female offender, whether she might be pregnant, the inclusion of behavioural traits strikes a familiar chord with the motif of '*lichnost' prestupnika*' that scholars such as Poznyshev and Lyublinsky, names frequently referenced in post-Soviet juridical literature, developed in their work in the decade prior to the October Revolution.

Possibly, the most radical departure from Soviet justice was the grounding principle of humanism. As one of the central tenets of the new Constitution – 'the dignity of man is protected by the state' (Art. 21) – the principle was reinforced in the Criminal Code in the form of a commitment to 'ensure the physical, psychological, material, ecological or other safety of man' (Art. 7).[60] More generally, as keynote topics for the judiciary, the ideals of humanism and *lichnost'* generated complementary research in monographs and articles published in specialist journals such as *State and Law*, *Jurisprudence*, *Legality*, and *Russian Justice*.[61] Analyses of, for example, the object of crime (*ob'ekt* versus *predmet*), criminal psychology, the meaning of *chelovek* and *lichnost'* – the preferred term in juridical vocabulary,[62] the subjective side of crime have all come under the banner of the 'humanist turn' in post-Soviet juridical science. As a qualified rejection of the Marxist–Leninist socially determined concept of man and morality ('everything which is useful for the construction of communism, for the Revolution'), new research has prioritized man's rights, freedom, values, and well-being as socially derived interests to be protected by law. However, by fixing their gaze squarely on man, some post-Soviet researchers were not only breaking with Soviet convention that treated the violated 'object' of crime as the abstract 'sum of social relations' (*sovokupnost' obshchestvennykh otnoshenii*), they were consciously reviving the humanist current in pre-Revolutionary juridical thought as pioneered by liberal reformers in the 1860s and championed by the next generation of scholars working with the tools of positivism and moral idealism. In a study of the object of crime, V.P. Emel'yanov, for example, anchored 'legally defended interests' in man as a flesh-and-blood bearer of rights and freedom:

> Objects of criminal assault may be life, health, personal worth, the natural environment, social and state establishments (their activities) and so forth – in short, anything which exists, that is tangible, and which may suffer real harm (...) and which is protected by law irrespective of the relation that one or another part of the population may have with it.

At the source of this idea, as Emel'yanov openly acknowledged, were Kistyakovsky and Belogritz-Kotlyarevsky who, after Liszt and Ihering, had defined the 'object of crime' as legally protected vital interests (and, correspondingly, conflated the object (*predmet*) and target (*ob'ekt*) of crime).[63] Interestingly, Naumov himself, who, in the more official context of his introduction to the 1996 Code labelled 'humanism' a European approach to criminal justice, could not resist inclusion of a national precedent in this regard: before the Revolution, this humanistic principle was, he claimed, a purely Russian phenomenon that found its most powerful expression in the work of scholars who combined their own classical inheritance, with its golden rule of nulla poena sine lege ('there is no penalty without a law') with some of the more fruitful innovations of the sociological school, notably, 'factors of criminality', affording the possibility to combat crime.[64]

How far the new Criminal Code succeeded in settling scores with the legacy of Soviet criminal justice and managed to answer the current social and economic dynamics of post-Soviet reality quickly became a divisive issue among theorists and practitioners. Theorists felt that the Code did not live up to its promise of greater humanism and, to this effect, signalled a number of shortfalls concerning provisions for establishing degrees of criminal responsibility and the individualization of punishment.[65] For practitioners, however, much of the new legislation was simply unworkable on the ground, and they quickly brought their grievances into the political arena. Indeed, almost as soon as the Code came off the press, objections were raised at parliamentary level. In the first year following the implementation of the code, the State Duma received 50 projects relative to 120 articles (roughly equivalent to one-third of the entire Code).[66] By March 2002, more than 160 projects proposing revisions and amendments to some 200 articles had been submitted for consideration by parliament. While many were demanding harsher penalties – including the death penalty for acts of terrorism – in the belief that 'might was right', others called for softer punitive measures in the case of less serious crimes so as to cope with the problem of overcrowded prisons and thereby bring the penal infrastructure as a whole in line with European standards.[67]

Criticism of the Code pressured its leading authors into defending, if only by reiterating, the gains they had originally made. While, of course, no ruling could be definitive, cast in stone once and for all, it was crucial, they argued, to preserve the body of legislation intact. Conceived as a kind of legal anchorage, the Code would, they hoped, afford stability to criminal law regulations in a society deep in the throes of economic, political, and spiritual change.[68] Conversely, the piecemeal amendments put forward in various projects to the Duma tended to ignore both the structural connections within the Code and underlying normative premises, and, if made law, risked undermining its overall coherence.[69] For Naumov and fellow compilers of the 1996 edition, the relatively low level of federal endorsement these new proposals ultimately received, producing only a small body of additional laws with partial changes to 50 articles, was proof that they were poorly focused and insufficiently grounded. However, neither defenders nor critics of the Code had an answer for the economic difficulties, which hindered, if not blighted, hopes for the smooth implementation of penal reform. If, statistically, the increase in the numbers of registered indictments could be taken as proof of the growing effectiveness of law-enforcing bodies, and, generally, of greater vigilance in combating crime, delays in constructing new prisons and detention centres to accommodate the ever-growing numbers of convicted criminals not only led to practical difficulties but shook the theoretical understanding of punishment as 'deprivation of freedom', prompting a major rethink of the politics of sentencing, especially with regard to less serious infractions such as economic crimes, first-time offenders, and breaches of the law through negligence. In order to free up prisons and colonies, authors of the Code now suggested that certain prison sentences could be substituted by fines or confiscation of property and that a more systematic provision for parole and suspended sentences should be introduced. Further decriminalization of minor infractions would also encourage greater discernment in determining degrees of criminal responsibility as part of the drive towards the humanization of punishment.

These recommendations were brought before a parliamentary hearing in March 2002 marking the first five years of the Code but also to answer widespread concern that the Code was inadequate to the task of containing crime.[70] A panel of experts featuring the familiar faces of S.G. Kelinga, N.F. Kuznetsova, A.V. Naumov and I.E. Zvegarovsky presented their findings to an audience of governmental and judicial officials. In his keynote speech, Naumov cleaved to his original defence of the value of the Code as an integrally conceived document that answered quite well the unfinished (and unpredictable) business of post-Soviet social and economic transition. But he also conceded the self-evident truth that more work needed to be done, especially in the field of economic crime, corruption, terrorism, and environmental abuses, namely the chief indices along the downward spiral of general lawlessness that has been plaguing the country since the mid-90s at least. What was required, he and other defenders of the Code argued, was a consultative body of specialists working in tandem with federal organizations to ensure more effective drafting and implementation of laws. And, of course, money: ultimately, the main difficulty that no one could resolve was the lack of financial resources available for the construction of an adequately and appropriately staffed penal system designed to encourage successful reintegration into society and prevent further lapses into criminal behaviour.

While specifications in the new Code may strike the outsider as common or garden, it should not be forgotten that in the Soviet Code, absence of strict guidelines for determining the severity of an offence, together with rigid ideological prescriptions, had generated terrible abuses of the judicial system undermining people's trust in the law. Clearly, the most difficult hurdle to overcome for reformers was an 'attitudinal one', a deeply ingrained suspicion of law and a stereotypical view of the retributive function of punishment. But, if dropping the qualifier 'socialist' when speaking of 'justice', or substituting 'universal human values' for 'democratic', had enormous symbolic resonance for the post-Soviet judiciary, it was unlikely, as contemporaries recognized, to move the hearts of post-Soviet citizens.[71] While one might applaud the spirit of fair mindedness and intellectual affinity with which specialists drafted the Code, for anyone with even the most superficial knowledge of present-day Russia, it does not require much critical judgement to suspect that formal protection of individual interests was – and is – extremely fragile. In an interview given for the journal *Juridical World*, a career style journal covering topics of interest to the professional, Professor Emeritus Vitalii Kvashis offered the poignant reminder that the legal consciousness and psychology of several generations of people in Soviet Russia had been impaired by the violence and cruelty associated with the class struggle, the destruction of war, and totalitarian ideology 'according to which human life means nothing'. Psychologically mutilated by extreme upheavals and with little example of true democratic values, the majority of the population is convinced that without brutality it is not possible to deal with criminality:

> It takes decades to cultivate such a level of legal awareness, and today, with the growth in crime never seen before, it has become even more primitive. Connected with this euphoria of brutality is the widespread criticism in society of the unjustifiably mild punishments handed out to the most dangerous criminals – all the more so since, in recent years, judicial practice has – exceptionally, given her history – become imbued with a liberal ethos. On the other hand, the demand for harsher punishment suggests that peoples' demands for security have not been met. In addition, the low level of protection given to the individual (rare in the civilized world) goes hand in hand with the alienation of citizens from the system of justice – whence the high numbers of unreported offences, absence of authority, and lack of trust in the system of justice.[72]

As Kvashis suggests, since the collapse of the Soviet Union, the new economic reality has created a huge rift between rich and poor, with detrimental consequences to social mores and morale on both sides of the divide. Poverty is said to be at the root of crimes involving theft, murder, and cot deaths.[73] First-hand observers of criminality speak of a fairly grotesque carnival of distorted values.

The accepted norms of civic behaviour, self-discipline, and social responsibility have been upturned, producing anti-social behaviour driven by greed and revenge, which is generally left unchecked by an inefficient, if not corrupt, judiciary and an unscrupulous militia reluctant to do its job. As the most visible law-enforcing body, the militia 'is not squeamish when it comes to bribes, or beating up suspects and detainees. Instead of hunting down criminals and crimes, as the law requires, the militia is prone to concealment depending on the potential risk to them involved.'[74] The number of offenders actually brought to justice is still proportionally very small: according to Borodin and Klebanov, in the year 2000, only one-tenth of crimes were registered, meaning that the reported number of crimes perpetrated against another individual (152,077) should in fact be closer to one-and-a-half million.[75] The stark conclusion these authors come to is that the government's economic policy has merely left the individual – a law-abiding citizen – more defenceless than ever before. Deepening social cleavages between rich and poor have left the elderly and the unemployed increasingly vulnerable to what appears to be state indifference, if not incompetence in ensuring security.

> The humanization of criminal legislation and the system of punishment is extremely important (...). I believe that, where justifiable, sentencing that does not involve loss of freedom should be practised more widely. Our main aim is to prevent further crime.
>
> (Vladimir Putin, 2002)[76]

In April 2002, President Putin endorsed recommendations for amendments to the Code put forward a month earlier.[77] The same spirit was carried over into the Code of Criminal Procedure, which came into effect in July of that year. Its underlying principles – publicity, legal justice, respect for human worth, rights, inalienability (of person and property), presumption of innocence – are intended to protect the defendant from physical or moral harm. More generally, of course, and by sheer force of reiteration, the overriding aim is to demonstrate that recognition of these rights in criminal procedure is the best way to ensure that a rule of law state may enjoy long-lasting stable foundations. For the moment, then, the liberal juridical thinkers seem to have ridden out the storm. That said, in the eyes of wary critics, if the principle of humanism in sentencing the criminal offender has been conceived as a means of protecting human rights inside the courtroom, outside it, ordinary law-abiding citizens have virtually no guarantees of protection at all.

Afterword

Post-Soviet legal culture and pre-revolutionary models

> Contemporary criminal legislation cannot be constructed from the ideas of a single school of thought. If it is to enjoy status as scientifically rigorous and contemporary, it must combine the best of classical and sociological ideas, and take into account more recent modifications.
>
> (A. Naumov)

> One must take note of the high degree of significance and actuality of our national historical experience in today's conditions of constructing norms (*normotvorchestvo*).
>
> (A.I. Aleksandrov)[1]

For students of Russian intellectual culture, the question of 'resources' is one most commonly flagged up for consideration in post-Soviet scholarship. The clear parallels with some of the premises of pre-Revolutionary juridical science, especially with regard to the subjective side of crime, together with the stock of terms such as 'legality', '*lichnost*', 'responsibility', 'humanism' associated with the Russian pre-Revolutionary liberal tradition more broadly, may, of course, be coincidental and best explained by the order of common sense, or as a response to international expectations. But, if we bear in mind that these concepts and principles formed part of an intellectual baggage that some legal scholars acquired as students of law during the Brezhnev era but did not broadcast, their inclusion in post-Soviet juridical discourse – indeed, even the official legislation – can also be interpreted as a conscious effort not only to exploit the achievements of a national intellectual patrimony but, where possible, stress its actuality.

A cursory overview of contemporary juridical literature reveals that the frequency of references to Kistyakovsky and Poznyshev as the two termini in the golden age of Russian legal culture is offset by a seemingly random selection of iconic figures, possibly the result of a chance encounter with their works, and, in many instances, 'second hand' knowledge dependent on post-Soviet reprints and anthologies of pre-Revolutionary legal thought. For Anatoly Naumov, it was the fortuitous discovery in the early 1960s of Tagantsev's seminal *Course* that triggered his interest in the pre-Revolutionary juridical tradition more generally and which he has brought to bear in his work ever since.[2] In the foreword to what is widely regarded as one of the most authoritative textbooks in criminal law in the last decade, Naumov's opening remarks are explicit acknowledgement of the legacy of late Imperial scholarship and of its relevance for the post-Soviet readership: 'As a single authored monograph, this *Course of Lectures in Russian Criminal Law* (...) continues the pre-Revolutionary tradition of Russian juridical science, the last such "Lecture Course" [as opposed to textbook – FN] written by Tagantsev in 1902.'[3] Since the collapse of the Soviet Union, the 1902 edition of Tagantsev's lecture course has seen two reprints: the first, an incomplete edition, was published in 1994 as projects for the new Criminal Code were underway; the second, dated 2001, contained a lengthy introduction by Naumov in which he stressed the contemporary significance of his elected mentor. Tagantsev's normative approach to law (*pravo*) did not reduce to an arid formulism but took stock of the flux inherent in the social context in which laws are made. He strongly opposed punishment based on analogous situations, an anomaly that was, however, written into the Tsarist Code as a prerogative for dealing with political crime, and which, in Soviet justice, became a mainstay resulting in the criminalization of the most anodyne gesture towards free thought. Tagantsev's rigorous separation of law and morality, his categorization of the object of crime (like Kistyakovsky he spoke of legally protected vital (*zhiznennye*) interests), and his analysis of imputability all fed into his concept of crime, the essence of which, as I discussed in the previous chapter, passed almost unchanged into post-Soviet legislation. If this was largely due to Naumov's persuasive input, the contemporary relevance of Taganstev's thought has also been acknowledged by others:

> His work represents a rich scientific inheritance that is vital in today's efforts to raise the intellectual level of criminal-juridical research. It contributes to a deeper understanding of criminal law problems, and provides an example as to how these should be set out in the new Criminal Code of the Russian Federation.[4]

For post-Soviet successors, then, it is the fusion of classical and sociological approaches associated with Tagantsev and his generation that represents the most suitable template for post-Soviet legislation. If the former, thanks to Feuerbach, established some of the theoretical categories of criminal law, encouraging the study of the subjective side of crime, guilt, and imputability, approaches to crime as a social, biological, and physical phenomenon prompted the construction of criminal law sanctions based on the principle of individualization. As I suggested in the previous chapter, both aspects have been consciously assimilated by compilers of the 1996 Code as guidelines on sentencing.

Naumov's indebtedness to Tagantsev for the rigour of his thought invites questions concerning the place of the pre-Revolutionary heritage in post-Soviet juridical thought and practice more broadly, whether familiarity with this legacy merely engages the interest of the antiquarian or whether it might actually shed light on present-day issues.[5] Certainly, the fad for re-editions, which was already popular during the Gorbachev era and which has grown in the decade since the fall of communism, is symptomatic of endeavours across the cultural and intellectual landscape to recover the more distant past so as to be able to renegotiate aspects of the more immediate legacy. And in this sense, criminal law is no exception. Koni, Tagantsev, Arsen'ev, Spasovich, and others have been awarded with posthumous celebrity status. This is, of course, not to suggest that they were completely effaced during the Soviet period: Brezhnev era scholarship, in particular, provides examples of historical theoretical studies of past masters which, if ideologically weighted with evaluations advanced in the light of current Marxist criteria, were often well referenced or rich in lengthy quotations.[6] Today, in their current revival, however, individual past masters have been accredited with the accolade of moral authority. Especially important is the consistency with which they applied the principles of justice in their work as lawyers and judges. Koni's constant reminder that the work of a judge must be guided by the 'prescriptions of positive law and the unconditional, universal demands of the moral law' has been picked up by post-Soviet reformers of criminal procedure, hopeful that it might help remedy stubborn vestiges of corruption in the courts.[7] Or, again, the almost ubiquitous celebration of Tagantsev – 'his personality and the multitudinous activities he managed in his career represent a massive achievement not only for Russian jurisprudence but for Russian culture generally' – expresses quite typically the present-day tendency to commemorate and salvage the past.[8] To much the same effect, tributes to pre-Revolutionary thinkers contain an 'actuality of the past' dimension, suggesting to the reader that if history does not repeat itself, the current situation in post-Soviet Russia does not present a set of entirely new circumstances.[9] And indeed, it is hard to avoid similarities in terms of the challenges each generation faced. In both periods, endeavours to reform meant having to raise public legal awareness and encourage trust in a profession whose reputation had been sullied by corruption, incompetence, and powerlessness before the administrative, and latterly, party institutions to which they were subordinated. Both before and after communism, efforts to institute trial by jury required a sustained campaign by a reform-minded judiciary to overcome opposition fed largely by a paternalistic attitude towards the Russian people and an inability to accredit them with a legal awareness.

The hagiographical component in post-Soviet assessments of the pre-Revolutionary heritage is not, of course, a recent invention; rather, it belongs to a practice of constructing traditions that pre-Revolutionary reformers themselves were conscious of and actively exploited in obituary notices and jubilee editions as a complementary, yet highly effective, way of instilling the values of legality, justice, and humanism in an audience that otherwise might be cautious or unreceptive. Indeed, a number of post-Soviet publications have simply reprinted some of these as forewords to selected works of an individual author.[10] However, if, in the pre-Revolutionary period, gestures of mutual appreciation aimed to garner greater esteem for the liberal reform movement, some post-Soviet commemorations of this heritage seem – ironically – given their choice of intellectual icons, to be motivated by nationalist sentiment. The upshot is that the liberal-cum-socialist ideas of certain original reformers, such as Chicherin, Shershenevich, Bogdan Kistyakovsky, to mention just a few, have now been enlisted to mark, somewhat crudely, Russia's differences with West European practices:

> We should familiarize ourselves and assimilate the experience of the traditional moral–juridical structure of Russia, that enabled her to preserve the health of the nation, sustain great power (*derzhavnost'*) for centuries until she stumbled on attempts to graft westernizing ideas of social order on to the Russian countryside. Such was the case with class hatred, and it is such again, today, as pseudo-reformers attempt to alter the collective (*sobornyi*) spirit of the Russian people, entice them with individualism and the cult of the body. Such a radical turn away from spirituality has quickly taken its toll in the juridical sphere: the criminalization of society is growing catastrophically.[11]

Ignorance of the original context in which 'master ideas' were elaborated and second-hand readings can, and do, result in misrepresentations of arguments or incorrect emphasis, and, sometimes rather amusingly, betray shallow knowledge of the author in question. (On more than one occasion, I have seen Solov'ev's famous denunciation of the death penalty, dated 1906, unwittingly implying that it was a sort of post-script composed in the grave.) But if this unfortunate, yet inevitable, consequence of constructing a pantheon of juridical masters, whose ideas are reproduced and condensed in pocket-sized anthologies or selected works, is a second-hand assimilation that can lead to the proverbial 'Chinese whisper' effect of distortions, and factual inaccuracies, it nevertheless signals the quest for a theoretical paradigm that might answer Russia's current needs in the domain of law.

Law, morality, and personhood – a Solov'evian echo in post-Soviet juridical thought

> For centuries, in Russia, the person (*lichnost'*) was suppressed by the institutions of serfdom and autocracy. There was no room for the growth of the feeling of citizenship, either in private, or in public relations. For the first time in Russian history the idea of *lichnost'* with attendant rights and freedoms protected by the law was put forward in the Judicial Statutes of 1864. But nothing was done in the sphere of civil and political rights. (…) The next fifty years witnessed pendulum swings between progress and reaction. (…) Only in February, 1917 did the 'light of freedom' glimmer in our land, when the Provisional government passed laws broadening our civil and political freedoms (of movement, press, association, the right to form political parties, etc.).[12]

The tragedy of Russian liberalism described here by Lyublinsky in 1917, while he waited in exile hoping to witness the rapid unravelling of Bolshevism, has acted as a warning call for some post-Soviet writers, who, in endeavouring to revive the person and humanism as leitmotifs of pre-Revolutionary liberal legal culture, must also reckon with its flaws that ultimately made it politically unworkable in Russia. Chernyshevsky, recall, saw it as doomed, because the assumptions it carried were too remote from Russian reality to make it viable, a case in point being the liberal concept of freedom which, as Lyublinsky's apologia implies, was repeatedly compromised by tsarist *proizvol*.

> The manner in which reformist liberals discussed natural law is often reminiscent of the perfunctory gestures we make when raising a toast to someone's health: moral energy was lacking. While the holiest of holies – the right of freedom – was ceremoniously honoured, it was never imputed to the state to *concede* these rights as 'sacred' or supra-temporal. Consequently, no matter how great the share of inalienable freedom a citizen might be allocated, that which he might be allowed to fight for with idealistic devotion depended upon criteria decided by the state. Whatever the petitions, recommendations, or civilian homilies which liberals addressed to the government, their legal claims tended to be couched in the language of gains to be had by the state. In other words, they were clever 'hypothetical imperatives' designed not to impinge on state supremacy.[13]

The author of these comments, the historian of philosophy, Erikh Solov'ev – a specialist in Kant and Lutheranism and a prominent *shestidesyatnik* – revisited the quarrel between Chicherin and his coincidental namesake, coming down firmly on the side of the latter in what he called a contest between standard liberal values predicated on assumed freedom (economic, material) and Christian morality, wherein inner 'spiritual freedom is experienced, or acts, as civic freedom'.[14] For this latter-day admirer, Solov'ev succeeded in addressing juridical nihilism where liberals had failed. Rather than subordinate rights to the state, as his liberal peers – the enlightened stewards – had done, Solov'ev rephrased human rights as the juridical application of Christian ethics. As Erikh Solov'ev rightly observes, both in his criticism of government policy and in his activism in favour of minorities and the peasantry, Solov'ev was a living example of the way Christian morality instigated appeals to admit civic rights and freedoms. However, in doing so, he posed an untenable threat to the state prerogative as custodian, which ultimately made him a 'dissident defender of rights'.[15]

Erikh Solov'ev's argument may be contested, and, indeed, other scholars generally bring into play an element that this author overlooks, namely that in his theocratic project, even if in later life he may have abandoned its utopian-style formulation, Solov'ev never lost sight of his vision of integral wholeness and the role he attributed to the state. But, this arguably does not lessen the contemporary significance of the relation he maintained between law and morality more specifically. Indeed, a small handful of legal thinkers more engaged with the philosophical premises of law rather than its practical implementation have recognized the intellectual achievement of pre-Revolutionary research in natural law, and the pertinence of Solov'ev's moral philosophical approach to juridical issues.[16] At the centre of their conceptual platform, they have placed the idea of the person urging that all concrete proposals for updating court proceedings should be designed to protect her rights. In his *Criminal Politics and the Criminal Process in the Russian State System*, A.I. Aleksandrov, for example, has constructed a comprehensive theoretical and historical defence of the rule of law state, the democratic principles of which, he argues, should be grounded in the idea of the good and of justice. These twin values encourage a healthy patriotism among citizens, respect for the law and other people's rights. Indeed, according to Aleksandrov, the development of law is conditional upon morality and should be actively promoted at state level in its 'propaganda' to instil democratic constitutional principles: 'Without these values, the further development of the rule of law in Russia is impossible.'[17] In making his case for the close ties between legal awareness, morality, and justice, Aleksandrov lifts and slightly transforms a number of easily recognizable Solov'evian motifs – law as a minimum of morality, realization of the good, the general good – to argue that the relation between law and morality provides the foundation of justice:

> Juridical law and normative law (*pravovoi zakon*; *pravo*) should not correspond merely formally, but in deed with justice. In this sense, the principle of law (*pravo*) is not universal equality; rather it is equality in obligation (*dolzhnoe*), in the realization of the good. Just and right is not the person who indiscriminately commits a crime, but who, in equal regard for all, refrains from doing so because he neither wishes it nor can do so out of moral principle.[18]

More than a mere paraphrase of Solov'ev's argument, the thrust of Aleksandrov's remarks honour the principles that drove Solov'ev in his defence of rights, namely his vision of the human person as a God-given 'end in herself' who should never be treated as a means.[19]

In his book, *Reforming the Russian Legal System*, published in 1996, Gordon Smith concluded on an optimistic note:

> Laws matter. Rights are now being recognized and new generations of Russians are growing up in a rapidly evolving culture in which justice and rule of law are not empty slogans masking authoritarian rule and the arbitrary exercise of power.[20]

At the time of writing, ten years on, I am hesitant to express the same optimism. Thwarted by the tsars, obstructed by Bolshevism, the Western-inspired secular model of liberalism with its message of freedom and rule of law seems again to be losing ground in the current political climate. As an alternative, the underlying message of Solov'ev's 'theological liberalism', which, if inspired by Christian morality, so readily translated into secular terms, perhaps merits to be heard in a society that still trades in religious pathos (to whatever ends) and views itself as post-Soviet, not post-Christian.

Notes

Introduction

1 Lyublinsky, 1906, foreword.
2 For discussions of late Imperial juridical culture, most of which deal primarily with civil law, see, for example, Smith, 1996, Ch. 1; Wagner, 1994; Kaiser, 1972; Kucherov, 1974; Crisp and Edmondson, 1989; Solomon, 1997; Baberowski, 1996; Wartenweiler, 1999. Legal historians of Russia have tended to focus on civil law, or confined research on the criminal justice system to the Soviet era. See, for example, Solomon, 1996. For more punctual studies dealing with various aspects of the penal system in Imperial Russia, see the Bibliography.
3 Lyublinsky, 1915, 5.
4 Hans Gäntzel's somewhat outdated book, *Wladimir Solowjews Rechtsphilosophie auf der Grundlage der Sittlichkeit* (1968) charts Solov'ev's intellectual development in his theory of law and morality but offers little contextualization, and in terms of critical engagement with his sources is quite timid. Andrzej Walicki's groundbreaking *Legal Philosophies of Russian Liberalism* (1987) contains an important chapter on Solov'ev's philosophy of law, as well as chapters on the ideas of those who both taught and practised law professionally, notably Boris Chicherin, Pavel Novgorodtsev, Leon Petrazhitsky and Sergei Gessen. However, Walicki does not address the implications of Solov'ev theory for criminal justice.
5 There exists a vast literature on Solov'ev, though his contribution to criminal justice has not received much attention. Recent studies examining his place as a 'voice of conscience' include van den Bercken *et al.*, 2000; Sutton, 1996 [Special Issue]; van der Zweerde, 2003; Valliere, 2000; Wozniuk, 1999; Gaut, 1998; de Courten, 2004; Schrooyen, 2006. Among the numerous publications (including new editions of Solov'ev's work) in Russia, see, for example, Borisova and Kozyrev, 2001. See also the fairly comprehensive bibliography of Solov'ev's works and studies on him by Kristi Groberg compiled for the Trans-National Vladimir Solovyov Society.
6 Important studies on the public sphere and liberalism include Clowes *et al.*, 1991; Timberlake, 1972; Fischer, 1958; Leontovitch, 1958. Laura Engelstein has done some of the most innovative work on liberalism as a set of values and attitudes across social groups. See Engelstein, 1992. Also by Engelstein, 1999. Recent Russian studies on liberalism include *Russkii Liberalism*, 1999; Pustarnakov and Khudushina, 1996.
7 Foucault, 1975; Norbert Elias, *Über den Prozess der Zivilisation. Soziogenetische und psychogenetische Untersuchungen* [1939] (Bern, 1969); Evans, 1997.
8 Evans, 1997, 14.
9 Ibid., 18.

1 Fathers and sons of legal reform

1 Fischer, 1958.

2 Spasovich was forced to resign his post as professor of Criminal Law in 1864 after the publication of his 'ideologically suspect' textbook on the subject. On this episode in Spasovich's career, see Smolyarchuk, 1982. Solov'ev was, in fact, only temporarily suspended from his university post in philosophy as *dotsent*, censured by the state authorities for his public condemnation of the death penalty. Although, six months later the ban was lifted, he did not resume a career as an academic.

3 On the emergence of *obshchestvennost'* and the press, see, for example, E. Clowes, Kassow and West, 1991; Brooks, 1985; Manning, 1982; McClelland, 1979; Balmuth, 2000.

4 For the most comprehensive account of juridical culture on the eve of reform, and of the leading ministerial and university figures that shaped it, see Wortman, 1976.

5 See Tagantsev, 1892. On Tagantsev, see Naumov (Introduction), 2001; Zagorodnikov, 1992. On Mittermaier, see, for example, Evans, 1996.

6 Arsen'ev, 1915, 118–119 cited in Wortman, 1976, 254. The *Journal of the Ministry of Justice* also inspired the founding of another specialist periodical, *Yuridicheskii Vestnik*, in 1860 by N.V. Kalachov, a former student of Redkin. See Wortman, 1976, Ch. 2.

7 Arsen'ev, 1905, an anthology of essays first published in *Vestnik Evropy* between 1880 and 1904; 1915. His theoretical works included essays on the Russian Bar and studies on contemporary French and German systems [*Predanie sudu i dal'neishii khod ugolovnogo dela* (1870) and *Sudebnoe Sledstvie* (1871)]. In the 1890s, Arsen'ev worked on the Brokgaus-Efron encyclopaedia, contributing the majority of articles on law. See Kel'ner, 1993, Ch. 3. For a detailed account of the history of *Vestnik Evropy*, see Gekker, 1911.

8 Cited by D.A. Tolstoi in a report on his appointment as Minister of the Interior in 1882. See Kelner, 1993, 209.

9 For a detailed account of the history of the creation of the journal, see Pogorelskin, 1971.

10 Textbooks on criminal justice reviewed by the journal include Tal'berg, 1889; Tagantsev, vyp. 3, 1890; N.D. Sergeevsky, *Russkoe ugolovnoe pravo: Posobie k lektsiyam* (3rd edn, SPb, 1896); Leventsim, 1897; *Sudebnye Rechi* by Spasovich, A.F. Koni. Among the most authoritative Western authors reviewed were Gabriel Tarde, chief spokesman for the sociological school of criminology, *Les transformations du droit. Etude sociologique* (Paris, 1893).

11 After this affair, Koni was transferred to the civil department, 'an area normally less sensitive for the government'. See Wagner, 1976, 376.

12 Arsen'ev, 'Politicheskii Protsess – 1869–1871', *Vestnik Evropy*, 11 (1871), discussed in Gekker, 1911, 239–240.

13 Afterword, *Svoboda Sovesti*, quoted by Koni in his obituary note, 'Konstantin Konstantinovich Arsen'ev (1837–1919)'. See Potapchuk, 2001, 7–20.

14 K.K. Arsen'ev, 'Programma russkikh liberalov', 4 and 6 (1882), and included in his collection of essays *Za chetvert' veka (1871–94)*, 84–109.

15 Modelled on the German *Realschule*, a 'Realist' education focused on science, rather than Greek and Latin, which formed the backbone of the 'Gymnasium' curriculum.

16 This, as Olga Crisp points out, had repercussions on the civil code, namely that a major difficulty in discussing peasant land tenure was

> how to isolate those features and legal disabilities which stemmed from an individual's status as a peasant or member of a legal estate (*soslovie*), and those which were connected with the specific manner of land-holding and the legal norms which governed it.

See O. Crisp, 'Peasant Land Tenure and Civil Rights Implications before 1906', in Crisp and Edmondson (eds), 1989, 33–64. On Arsen'ev's links with the zemstvo liberals, see Pirumova, 1977, Ch. 5.

17 Arsen'ev, 'Liberalizm, kak istochnik vsyakikh zol', 9 (1890), republished in *Za chetvert' veka*, 451–459. Arsen'ev took up the cause of religious tolerance (in the borderlands) in a number of articles, which were subsequently published in his first volume of collected essays in 1905 (see note 7 above).
18 Arsen'ev, 1890, 436–443.
19 See, for example, *VE*, 1 (1887) 348–356; 'Administrativno-karatel'naya vlast' zemskikh nachal'nikov', 6 (1894), 809–826; 'Novaya kritika suda prisyazhnykh, 3 (1896), 390–406, 5 (1896), 358–370, 6 (1896), 775–791, 7 (1896), 400–417; 'Zhelatel'nye popravki v fynktsionirovaniya i ustroistve suda prisyazhnykh', 5 (1897), 349–353. On land captains and counter reform, see T.S. Pearson, 'The Origins of Alexander III's Land Captains: A Reinterpretation', *Slavic Review*, vol. 40, 1981, 384–403, and *Russian Officialdom in Crisis: Autocracy and Local Self-Government, 1861–1900* (Cambridge, 1989), also by Pearson.
20 Arsen'ev, *VE*, 1, (1894), 459.
21 Arsen'ev, 'Programma russkikh liberalov', and V. Vodorozov, 'Liberal'naya partiya', Brokgaus-Efron, *Entsiklopedicheskii Slovar'*, vol. 34, 1896, 633–634.
22 See Zaionchkovsky, 1970, 275.
23 K.K. Arsen'ev, 'Liberalizm, kak istochnik vsyakikh zol', *VE*, 9, 1890, in Arsen'ev, 1915, 451–459.
24 See Kel'ner, 1993, 260.
25 Chernyshevsky, 'Bor'ba partii vo Frantsii pri Lyudovike XVIII i Karle X', *Sovremennik*, 8 (1858), quoted from W.J. Leatherbarrow and D.C. Offord, *A Documentary History of Russian Thought* (Ann Arbor, 1987), 205.
26 Dostoevsky, *Letters and Reminiscences* (New York, 1923), 39. Cited in Timberlake (5). See also his *Winter Notes on Summer Impressions* (1863) for an account of the negative impact of Western civilization on spiritual values.
27 Cited in Timberlake, 1972, 5.
28 Chicherin, *Sobstvennost i gosudarstvo* (Moscow, 1882), cited in Crisp, 1989, 35. For a discussion of more popular perceptions of property as privilege, see R. Wortman, 'Property Rights, Populism, and Russian Political Culture', in the same volume.
29 V.S. Solov'ev, 'Ekonomicheskii vopros s nravstevennoi tochki zreniya', *VE*, 12, 1896. Discussed below.
30 My references are taken from the French translation: Vl. Solov'ev, *La Justification du bien* (trans. T.D.M.) (Geneva, 1997), 338.
31 Ibid., 330.
32 Ibid., 351.
33 Ibid., 342.
34 Incidentally, on this point, Solov'ev made a concrete proposal to reduce the number of working hours for manual labour. A shorter working week, he reasoned, does not necessarily mean a decrease in production.
35 Solov'ev, *Tri Razgovora* (1899–1990), 'Vtoroi Razgovor: Politik'.
36 Vl. Solov'ev, 'Idoly i Idealy' in Natsional'nyi Vopros v Rossii, vol. 2 (1891) in *V.S. Solov'ev. Sochineniya v dvukh tomakh*, vol. 1 (Moscow, 1989), 624.
37 See *Solov'ev: Pis'ma*, vol. IV (pod. Red. E.L. Radlova) (Pbg., 1923), 34. (My thanks to Pauline Schrooyen for helping me track down this reference.) On Solov'ev's political affinities and differences with the *Vestniki*, see also Kel'ner, 1993, 225–227. For a contemporary account of Solov'ev's intellectual relations with the Slavophiles, see Milyukov, 1903, 295–308. (This text was originally a public lecture given in 1893.) See also Gaut, 1998, 77–94.
38 Writing in 1897, the populist-democrat V.G. Korolenko identified a number of core

principles defended by the *Vestniki*, which afforded the journal a degree of 'ideological' coherence: a healthy civic life in which the law and the inalienable rights of the person are respected; an independent court of law; development of local self-government; religious tolerance; freedom of speech and the press; and education for all. See Kel'ner, 1993, 258.

39 See D.N. Shipov, *Vospominania i dumy o perezhitom* (Moscow, 1918), 131–155. Given the passing similarities, and shared impulse in Slavophilism, it is curious that Solov'ev seems to have had little to do with Shipov, except possibly via the intermediary of S.N Trubetskoi, another 'zemstvo liberal' and close friend of Solov'ev. Virtually all Shipov's closest allies rejected his concrete proposal to reinstate the pre-Petrine 'zemskii sobor'.

40 Cited in V.I. Smolyarchuk, *A.F. Koni i ego okruzhenie* (Moscow, 1990), 273.

41 See the various obituary accounts by, among others, Koni, Spasovich, and Arsen'ev, of Solov'ev published in *Vestnik Evropy* over the course of several months following the death of Solov'ev in July 1900. (References are given in Chapter 4 below.) Arsen'ev's comment comes from a letter addressed to Stasyulevich, cited in Kel'ner, ibid., 226 note.

42 Koni went so far as to compare the writings of Solov'ev with those of Aksakov in *Den'*, *Rus'*, and *Moskva*: A.F. Koni, 'Pamiati Vladimira Sergeevicha Solov'eva', pamphlet, 1901, 28–29.

43 The literary historian, A.N. Pypin, wrote on the liberal tendencies embedded in Slavophilism in much this vein. See Balykin, 1996.

44 Cf. Zimmerman, 1980, 7. Vodorozov in a supplement to his 1896 article, which appeared in a new edition of the Brokgaus-Efron *Entsiklopedicheskii slovar'*, wrote that after the 1905 revolution there were no clear boundaries between liberalism and socialism. Any differences at all were a matter of temperament. Cf. Timberlake, 1972.

45 See Wartenweiler, 1999, Ch. 1.

46 See, for example, A.A. Bogdanov, *Liberaly i Sotsialisty* (SPb., 1905) for an application of the labels of 'Old' and 'Progressive'.

47 Wartenweiler, 1999, 90–91.

48 On this theme, see Zimmerman, 1980, 1–20.

49 Inspired by Montesquieu (*Esprit des Lois*) and Beccaria (*Dei delittie della pene*), the term *grazhdanin* had figured prominently in Catherine the Great's *Nakaz*. The 'Instructions' painted a vision of a just society in which everyone, including the monarch, would be subject to the law and enjoy political freedoms as well. See Tolz, 2001, 54.

50 According to Boris Mironov, however, the conservative view of power and authority (from Karamzin to Tikhomirov) mirrored best the view of the people and served as the best form of protection against the threat of Russia's Europeanization. Mironov, 1999, 216.

51 Founded in 1872, it was initially more moderate, but by the 1890s it had become staunchly reactionary. It featured some comically crude caricatures of 'progressive' intellectuals, including a memorable one of 'Mr. Solov'ev', a liberal par excellence.

52 M. Reisner, for example, defined the 'citizen' as endowed with 'independent action, moral independence and responsibility'. Brokgaus-Efron *Entsiklopedicheskii slovar'*, vol. 16, 390. Cited in David Wartenweiler, 1999, 7. Vladimir Wozniuk argues that Solov'ev's essays on politics, law, and ethics should primarily be seen as a defence of human rights. See Wozniuk, 1999.

53 Engelstein, 1999, 235. If, intellectually, individualism was loaded with unsavoury connotations; in practice, there was, however, during the Silver Age, as Mironov suggests, a certain fascination with the cultivation of 'image statements' – quizzical dress, eccentric life style, and other such affectations – designed to draw the spectator's eyes to difference rather than conformity and thus make the individual stand out from the crowd. Mironov, 1999, 288.

2 Reforming criminal law (1864–1903)

1 Quoted by Kistyakovsky, 1909 in his contribution to the *Vekhi* collection. See Shatz, 1994.
2 'Ustav ugolovnogo sudoproizvodstva', *Svod Zakonov Rossiikoi Imperii*, vol. XVI, pt. 1 (ed. 1892), cited in Szeftel, 1958, 2. See also *Ustav ugolovnogo sudoproizvodstva*, compiled by Prof. M.N. Gernet (Moscow, 1916), 'Obshchie Polozheniya'.
3 Arsen'ev, 'Vnutrennoe Obozrenie', *Vestnik Evropy*, 10, (1898), 794.
4 Statute on prevention and suppression of crimes, cited in Szeftel, 1958, 8.
5 Engelstein, 1992, 20.
6 Szeftel, 1958, 5.
7 Police surveillance was established by the Ordinance of 12 March 1882. The state of emergency had two measures of containing disorder and maintaining public tranquillity – a reinforced protection (*usilennaya okhrana*) and 'extraordinary protection' (*chrezvychainaya okhrana*). The first could be declared by the Minister of the Interior, while 'extraordinary protection' required the tsar's approval. See, Fuller, Jr, 1982, 291. See also, Daly, 1995. and Waldron, 1995, 1–25.
8 Szeftel, 1958, 9. According to William Fuller, between 1881 and 1903, military courts tried between 200 and 1,000 civilians a year. Ibid., 290, 295.
9 Wortman, 1976, 277–283.
10 Ibid., 283.
11 'Vnutrennoe Obozrenie', *VE*, 6 (1894), 824.
12 Ulozhenie o nakazaniyakh ugolovnykh i ispravitel'nykh [1845], art. 1. Cf. Mironov, 1999.
13 For recent post-Soviet histories of the criminal and penal codes in the Imperial era, see, for example, Naumov, 2004, 60–115; Konyakhin, 1845–1996.
14 Mironov notes that 1,415 articles detailed crimes in connection with state funds, 74 in connection with the government, 19 against the state, 32 on religious grounds. Mironov, 1999, 24.
15 Wortman, 1976, 10–11. On the scale of punishments, see, for example, Wood, 1989, 215–233. See also 'Lestnitsa Nakazanii', in Brokgaus-Efron, *Entsiklopedicheskii Slovar'*, vol. XXXV, 177–182, and Mironov, 1999.
16 Wood, 1989, 223; 1980.
17 Often rendered in French as 'maison de force'. Stemming from old Russian *mery* (corrective measures), the term has euphemistic associations in popular etymology, linking 'smirenie/smiritel'nyi' (restrain, subdue) with *mir* (peace, reconciliation). The institution was phased out in the 1880s as part of the wider programme of prison reform. My thanks to Alfred Sproede for unravelling the etymology.
18 Foinitsky, 1889, 283–284, cited in Wood, 1989, 223. On Foinitsky's theoretical approach to crime and punishment, see below, Ch. 3.
19 Gernet, 1913, 144–147.
20 Ibid., 147.
21 Ukaz, 1754, cited in Wood, 1989, 216, n. 6.
22 Murav'ev, 1874, 91; Mironov, 1999, 30–31.
23 Murav'ev, 1874, 86f.
24 Ibid., 89–90.
25 Ibid., 93.
26 Gernet, 1913.
27 Murav'ev, 1874. See note 22 above.
28 Ibid., 94–102
29 Ibid., 109–110.
30 Ibid., 110. Further objections to the practice took into account the psychological makeup and background of the offender to argue that the greater one's sense of personal honour, the more painfully one experienced humiliation. By contrast, a

shameless, thick-skinned or stupid person was less likely to experience guilt and shame in the same way. The whole point of the exercise was therefore lost on him.

31 Dril', 1883, 253. On the legal culture of the peasantry, see, for example, Frierson, 1987. Also by Frierson, *Peasant Icons: Representations of Rural People in Late Nineteenth Century Russia* (Oxford, 1993). Burbank, 2004. G. Popkins, 1999, 57–87. Also by Popkins, Jan. 2000 and 2000. (My thanks to Gareth Popkins for generously supplying me with copies of his work.)
32 S.V. Pakhman, 'Ocherk narodnykh yuridicheskikh obychev Smolenskoi gubernii' [1900], cited in Frierson, 1987, 59.
33 A.N. Engel'hardt, *Iz Derevni: 12 pisem, 1872–1877* (Moscow, 1937), cited in Mironov, 1999, 67–68.
34 M.A. Dmitriev, *Glavy iz vospominanii moei zhizni* (1864–1866), cited in Mironov, 1999, 67.
35 Frierson, 1987, 58.
36 Ibid., 66.
37 See Popkins, 2000.
38 See Frierson, 1987, 65.
39 See R. Wortman, 'Property Rights, Russian Populism, and Russian Political Culture', in Olga Crisp and Linda Edmondson (eds), *Civil Rights in Imperial Russia* (Oxford, 1989). Popkins, 1999.
40 Ivan Strakhovsky, *Krestianskie prava i uchrezhdeniya* (SPb., 1904). See review of this book in *VE*, 2 (1904), 394–399.
41 Popkins, 1999, 68–69.
42 Wortman, 1976, 3.
43 See 'Vnutrennoe Obozrenie', *VE*, 12 (1884), 846–865.
44 This ambitious undertaking was broken into four sub-committees: the judicial system in general; criminal procedure; civil procedure; and local court establishments. See 'Vnutrennoe Obozrenie', *VE*, 7 (1896), 400–417.
45 N.V. Murav'ev speech dated 1894, cited in *Sudebnye Ustavy, 20 XI 1864 (za 50 let)*, 2 vols and suppl. (Pg., 1914), 689.
46 'Vnutrennoe Obozrenie', *VE*, 6 (1900), 770, and *VE*, 1 (1901), 367–383. See also Koni, 'Posleslovie', 2003, 336–339.
47 'Vnutrennoe Obozrenie', *VE*, 10 (1898), 796.
48 'Vnutrennoe Obozrenie', *VE*, 2 (1897), 820.
49 Various degrees of non-indictable 'irresponsibility' (*sostoyanie nevmenyaemosti*) – drunkenness, simpleton, old age, sleepwalking – had been integrated into the Penal Code (1845) with set age limits (for example, a child under the age of ten could not be held accountable for a legal infraction), but the criteria used to determine insanity were token and arbitrarily informed.
50 For a critique of this categorization, namely that it did not go far enough by differentiating between ordinary and political crimes or by breaking down the former category into minor and serious instances of 'criminal foul' [*ugolovnaya nepravda*] falling to the respective jurisdictions of local and high court authorities, see Przheval'sky, 1896 and 1897). See also 'Vnutrennoe Obozrenie', *VE*, 2 (1897), 819–827.
51 Naumov, 2004, 102.
52 Murav'ev, 1874, 85; Mironov, 1999, 35.
53 Gernet, 1961, 9–56.
54 Cf. Mironov, 1999, 15. Human denigration was also part of the course in eighteenth-century Prussia, however: 'At his Majesty's pleasure, a person (bearing a petition) may be hanged alongside a hound.' Tagantsev, *Russkoe ugolovnoe pravo*, cited by Solov'ev in his chapter on law and morality in *Opravdanie Dobra* (1897).
55 Walicki, 1987.
56 Kistyakovsky, 1994, 95.
57 Mironov, 1999, 216.

58 Pobedonostsev, 1965, 85–86.
59 Mironov, 1999, vol. 2, 20; Wagner, 1994.
60 Engelstein, 1999, 227.
61 Arsen'ev, 'Vnutrennoe Obozrenie', *VE*, 1, 1899, 348.
62 'Vnutrennoe Obozrenie', *VE*, 1 (1901), 367–383.
63 For example, Korsakov, 1896; *Sochineniya V.D. Spasovicha* (1890–1900); *Sbornik statei N.M. Korkunova (1877–1897)* (SPb., 1898); Arsen'ev, 1904.

3 Theorizing crime and punishment

1 V. Przheval'sky, 'Reforma ugolovnogo zakonodatel'stva.' Speech read before an audience of the Moscow Juridical Society (13 iii 1888), published in *Yuridicheskii Vestnik*, 4, (1888), 568–581; Tagantsev, *Russkoe ugolovnoe pravo*, cited from 2nd edn (1887–1892), vol. 3, 1024.
2 See Engelstein, 1999, 227–228.
3 Pre-Reform jurists frequently cited include L. Tsvetaev, *Nachertanie teorii ugolovnykh zakonov* (M., 1825); P. Guliaev, *Russkoe ugolovnoe pravo* (SPb., 1826; 2nd edn, 1833); S. Barshev, *O mere nakazanii* (Moscow, 1840). On the eve of Reform, juridical science relied almost exclusively on S.I. Barshev's *Obshchie nachala teorii i zakonodatel'stva o prestupleniikh i nakazaniiakh* (M., 1841), and a *Praticheskoe rukovodstvo*, compiled by N.I. Stoyanovsky (1852).
4 Monographs and articles dating from the early Reform period include Spasovich, 1863; P. Kalmykov, *Uchebnik ugolovnogo prava* (1866) S. Budzinsky, *Osnovnye nachala ugolovnogo prava* (1870); Neklyudov, 1875; Kistyakovsky, 1875; A. Lokhvitsky, *Kurs russkogo ugolovnogo prava* (1867); M. Dukhovsky, *Zadacha nauki ugolovnogo prava* (1872); N. Tagantsev, *Kurs ugolovnogo prava* in 3 pts: (1874–1880); Sergeevsky, 1879.
5 The most frequently cited works include Sergeevsky, 1887; Tagantsev, 1887–1892; Foinitsky, 1884. Surveys and bibliographical studies of current literature include Sergeevsky, 1893; Povorinsky, 1896; Tregubov, 1894–1908; Esipov, pre-1905; Gernet, 1913. Specialized journals launched in the period include *Yuridicheskaya Letopis'* (1890-), *Yuridischeskaya Bibliografya* (1884-), *Zhurnal Grazhdanskogo i Ugolovnogo Prava*, the official *Zhurnal Ministerstva Yustitsii*, and *Yuridicheskii Vestnik* (SPb., 1860–1861, re-launched in 1867 under the auspices of the Moscow Juridical Society. From 1884, it was published by the juridical faculty of St Petersburg University and finally closed down in 1892.)
6 Slominsky, 1895, 782.
7 A.F. Koni, 'Vladimir Danilovich Spasovich (1829–1907)' (obituary), in *V.D. Spasovich. Izbranniye trudy i rechi* (Tula, 2000), 8. For a detailed account of his brush with the third section, see Smolyarchuk, 1982, 93–99.
8 Kistyakovsky, 1867. Kistyakovsky (1833–1885) was professor at Kiev University from 1864 to 1885 and president of the Kiev Juridical Society. He worked on juvenile crime and customary law.
9 Foinitsky, 1884. Cited in Kashepov *et al.*, 1998, 541.
10 Wagner, 1994, 35.
11 Texts by Feuerbach cited in Russian literature include his *Revision der Grundsätze und Grundbegriffe des positiven peinlichen Rechts* (1799–1800), in which he analysed the problem of liability (differentiating between dolus (*zloi umysl*) and culpa (*neostorozhnost'*) as basic forms of guilt, and his *Lehrbuch des gemeinen in Deutschland gültigen peinlichen Rechts* (14th edn, 1848). Russian translations of Feuerbach's work provided the basis for the teaching programme in Russia in the early Reform period: *Pravo Ugolovnoe: Filosofskaya ili vseobshchaya chast'* (1810); *O Prestupleniyakh i nakazaniyakh* (1811); *O protsesse* (1821). See Arsen'ev, 1902, 504–509.

See Vul'fert, 1897, 469–479, for a comprehensive overview of absolutist, psychological and sociological theories of punishment.

12 N.D. Sergeevsky, *Russkoe ugolovnoe pravo*, quoted from the 1911 edition in Levitsky, 2004, 109.

13 My account of the anthropological and sociological theories of crime and punishment draws primarily on V.D. Spasovich, 'Novye napravleniya v nauki ugolovnogo prava' (*VE*, 1891), published integrally in Spasovich, 1896, 211–300. Critical evaluations of the anthropological school include Sergeevsky, 1882, 209–221; 1879, 1883, 1893. For more positive accounts, see Prof. Vul'fert, 'Antropologo-pozitivnaya shkola ugolovnogo prava v Italii, 1887–1893; D. Dril', 'Psikhologiya Prestupnosti' *Yuridicheskii Vestnik*, 1887 (2, 264–305; 3, 407–436; 4, 601–630; 5–6, 163–211; 11, 345–394; 12, 541–579). Also by Dril': 'Antropologicheskaya shkola i eya kritiki. Zametki po povodu statej g. Obninskogo, *Yuridicheskii Vestnik*, 12, 1890, 579–599. I. Zakrevsky, 'Ob ucheniyakh ugolovno-antropologicheskoi shkoly', *Zhurnal grazhdanskogo i ugolovnogo prava*, 1, 1893. Zakrevsky also published a monograph under the same title. See Khar'kov, 1893; Belogritz-Kotlyarevsky, 1892.

14 Spasovich, 1896, 226–228. Spasovich analysed Ferri's: *La teoria della imputabilita, e la negazione del libero arbitrio* (2nd edn, 1879); *I nuovi orrizonti del diritto e della procedura penale* (2nd edn, 1884).

15 *I nuovi orrizonti del diritto e della procedura penale* summarized by Spasovich, 1896, 220–221.

16 Tarde's major works on criminology include *La criminalité comparée* (1886), *Les lois de l'imitation* (1890), and *La philosophie pénale* (1890). He was also known for his work as an archaeologist and economist. See Spasovich, 1896, 252ff.

17 Tarde's theory of the 'milieu' (*sreda*) as summarized by Foinitsky, 'Faktory Prestupnosti', *Severnyi Vestnik*, 8 (1894), quoted from Kashepov *et al.*, 1998, 595.

18 Main works by Neklyudov include *Ugolovno-statisticheskie etyudy* (SPb., 1865) and *Ugolovnoe pravo* (SPb., 1875). Works by Dril' include Maloletnie Prestupniki (Moscow, 1884) and *Prestupnost' i Prestupniki* (SPb.,1895). See also note 13 above. For a less imaginative rehash of anthropological theories, see R. Mintslov, 'Osobennosti klassa prestupnikov', *Yuridicheskii Vestnik*, 12 (1881), 1–22.

19 Spasovich, 1896, 211; 219–220.

20 Tagantsev, *Russkoe ugolovnoe pravo* (Introduction) cited in Kashepov *et al.*, 1998, 474; 1892, 828.

21 Cf. I. Foinitsky, 'Faktory Prestupnosti', *Severnyi Vestnik*, 8, 1894, cited in Kashepov *et al.*, 1998, 587–588.

22 Ibid., 592.

23 See his comments on M. Dukonsky, a young docent at the Yaroslav lycee, who, in 1872, presented a statistically based study of crime for his master's degree. Tagantsev, Jubilee Speech, 1892, 827.

24 Tagantsev, Kurs russkogo ugolovnogo prava (2nd edn, SPb., 1887–1892), cited in article by Arsen'ev, 1899, 847.

25 *Kurs russkogo ugolovnogo prava*, in Kashepov *et al.*, 1998, 489, 496.

26 Tagantsev, 1887–1892, 479; 1892, 826.

27 *Kurs*. (3rd edn, 1902), 16, quoted from Levitsky, 2004, 44.

28 *Kurs*, in Kashepov *et al.*, 1998, 479.

29 Arsen'ev, 1902, 504.

30 Belogritz-Kotlyarevsky, 1892, 47. See also, M.N. Gernet, *Ugolovnoe pravo. Chast' obshchaya* (lectures read at the People's University, Kherson, 1913), Ch. 3.

31 Belogritz-Kotlyarevsky, 1892, 47.

32 N.D. Sergeevsky, *Russkoe ugolovnoe pravo* (1887), quoted from 1911 edn, in *Russkie i zapadnoevropeiskie uchenye…*, 109.

33 Belogritz-Kotlyarevsky, 1892, 43–44.

34 See below, Ch. 5.

35 Articles by Foinitsky on the prison question include 'Ssylka ili tiur'ma?', Foinitsky, 1881, 686–698, and several contributions to the state-sponsored *Sbornik Gosudartsvennikh Znanii* (1874–1879): Tiur'emnaya Reforma i tiu'movedenie'; 'Tiur'emnaya statistika na Zapade'; 'Russkaya karatel'naya sistema'. See 'Ivan Yakovlevich Foinitsky. Zhizn' i Tvorchestvo (1847–1913), in Kashepov *et al.*, 1998, 513–529.

36 Foinitsky, 'Ugolovnoe pravo, ego predmet, ego zadachi', *Sudebnyi Zhurnal* (1873), cited by Tagantsev (*Russkoe ugolovnoe pravo*, Introduction) as an opinion diametrically opposed to his own. See Kashepov *et al.*, 1998, 493. Foinitsky's definition was also cited by Arsen'ev, 1899, 848.

37 Foinitsky, 1889, 42–43.

38 Ibid., 94–95.

39 Ibid., 66.

40 Organized charitable work to safeguard the prisoner's return to normal life had existed in England since the beginning of the nineteenth century (a Society for the improvement of prison discipline was founded in 1816). In Russia, prison trusts (*obshchestvo popechitel'noe o tiur'makh*) were semi-governmental bodies (dating from 1819) which, if comparable in their mandate to ensure the physical and moral well-being of the detainees, did not provide care for prisoners once they had completed their term. See Gernet, 1913, 131ff.

41 The influence of Howard's work, 'The State of Prisons in England and Wales' (1777), is suggested by Spasovich in a paper given at the IV International Penitentiary Congress in St Petersburg, 1890. See his 'John Howard (1729–1790)', in Spasovich, 2000, 347–358. Another major influence on Foinitsky, and his contemporaries, was, of course, Cesare Beccaria whose *Dei delittie delle pene* (1764) was translated into Russian several times during the course of the nineteenth century and at least three times (1878, 1879, and 1889) as Foinitsky began his own work in the field.

42 Dostoevsky, *Notes from the House of the Dead* (1861), cited in Wood, 1989, 225.

43 See Gernet, 1913, 112. Also by him on the prison question: Gernet, 1961.

44 Foinitsky, 1874.

45 Ibid., 99.

46 Ibid., 43.

47 Ibid., 128–129.

48 Foinitsky, 1875, 161.

49 Ibid., 166.

50 Ibid., 177–178.

51 *Ugolovnoe Ulozhenie. Proekt redaktsionnoi kommisii* (SPb., 1895), paragraphs 24 and 23.

52 Foinitsky, 1889, 500; Gernet, 1913, 131.

53 For comment on this monograph as an historical account of Russia as 'the classical land of corporal punishments', see Wood, 1989. See also Adams, 1996.

54 'Individual'nost' nakazaniya', Foinitsky, 1889, 50ff.

55 Ibid., 67.

56 Ibid., 60–61.

57 Foinitsky's younger contemporaries who worked with a combination of sociological and anthropological elements included P. Pustoroslev, *Analiz ponyiatiya o prestuplenii* (Moscow, 1892); E. Tarnovsky, 'Prestuplenie protiv zhizni i usloviia obshestvennogo byta', *Yuridicheskii Vestnik*, 8, (1887), 481–584.

58 For Tagantsev's objections, see *Lektsii po russkomu ugolovnomy pravu. Chast' obshchaya.* vyp. III (SPb., 1890), Section 777, 1202–1205, cited in Esipov, 1894, Ch. 3, together with Foinitsky's counter-argument.

59 Kistyakovsky, *Elementarnyi uchebnik obshchego ugolovnogo prava* (posthumous edn, Kiev 1891), 697; Spasovich, 1863, 179.

60 Tagantsev, *Russkoe ugolovnoe pravo* (3rd edn, SPb., 1902), vol. 1, 956.

61 Arsen'ev, 1900.

62 Murav'ev, 1874, 79.
63 For detailed analysis of this question, see A. Walicki, *A History of Russian Thought from the Enlightenment to Marxism* (Oxford, 1980), and Walicki, 1987.
64 Pobedonostsev, 1965, 89.
65 S. Barshev, *Obshchie nachala teorii i zakonodatel'stv o prestuplenijakh i nakazaniakh* (Moscow, 1841), 2, 9. Despite upholding the accepted retributive function of justice, Barshev did, exceptionally for the pre-Reform generation, analyse in some depth the concept of liability. See Arsen'ev, 1899, 847–850.
66 Cf. A.E. Presnyakov, *Apogei samoderzhaviya: Nikolai I* (Leningrad, 1925), 13, cited in T.A. Kapustina, 'Nicholas I', in Donald J. Raleigh, *The Emperors and Empresses of Russia. Rediscovering the Romanovs* (Armonk, New York, London, 1996), 262.
67 Foinitsky, 1889, 187–188.
68 Foinitsky, cited in Gernet, 1909, 266.
69 Tagantsev, 1887, vol. I, 30ff. See also, A. Naumov (Introduction) in Tagantsev, 2001, 13.
70 Sergeevsky, *Russkoe ugolovnoe pravo (posobie k lektsiiam)* (SPb.,1887), 85.
71 Ibid., 83–84.
72 Tagantsev, *Russkoe ugolovnoe pravo*, cited in Kashepov *et al.*, 1998, 496.
73 Arsen'ev, 1902, 506.
74 Sergeevsky, 1893, 15.
75 Western literature, most in view, in Russia in the late 1890s included Franz von Liszt, *Das Verbrechen als social-pathologische Erscheinung* (Dresden, 1899). Russian translations of works by Adolfe Prins include *Prestupnost' i obshchestvo* (Moscow, 1896) and *Prestupnost' i repressiya* (Moscow, 1898).
76 Davydov, 1900, 95.
77 Vorotynsky, 1901, 33.
78 Ibid., 16.
79 Davydov, 1900, 106; Vorotynsky, 1901, 29–30.
80 Arsen'ev, 1902, 507. See also Koni, 1902, who argued that in their more moderate claims the anthropological and sociological schools did not contradict the premises of old school classicists.

4 Solov'ev as a philosopher of law

1 Quoted from the translation by Wozniuk, 2000, 211–212.
2 The September issue carried obituary notices by Arsen'ev, Evgeny Trubetskoi, L. Slominsky, *VE*, 9, 401–426. Other retrospective accounts of his life, cited below, include P. Struve, 'Pamyati Vladimira Solov'eva', *Mir Bozhii* 9, 1900; V. Spasovich, *VE*, 1, 1901, 211–238; Koni, 1903.
3 Letter from Koni to Stasyulevich (2 viii 1900). Stasyulevich called him a 'human soul' (*dusha cheloveka*) (letter to Zhemchuzhnikov (10 ix 1900). Both letters in Lemke, 1911–1913, vol. 2.
4 Letter from Koni to Chicherin (12 ii 1901) in 1969, 169. For this reason, as Koni explained, he had decided to accept an invitation to give a public lecture (his 'oraison funèbre', as he called it) at a joint meeting of the Department of Russian Language and Literature and the Section of Fine Arts in January 1901. The speech was published in *Vestnik Evropy* (see above, note 2) and as a separate pamphlet in 1903.
5 Solov'ev published several articles on the famine in which he was highly critical of government ineptitude to provide necessary relief. See Solov'ev, 1891; 1892. For commentary on Solov'ev's views on social reform, see, for example, Erikh Solov'ev, 2003, 115–139; Zimmerman, 1980, 1–20; Paul Vallière, *Bukharev, Soloviev, Bulgakov. Orthodox Theology in a New Key* (Michigan, 2000).
6 'La question sociale en Europe' (1892). Quoted from the translation by Vladimir

Wozniuk, 2000, 32. An inchoate concept of human dignity is present in essays written in the 1880s, including, *Dukhovnye osnovy zhizni* (1882–1884) where he variously expounded in a Kantian vein on the idea of personal autonomy, or spoke of the divine significance of human beings. cf. Paul Vallire, *op. cit.*

7 Solov'ev, *Opravdanie Dobra*, cited in Walicki, 1987, 195.

8 Zimmerman, 1980, 7. See also Walicki's chapter on Solov'ev in Walicki, 1987. On Solov'ev's engagement as a social reformer, see J. Sutton, 'Vladimir Solov'ev, Moral Philosophy and "Sound Politics"', *SEET*, vol. 52, 4 (December 2000), 309–326. Also, see Sutton, 1988.

9 Wozniuk, 1999, 43–44. See also Gaut, 1998.

10 E. Trubetskoi, *VE*, 9 (1900), 415.

11 Quoted from his volume of selected articles, P. Struve, 1902, 199.

12 Ibid.

13 Ibid., 198–199. One might object to Struve's rather harsh assessment on the grounds that, in Solov'ev's work, the distinction between 'publististic' essay as an example of applied ethics and philosophical theory was rarely rigorously observed. Indeed, the history of *Opravdanie Dobra*, which started life as a series of journal articles, is a case in point. This overlapping of genres was, of course, widely practised by Russian thinkers in the nineteenth century.

14 Solov'ev, *VE*, 4 (1894), 785–795, *VE*, 11 (1894), 345–365, *VE*, 12 (1894), 802–817; *VE*, 3 (1895), 212–235, *VE*, 11 (1895), 323–336, *VE*, 12 (1895), 803–814. Others appeared in the journal of the Moscow Philosophical Society, *Voprosy Filosofii i Psikhologii.*

15 Spasovich, *VE*, 1 (1901), 230.

16 Koni, 1903, 684.

17 Struve, 'Filosofiya ideal'nogo dobra ili apologiya real'nogo zla?' (1897), cited from the revised version, 1902, in *Na raznye temy*, 188, 191.

18 Koni, letter to Chicherin, 1901.

19 Koni, 686.

20 Spasovich, *VE*, 1 (1901), 232.

21 Letter to Stasyulevich, cited in Kel'ner, 1993, 226n.

22 Arsen'ev, *VE*, 9 (1900), 407.

23 *Pravo i Nravstvennost'*, in Wozniuk, 2000, 202.

24 Vladimir Solov'ev, *La Russie et L'Eglise Universelle* (1889), cited from 4th edn (Paris, 1922), xxiii, in Valliere, 2000, 173–174.

25 For a summary of Solov'ev's concept of free theocracy, see, for example, Valliere, 1922, 132–133.

26 'O Khristyanskom gosudarstve i obshchestve', *Dukhovnye osnovy zhizni*. Quoted from the translation by Wozniuk, 2000, 25.

27 Ibid., 25 and 26.

28 *Kritika otvlenchennykh nachal*, Chs XVIII, XIX, and XX. For a comprehensive analysis of Solov'ev's theory of law and morality, seeWalicki, 1987, Ch. 3.

29 '*Pravo vyrazhaet soboyu lish' otritsatel'nyu storonu nravstvennogo nachala*', Ch. XX. Quoted from the Brussels rpt. edn. of *Sobranie sochinenii Vladimira Sergeevicha Solov'va*, eds S.M. Solov'ev and E.L. Radlov, vol. 2 (1970), 156.

30 *Kritika*, Ch. XX. See Walicki, 1987, 156–157.

31 Cf. Walicki, 1987, 181ff. See also Walicki, 1991, 32.

32 'Indeed, one finds a clear correspondence between the principle of law and man's moral nature in the quality of justice/fairness, viz, the lowest, negative degree of moral worth or virtue, the supreme, most positive degree of which is conveyed through sympathy and love ... in the name of a shared goal.' *Kritika*...157.

33 Walicki, 1987, 204.

34 *Pravo i Nravstvennost'*, quoted from Wozniuk, 2000, 136, 146–148, and 150–151.

35 *Opravdanie Dobra*, quoted from the revised French edn (Geneva, 1997), 397.

36 Solov'ev, 1895, 212–235.
37 Wozniuk, 2000, 169–170.
38 Ibid., 213. Implying 'truth-justice', *pravda*, in this instance, is truly the operative word.
39 Ibid., 204 and 207.
40 Ibid., 205.
41 Ibid., 211 and 210.
42 Kuchinsky, 1897.
43 Wozniuk, 2000, 209–210.
44 Ibid., 193.
45 Mokrinsky, 1902, 122–123.
46 Mokrinsky, cited in N. Sorochinsky, 1905, 56 note.
47 See B. Chicherin, *Mistitsizm v nauke* (Moscow, 1880). In their polemics of 1897, Chicherin reiterated many observations pertaining to Solov'ev's concept of the state and law that he had made in this first review.
48 Chicherin, cited in Gol'tsev, 1898, 52.
49 B. Chicherin, 'O nachalakh etiki, *Opravdanie Dobra*, Nravstvennaya filosofiya Vladimira Solo'eva. *Prava i Nravstvennost'*, Ocherki iz prikladnoi etiki, ego zhe: V. Solov'ev, 'Mnimaya Kritika. Otvet B.N. Chicherinu'; B.N. Chicherin, 'Neskol'ko slov po povobu otveta g. Solov'eva; V. Solov'ev, 'Neobkhodmye zamechaniya na 'Neskol'ko slov' B.N. Chicherina in *VFP*, 4 (Sept.–Oct., 1897). My quotations are taken from the integral edition, published in the Soviet philosophical journal, *Voprosy Filosofii*, 'Polemika B.N. Chicherina i V.S. Solov'eva 1897g', *VF*, 1989 (9: 69–84; 10: 88–100; 11: 82–97; 12: 89–96) and 1990 (1: 100–108; 2: 88–103; 3: 74–87; 4: 69–75). Citation: 12 (1989), 95.
50 Ibid., 12 (1989), 95.
51 Ibid., 1 (1990), 101.
52 Quoted from Gol'tsev, 1898, 50 and 53. Chicherin had, in fact, voiced the same objection in his earlier critique of Solov'ev's doctoral thesis, *Kritika*. B. Chicherin, *Mistitsizm v nauke* (Moscow, 1880), 68ff.
53 B. Chicherin, 12 (1989), 93.
54 Ibid., 1 (1990), 103–104.
55 For comment on the contrasts and unwitting overlaps between Solov'ev's and Chicherin's view of human society, see Valliere, 2000 and Walicki, 1987. Valliere, for example, argues that, as a Hegelian, Chicherin did in fact subordinate the separate spheres of human and social activity to a higher principle and cites passages from Chicherin's early period to bear out this claim.
56 Chicherin, 1 (1990), 104.
57 Solov'ev, 'Mnimaya Kritika', 2 (1990), 92 and 98.
58 Chicherin, *Filosfiya Prava* (1900), cited in Mikhlin, 2000, 160.
59 Solov'ev, 1895, 225.
60 Comments by P. Mokievsky, writing for the populist journal *Russkoe Bogatstvo*, cited by N. Gorodensky in his own lukewarm assessment of *Opravdanie Dobra* (2nd edn). See Gorodensky, 1899.
61 Wozniuk, 2000, 138 and 154.
62 Ibid., 160–161 and 139.
63 Ibid., 186.
64 In the conclusion to 'Printsip nakazaniya s nravtsvennoi tochki zreniya', Solov'ev somewhat elusively mentioned that 'the moral principle of punishment has been endorsed by some theologians, philosophers and jurists'. See Solov'ev, 1895, 234.
65 The legal positivist Gabriel Feliksovich Shershenevich (1863–1912) was professor for State Law at Kazan University from 1895 until 1906 when he was named to the Chair at Moscow University. Member of the Kadet party, his major theoretical works include a three-volume *Obshaya teoriya prava* (Moscow, 1910–1912).

66 The piece in question was entitled 'Opredelenie poniatiya o prave'. However, in a monograph entitled *Ponyatie o prave* (Kazan, 1896), he mentioned Jellinek and Hoffding in connection with the question of the social dimension of ethics (p. 25). He also developed his own view on the character and goals of legal and moral norms, pointing out that criminal law most effectively brings to view the intricate relation between them. The former deals with motives for behaviour only in the event of a breach of norms leading to censure, whereas the latter concerns both observance and breaches of norms eliciting both approval and censure (*odobrenie, poritsanie*). Ibid., 50.

67 Jellinek, *Die Socialethische Bedeutung von Recht, Unrecht und Strafe* (1878). In his major work, *Obshchaia teoriya prava*, Shershenevich also mentions Solov'ev and Gumplowicz (after the 1910 Russian translation of the latter's book *Obschee uchenie o gosudarstve*) as proponents of this view. I am grateful to Anita Schluechter for providing me with this information.

68 For Walicki, that Jellinek's theory should have been classified as belonging to legal positivism when he included an ethical component was not entirely appropriate. He argues that it would be more accurate to regard him as a proponent of the psychological school, which in Russia was associated with Leon Petrazhitsky. Walicki, 1987, 314, 201.

69 Shershenevich, 1897, 470.

70 Ibid.

71 Solov'ev, 1897, 483.

72 Esipov bases his claims on the following works: Feuerbach, *Revision der Grundsätze und Grundbegriffe des positiven peinlichen Rechts* (1800); Köstlin, *Neue Revision der Grundbegriffe des Criminelrechts* (1845). References are taken from the article version of this chapter, which later appeared in monograph form: Esipov, 1893.

73 Ibid., 25. Obliged, however, to countenance the socio-political contingencies of his day, Spasovich promptly complemented this purely theoretical definition with a more 'usable' equivalent – 'crime is prohibited by laws backed by punishment'. As Esipov put it, the second definition 'although only apparently (*xotya povidimonu*) complied more readily with the actual (*zhiznennye*) goals of law'.

74 Ibid., 33.

75 Ibid. Foinitsky and Sergeevsky were '*oponenty'* at Esipov's defence of his master's dissertation (on arson) in 1892. The defence was chaired by Tagantsev.

76 Ibid., 24, 26, and 27.

77 Ibid., 43, 47, and 45.

78 Cited in Tagantsev, *Russkoe ugolovnoe pravo* (1902 edn). See Kashepov *et al.*, 1998, 485.

79 Esipov, 1907, 14. Prior to this, in his thematic bibliographical compilation of criminal law literature, Esipov included a section entitled 'Sin and Morality'. Comprising studies focusing on crimes against faith [for example, Belogritz-Kotlyarevsky, *Prestuplenie protiv religii* (1886), Pustoroslev. 'Prestuplenie i prostupki protiv very' (lecture, 1902)], it also contained two works that analysed crime from a moral religious perspective – his own and Solov'ev's. Esipov, nl.ndg, but no later than 1905.

80 V.V. Esipov, Nravstvennost' i Pravo, Ch.1, 'Khristianskaya etika i pravo', in *Nravstvennost' i Pravo*, 14.

81 Ibid., 12.

82 Ibid., 58. Esipov refers to C. Gide, *Justice et Charité* (Paris, 1899) and G. Belot, *Charité, selection* (sic.), *morale sociale* (Paris, 1899).

83 Ibid., 52.

84 Walicki, 1987, 210; Evtuhov, 1997, 10.

85 Kistyakovsky, 1915. Cited in Al'bov *et al.*, 1997, 321. Unlike his father, Alexander, Bogdan Kistyakovsky (1868–1920) specialized in state and administrative law. Until

1912, when he began teaching at the Demidov lycee in Yaroslavl, his teaching had been patchy, second to his editorial work on the journals *Yuridicheskii Vestnik* and *Kriticheskoe obozrenie*. He was named Professor at Kiev University in 1917.

86 I.V. Mikhailovsky, *Ocherki filosofii prava*, in *Russkaya filosofiya prava: Filosofiya very i nravstvennosti* (SPb., 1997), 243.

87 Ibid., 280.

88 Ibid., 285.

89 Ibid., 248.

90 Shershenevich, *Obshchaya teoriya prava*, vol. I (1911), cited in Mikhailovsky, ibid., 249.

91 Walicki, 1987, 209.

92 Aleksandr Semenovich Yashchenko (1877–1934) specialized in state and international law. After graduating from Moscow University in 1900, he was assigned to the Chair of International Law. In 1907, he obtained the degree of *privat-dotsent* and, two years later, was named Extraordinary Professor in encyclopaedia and philosophy of law at Yurev (Tartu) University. He transferred to St Petersburg University in 1913 as a full professor. Residing in Berlin at the moment of the October Revolution, Yashchenko decided not to return to Russia and became active within the Russian émigré community. In 1924, he was appointed to the Chair in International Law at the University of Kaunas. See A.P. Al'bov, 'Introductory Essay', in *A.S. Yashchenko: Filosofiya prava Vladimira Solov'eva. Teoriya federalizma* (SPb., 1999), 5–16.

93 A.S. Yashchenko, *Teoriya Federalizma. Opyt sinteticheskoi teorii prava i gosudartsva* (*YUR'EV*, 1912). Quoted from reprint, edited by V.P. Sal'nikov, A.P. Al'bov, and D.P. Maslennikov, *A.S.* (SPb., 1999) 105–106. In this section, from which these quotations are taken, Yashchenko develops his theory of the foundation of ethics 'absolute in principle, synthetic in content', 99–106.

94 Ibid., 108n.

95 Ibid., 105–106.

96 Ibid., 133.

97 Mikhailovsky, 1997, 253–254.

98 V. Solov'ev, 'Mnimaya Kritika', *VF*, 3 (1990), 3, 83.

99 See Koni's letter to Chicherin, note 4 above.

100 Koni, 1902. Read before a class at the Aleksandrovskoe lycée, it was originally planned as the opening lecture in a course entitled *Sudebnaya Etika*, but the series was cancelled as per Minister of Justice Murav'ev's instructions.

101 Ibid., 21.

102 Novgorodtsev, 1909, 15–16.

103 Novgorodtsev, 1902, Foreword.

104 On responses by contemporaries to *Vekhi*, see, for example, L. Schapiro, '*The vekhi group and the mystique of the revolution*', SEER, 44 (Dec. 1955), 6–76; Gaidenko, 1993, 16–46.

105 M. Gershenzon, *Vekhi*, preface to the 1st edn (Moscow, 1909).

5 Criminal justice in the age of revolution (1900–1917)

1 Among Russian contemporaries, Foinitsky was regarded as Liszt's closest follower. See Arsen'ev, 1899. Main works by Liszt translated into Russian include *Lehrbuch das deutschen strafrechts* (1st edn, Berlin, 1881, 10th edn, 1900); *Der zweckgedanke im strafrecht* (Berlin, 1882/3), translated into Russian in 1895, *Nakazanie i ego tseli* (SPb., 1895). The 'Lehrbuch' title was modified in Russian as *Uchebnik ugolovnogo prava* (Moscow, 1903). I have not been able to trace the original German titles for the following Russian versions: *Zadacha ugolovnoi politiki* (SPb., 1895); *Prestuplenie kak sotsial'no-psikhologicheskoe yavlenie* (4th edn, SPb., 1903).

2 Tagantsev, 1887–1892, itself an extensive reworking of an original lecture series published in 1874, was re-edited in a two-volume format in 1902. Vl. Sluchevsky's *Uchebnik*, first published in 1892, was republished in 1895, 1910, and 1913, while the sixth edition of Sergeevsky, 1887, appeared in 1905.
3 Walicki, 1987, 6.
4 Trubetskoi, 1909, 23–26.
5 Bulgakov, 'Tserkov i Gosudarstvo', *Voprosy Religii*, 1 (1906), cited in Zimmerman, 1980. For assessments of Solov'ev's thought, including its legal philosophical dimension, by contemporaries and immediate successors, see: Novgorodtsev, 1909, 317; Trubetskoi, 1913; Bulgakov, 1903, 195–262.
6 Gernet *et al.*,1906 (Preface). This textbook, which was intended for gymnasia and Institutions of Higher Education for Women, ran into several editions. My references are based on the third edition, 1910.
7 Gernet *et al.*, 1906, Preface.
8 Gernet, 1908. The aim of this collection of essays containing contributions by Western authors was to familiarize Russian readers with social–democratic views of criminality and socialism.
9 Belogritz-Kotlyarevsky, 1903. He intended the book as a complement to Foinitsky's authoritative *Kurs ugolovnogo sudoproizvodstva*, first published in 1884.
10 Ibid., 5. Belogritz-Kotlyarevsky's breakdown of the criminal into four types – incorrigible, corrigible, one-offs, and professional – took its cue from the anthropological school.
11 Ibid., 5, 67–68.
12 See, for example, Gogel', 1906; a collection of essays previously published in specialist journals; Chubinsky, 1905 (2nd edn 1912); Poznyshev, 1908.
13 [Anon], 1911, 4.
14 Chubinsky, 1912, 208–210.
15 Belogritz-Kotlyarevsky, 1903, 49. Interestingly, in support of this argument, Belogritz-Kotlyarevsky referred to an early piece by his immediate contemporary, Chubinsky ['Obshchaya kharakteristika novykh uchenii v ugolovnom prave' (1898)]. However, by the time Chubinsky came to write his major work on 'criminal politics' seven years later, he was advocating inclusion of the moral dimension in criminal justice.
16 Gogel', 1910, 22; 1906, 64–69 and 196–203, where he listed specialized associations set up to raise the level of social morality.
17 Chubinsky, [1905] 1912, 278–293.
18 Ibid., 281, and cited in Esipov, 1907, 52.
19 Belogritz-Kotlyarevsky, 1903, 252–253.
20 Poznyshev, 1912, 77.
21 Poznyshev, 1904, xi–xii; 362, 367, 361.
22 Poznyshev, 1908, 258.
23 Poznyshev, 1912, 139.
24 Poznyshev, 1911, 40ff.
25 Ibid., VIII, 1911, 214.
26 Ibid. Other categories included the emotionally weak, the professional criminal, those sensitive to abuse of alcohol, and 'composite types' where moral underdevelopment might, for example, be exacerbated by alcoholism.
27 Poznyshev, 1911, VII, 71; VIII, 230–231.
28 Poznyshev, 1908, 127.
29 Poznyshev, 1904, 358.
30 Poznyshev, 1908, 126.
31 For one of the best accounts of Russian culture between the Revolutions, see the classic study by Billington, 1970. Billington analyses the complex spirit of the Silver

Age through the prism of conflicting paradigms – 'decadence', Promethianism, and religious sentiment.

32 Vladimirov's first major work, *Uchebnik russkogo ugolovnogo prava* (Kharkov) was published in 1889. My account is predominantly based on his essay (Vladimirov, 1903), which was later incorporated as an appendix into a second textbook, Vladimirov, 1908.

33 'Ugolovnyi zakonodatel' kak vospitatel' naroda', cited in Vladimirov, 1908, 236–237.

34 If not quite a volte-face on his earlier views, Vladimirov's remarks on punishment made after 1900 definitely saw a re-emphasis, shifting from moral indictment, namely punishment, as revenge, should moralize the criminal and must involve suffering in order to redeem the material loss inflicted on his victim, to that of moral education.

35 Vladimirov, 1908, 63.

36 Ibid., 5. Vladimirov contended that the best definition of morality could be found in Paul's first epistle to the Corinthians (1, 13) on charity:

> I may have utter faith, so that I can move mountains, but if I lack charity, I count for nothing (…). Charity is patient, is kind; charity feels no envy; charity is never perverse or proud, never insolent; does not claims its rights, cannot be provoked, does not brood over an injury; takes no pleasure in wrong-doing, but rejoices at the victory of truth.

37 Ibid., 24, 64.

38 Ibid.

39 Chubinsky, [1905] 1912, 286.

40 On this point, Chubinsky alluded to the Danish Code (1866) where such 'crimes' incurred a heavy fine or imprisonment. Ibid., 293. It is worth noting here that although in his discussion of the relationship between law and morality, Chubinsky typically deferred to Jellinek's formula with Solov'ev as a national proponent of the same thesis. He also elaborated on Solov'ev's etymological and historical argument in favour of the inextricable link between law and morality, namely that in many languages, moral and juridical concepts are expressed either in identical terms or in words derived from a single root. Ibid., 281.

41 Novgorodtsev, 1902, Preface.

42 Ibid., 279–280.

43 Mokrinsky, 1906, 22. See also Mokrinsky, 1903.

44 Mokrinsky, 1906, 24–26n.

45 Walicki argues that in his interpretation, Novgorodtsev deferred to Petrazhitsky. Walicki, 1987, 293.

46 Mokrinsky, 1906, 31.

47 Ibid., 32. Like many of his contemporaries, Mokrinsky paired Solov'ev with Tolstoi, preferring the anarchic stance of the latter for its dogmatic consistency to the naïvety of the amateur juridical thinker.

48 Here, Mokrinsky uses the shorthand version of the adage 'The welfare of the people shall be the supreme law' (Salus populi suprema lex esto).

49 Ibid., 35–36. Again, Mokrinsky has the citation in Latin: 'bellum omnium contra omnes'.

50 Ibid., 29–30n. The last point, with its utopian ring to it, was directly inspired by Petrazhitsky, even as the justification of criminal justice in a morally imperfect world echoes Solov'ev's thought as well.

51 Walicki, 1987, 216. Works by Petrazhitsky, 1905, 1907, and 2nd edn, 1909–1910 were most often cited in contemporary literature.

52 Petrazhitsky, 1906, in Walicki, ibid., 257.

53 For clarification of Petrazhitsky's stock of terms, see Walicki, ibid., 251–252.

54 Lyublinsky, 1907. My references are based on his collection of essays. See Lyublinsky, 1915, 25–32. Main works by him are Lyublinsky, 1906; Lyublinsky, 1914, 1–27; Lyublinsky, 1915, 1–40.
55 Poznyshev, 1908, 114–121.
56 Chubinsky, [1905] 1912, 264.
57 Ibid., 262.
58 Prof. Vladimirov, 1908, 384.
59 Lyublinsky, 1915, 24. Fortunately, as Lyublinsky notes, this ludicrous proposal got no further.
60 Lyublinsky, 1906, 49–50.
61 Wozniuk, 2000, 184.
62 Spasovich, vol. 8, 1891, 286–287.
63 Bryner, 1990. For pre-Revolutionary histories of the death penalty in Russia, see, for example, Kistyakovsky, 1879; Viktorsky, 1912; Gernet, 1913.
64 See Rawson, 1984, 30–32.
65 Belogritz-Kotlyarevsky, 1903, 256.
66 Daly, 2005, 163–164.
67 Daly, 2002, 62–100. See also ibid. 164.
68 On the spectacle of 'civil execution', see above, Ch. 2.
69 Rawson, 1984.
70 V.S. Solov'ev, '*Publichnaya lektsya, chitannaya Professorom Solov'evym v kreditnom obshchestve*', March 1881; L. Tolstoi, 'To the Emperor Alexander III' (8–15 March 1881) in R.F. Christian (trans. and ed.), *Tolstoy's Letters*, vol. II (London, 1978).
71 Solov'ev, ibid. Quoted from *V.S. Solov'ev. Sochineniya v dvukh tomakh*, vol. 1 (Moscow, 1989), 42.
72 Tolstoi, 1978, 343.
73 V.D. Spasovich, 1891, 287.
74 Mittermaier, *Smertnaya kazn' po rezul'tatam nauchnykh isledovanii uspekhov zakonodatel'stva i opytov* (1864). See Sergeevsky, 1887, 164.
75 Tagantsev, 'Jubilee Speech', 1902, 821.
76 Kistyakovsky, 1867, Ch. 6.
77 Kistyakovsky, 1875, 715.
78 Kistyakovsky, 1867, 276.
79 On emergency rule, see above, Ch. 2.
80 Sergeevsky, 1879; Spasovich, 1863, 184.
81 Sergeevsky, 1887, 164.
82 Tagantsev, 1887–1892, 1123–1126.
83 Foinitsky, 1889, 50–51; 162.
84 Spasovich, 1891, 287; Foinitsky, ibid., 152–153; Sergeevsky, 1887, 114–115.
85 Arsen'ev, vol. XXXa 1900, 499. Kuz'min-Karavaev, 'Smertnaya Kazn' po voenno-ugolovnom zakonam', 1900, 500. See also, Fuller, 1982, 288–305.
86 Tarnovsky, 1917. Cited in Al'bov, 1997, 328.
87 Gessen, 1912, 188–189. Sergei Gessen (1887–1950) was the illegitimate son of Iosif Gessen, editor of *Pravo*. Gessen completed his education in Heidelberg and Freiburg, where he attended lectures given by Windelband, Jellinek, Lask, Meinecke, and Heinrich Rickert. In 1913, he became *privat-dotsent* at the University of St Petersburg, and in 1917 he was named Professor at Tomsk University, where he lectured on logic, ethics, history of philosophy, and philosophy of law. After years of migrating across Europe as an émigré (Germany, Prague), Gessen finally settled in Warsaw. Walicki was one of his pupils. See Walicki, 1987.
88 Gessen, 1912, 197–198 and 191.
89 Ibid., 232.
90 Ibid., 215; 218–219.

91 Ibid., 228.
92 Ibid., 193n.
93 Ibid., 228.
94 Solov'ev, *Law and Morality*, in Wozniuk, 2000, 183; 180–181.
95 Ibid., 174.
96 *Kritika otvlechennykh nachal* (1880), cited in Valliere, 2000, 132.
97 Solov'ev, *Law and Morality*, in Wozniuk, 2000, 184.
98 See Lentin, 1982, 128–137.
99 Article 91 stated that 'under extraordinary circumstances military crimes committed in peacetime could be punished according to the laws of wartime, if doing so was considered necessary for the preservation of military discipline'. Article 279 specified that 'in wartime, (. . .), military personnel could, under extraordinary circumstances, be sentenced to death for the non-military crimes of murder, rape, robbery, looting, or arson'. See Rawson, 1984, 34. A law of 9 August 1878 applied Article 279 to the civilian population. See also Belogritz-Kotlyarevsky, 1903, 255.
100 Rawson, 1984, 41; 47. A total of 1,959 cases received the death sentence, but 619 were commuted to katorga. Gernet, 1913, gives the number of death sentences passed in countries of Western Europe for the same year: Germany – 31 condemned; France – six executions and 43 commuted sentences; England – 13 executions and eight commuted sentences; Spain – 47 executions and two commuted sentences. Proportionately, however, the number of sentences actually passed dropped in the final decade of Imperial rule. Mironov gives the following figures: between 1826 and 1905, 1,397 people were condemned to death, 64 per cent of which were carried out; between 1905 and 1913, out of 6,871 convictions, 43.4 per cent were carried out. Mironov, 1999, vol. 2, 34. Davydov gives slightly different figures: between 1866 and 1892, there were 134 convictions, of which 44 were carried out; 83 of the 134 sentences were passed by the military courts. 1879 – 'the year of terror' – saw 22 convictions, of which 16 were carried out. Between 1888 and 1892, there were no executions. N.V. Davydov, 'Smertnaya Kazn', in Gernet *et al.*, 1906, 67–74.
101 Wheatcroft, 2002, 45.
102 P.I. Lyublinsky, 'Otnoshenie k smertnoi kazni russkogo obshchestvennogo mneniya', originally a conference given at the International Penitentiary Congress, Washington, 1913, in Lyublinsky, 1915, 276–285.
103 V.D. Kuz'min-Karavaev, 'Spravka o smertnoi kazni' po russkomu pravu', *Pravo*, 8 (26 ii 1905) in Kuz'min-Karavaev, 1907, 34–42.
104 Lyublinsky, 1913.
105 Lyublinsky, 1906, Foreword.
106 Zhizhilenko, 1914, 195.
107 N.N. Rozin, 'O Smertnoi kazni', *Pravo*, 1906. This essay along with a number of other 'keynote pieces' from this and other liberal juridical journals were later included in an anthology, again at Gernet's initiative (himself a contributor to *Pravo*) in *O Smertnoi kazni. Mneniya russkikh kriminalistov. Sbornik s prilozheniem ukazateli literatury na russkom yazyka o smertnoi kazni* (Moscow, 1909). My quotations from Rozin's essay are taken from this edition (39). Some contributions, such as that by A. Zhizhilenko (Prof. St Petersburg University) arguing that the premises on which the death penalty was traditionally justified (revenge and deterrence) no longer carried muster, were especially commissioned for this collection. Other (living) contributors included Poznyshev, N.V. Davydov, Kuz'min-Karavaev, and Chubinsky.
108 Mokrinsky, 1906, 3, cited in Gernet, 1909, 45–46.
109 In addition to Gernet, 1909, see, for example, Nabokov, 1904; Kuz'min-Karavaev, 1907. Volume 2 contained many of his Duma speeches in support of the original 1906 bill to abolish the death penalty. See also Tagantsev, note 112, below.

110 Kuz'min-Karavaev, 'Rech' v zasedanie Gosudarstvennoi Dumy 19-go Iuonya 1906', 1907, vol. 2, 370.
111 Kuz'min-Karavaev, ibid., May 1906, 349.
112 Tagantsev, 'Po zakonoproeektu ob otmene smertnoi kazni', an address before the State Council, 27 June 1906, in Tagantsev, 1913. It is important to note that some of these condemnations of the death penalty were read in certain quarters as covert approval of the revolutionary movement. Indeed, Duma representatives received death threats. Gernet reported concerns published in the official governmental newsletter, *Pravitel'stvennyi Vestnik*, that abolition would lead to increased instances of *samosud* and lawlessness in the villages. Gernet, 1909. Cf. Shishov and Paffenova, 1989, 142.
113 Nabokov, in Gernet, 1909, quoted from Shishov and Paffenova, ibid., 206–209.
114 S. Witte, *Vospominaniya*, vol. 3 (Moscow, 1960), 61–62, cited in Naumov, 2004, 365–366.
115 Rawson, 1984, 49. The first five months of 1906 saw 600 executions ('Rech' v zasedanii gosudarstvennoi dumy 3 maya 1906g. pri obsuzhdenii otvetnogo adresa', in Kuz'min-Karavaev, *Iz epokhi osvoboditel'nogo dvizheniya*, vol. 2 (SPb., 1907), 349, and Gernet notes that between 19 August 1906 and 20 April 1907, 683 executions were carried out by military field courts. See Gernet, 1913, 144.
116 Gernet, 1909, in Shishov and Paffenova, 1989, 141.
117 See above, notes 109 and 112. The collection of essays by Tagantsev, *Smertnaya Kazn'*, was intended for publication in 1910. But publication was stalled, and it appeared three years later in 1913.
118 Gernet *et al.*, 1906. The collection comprised a mixture of excerpts of scientific and popular articles calling for the abolition of the death penalty, which first appeared in leading thick journals such as *Russkoe Bogatstvo, Russkaya Mysl', Mir Bozhii, Obrazovanie, Moskovskii Ezhenedel'nik, Vestnik Evropy, Polyarnaya Zvezda,* and *Vera i Razum*.
119 Jellinek, letter Heidelberg, 4 April 1906 in Gernet *et al.*, 1906, Appendix.
120 Gernet *et al.*, 1906; 1907, 250.
121 Solov'ev, *Law and Morality* in Wozniuk, 2000, 182.
122 Gernet *et al.*, 1907, 201, 181, and 210.
123 V.V. Rozanov, excerpt from his *Lukavye Slova* in Gernet, 1906. Quoted from Shishov and Paffenova, 1989, 247.
124 Gernet, 1906, 113–114.
125 N.V. Davydov, 'Smertnaya Kazn', in Gernet *et al.*, 1906, 67–74.
126 Gernet, 1909, in Shishov and Paffenova, 1989, 143.
127 The 1908 movement was in fact the second attempt to forge a league. A first attempt, at the initiative of public figures and Duma representatives in St Petersburg, was made during the first eight-month period of emergency rule. See Tagantsev, 1913. Lyublinsky, 1913.
128 Recounted by Tagantsev in his *Smertnaya Kazn'*.
129 S.S. Goncharov and Father Butkevich cited by Tagantsev in his 1906 speech to the State Council, 172–173. See also Lyublinsky, 1913.
130 Tagantsev, 'Otmena smertnoi kazni', *Zhurnal Mininisterstva Yustitsii* (March, 1917), 9–14.
131 Gernet, 1913, 55.
132 Gernet, 1909 (Foreword).
133 Malinovsky, 1908, 1910.
134 Ibid., vol. 2, 97.
135 Ibid., 2. Malinovsky listed 17 short stories published between 1908 and 1910 including L. Andreev, *Razskaz o semi poveshennykh* (SPb., 1908); V. Anuchin, 'Kazn' Yakoba Steblinskogo', *Russkaya Mysl'*, 6 (1908); M. Artsybashev, 'Skazka starogo prokurora', *Sovremennyi Mir*, 12 (1908); V.G. Korolenko, 'Bytovoe yavlenie',

Russkoe Bogatstvo, 3–4 (1910); Iv. Prishvin, 'Palach', *Obrazovanie*, 12 (1908). Ibid., 74.

136 Nabokov in Gernet, 1909, quoted from Shishov and Paffenova, 1989, 208.

137 L. Andreev, *Rasskaz o semi poveshennykh* (English trans: London, 1909). My thanks to Katia Dmitrieva for drawing my attention to Andreev's work.

138 Lev Tolstoi, 1908. Quoted from I. Malinovsky, 1908, 1910, 53–73. In this period, Tolstoi addressed the issue of the death penalty on several occasions: 'Thou shalt not kill' (*Ne ubii*), 1907, and 'Christianity and the Death Penalty' (*Khristianstvo i Smertnaya Kazn'*), 1909. For the integral English translation of Tolstoi's piece, see 1989, 202–212.

139 Ibid., Malinovsky, 1908, 64.

140 Quoted from the English translation, 208.

141 Ibid., 211.

142 Solov'ev, *Law and Morality* in Wozniuk, 2000, 167.

143 Ibid., 176.

144 Koni, 'Posleslovie', 2003, 342–343.

145 See below, Ch. 6.

6 Rehabilitating law: criminal justice after communism

1 Shishov and Paffenova, 1989. Co-edited (with T.S. Paffenova) and introduced by Professor O.F. Shishov, a renowned critic of the death penalty.

2 On perestroika and new thinking, see, for example, Brown, 1997; Brown and Shevtsova , 2001; Sakwa, 1990; Dallin, 1992; Daniels, 1995; Miller, 1993; White, 1992, 1993.

3 Kelinga has continued to play a major role in the process of criminal justice reform, both as a member of Yeltsin's Presidential Committee for Clemency, set up in 1992, and in the commission for drafting the new Criminal Code. I am grateful to Dmitry Sergeev for drawing my attention to this publication.

4 Kelinga, 1989, 6–7.

5 Ibid., 8–9, and cf. 330.

6 Nina Andreeva, 'I Cannot Forego Principles', *Sovetskaya Rossiya*, 13 March 1988, cited in David Lane, *Soviet Society under Perestroika* (London, 1990), 114.

7 Kelinga, 1989, 327–331. On Soviet criminal justice, see Solomon, 1996.

8 The Amnesty International text gives the following figures for the first three years of Gorbachev's leadership: in 1985, 67 sentences were handed down, 34 of which were carried out; in 1986, 35 sentences were handed down, 14 of which were carried out; in 1987, nine out of a total of 61 sentences were carried out.

9 Cf. Smith, 1996, 143–144.

10 Of the 18 capital offences still listed, nine were for crimes against the state, five of an economic nature, with only four involving an individual victim (Criminal Code, Art. 23). See also A.I. Pristavkin, in Kvashis, 2000, 42.

11 Kelinga, 1989, 327–331. Gordon Smith notes that, as early as 1985, legal scholars 'anticipating the more tolerant atmosphere of the Gorbachev era' had drafted a 'Theoretical Model of a Criminal Code', which in fact served as the template for the draft criminal code widely circulated in 1988. Smith, 1996, 152.

12 Ibid., 16.

13 *Constitution of the Russian Federation*, Article 20. Cited in Smith, 1996, 243. Thereafter, Article 20 became a point of reference for committed abolitionists as they confronted mounting criticism against the moratorium in 1999. See, for example, the comments by the Minister of Justice, P.V. Krasheninnikov, in *Vserossiiskaya konferentsiya po problemam otmeny smertnoi kazni*, 48–52.

14 Zhil'tsov and Mal'ko, 2001, 425.

15 Ibid., 443. In other words, between 1992 and 1994, 90 percent of capital offenders

were pardoned. According to Pristavkin, between 1991 and 1996, 163 people were executed, reaching its highest level in the two years between 1995 and 1996 – that is, in connection with events in Chechnya when 139 offenders were shot. See R.M. Tsivilev, 'Smertnaya kazn' v Rossii: Nemnogo statistiki', in *Vserossiiskaya konferentsiya*…, 159, who gives the number of executions for the period 1985–1996 at 407. If the early years of Yeltsin rule witnessed a significant drop in the number of executions (one execution in 1992 and four the following year), they soared to 86 in 1995.

16 Cf. Zhil'tsov and Mal'ko, 2001, 433.

17 Ibid., 424.

18 Ibid., 437.

19 In 1996, there were 53 executions, with the last ever execution carried out in August of that year. The sentence, as such, continued to be handed down, however. Thus, in 1997, there were 108 capital offenders, and in 1998, the number decreased marginally to 77. The 1999 moratorium concerned both the sentence and the institution of the death penalty.

20 'O vnesenii izmenenii v stati 184 i 185 Ugolovnogo-ispolnitel'nogo kodeksa Rossiiskoi Federatsii' (8 January 1998). See Naumov, 2004, 368.

21 The right to a trial by jury was guaranteed in the new Constitution (Arts 19, 20, and 46) and the Code of Criminal Procedure (Arts 41 and 42). See. R.M. Tsivilev, *Vserossiiskaya konferentsiya*…, 158.

22 Separate from the hierarchy of regular courts, the Constitutional Court of the Russian Federation was established in July 1991 and, according to Gordon Smith, represents yet another achievement in Gorbachev's programme of legal reform that Yeltsin later adapted to the post-Soviet environment. Smith, 1996, 133.

23 Smith, 1996, 226.

24 M.I. Baitin, *Sushchnost' prava: Sovremennoe normativnoe pravoponimanie na grani vekov* (Saratov, 2001), cited in Zhil'tsov and Mal'ko, 2001, 426.

25 The Criminal Code (Pt 2, Art. 43) identifies three criteria of punishment – *kara* (punishment), correction, and prevention – which, clearly, the death penalty cannot fulfil. See Borodin, 2001, 59.

26 S. Kelinga in Kvashis, 2000, 73.

27 Kelinga, 1989, 16.

28 See G.M. Min'kovsky, *Izvestiya*, 14 May 1988, cited in A.S. Mikhlin, whose analysis of the data shows that respondents with higher education believed that the death penalty was necessary as a safeguard but that its use should be restricted. Mikhlin, 2000, 161.

29 The number of registered murders, which in 1994 totalled 32,286 and came down slightly in 1999 to 31,100, are still incomparably higher than the number of crimes committed in Western Europe, where abolitionists relished to point out that the death penalty does not exist.

30 Russian speakers included A.I. Pristavkin, president of the Presidential commission for clemency, P.V. Krasheninnikov, Minister of Justice, S.G. Kelinga, and F.M. Burlatsky, both at the Institute of State and Law, V.V. Borshchev, vice-president of the State Duma Committee on questions of social cohesion and religious affairs. 'Defender-apologists' of the death penalty were represented by researchers attached to the Ministry of the Interior and the General Procuracy – A.D. Boikov and A.S. Mikhlin. Foreign experts included Derrick Evans, deputy general secretary of Amnesty International, Andrew Cole, director of the International Centre for Prison Studies, London University, Sergio Delia, secretary of the League of Citizens and Parliamentarians for the abolition of the death penalty worldwide. (It may be no coincidence that in his Christmas Encyclical, November 1998, Pope John Paul II had called for a worldwide moratorium on the death penalty.)

31 The monograph by Zhil'tsov and Mal'ko, already cited, is one such example. See also Mikhlin, 2000; A. Yu. Kizilov, 2003. Articles on the death penalty published in specialist journals include, besides those already mentioned, Nikiforov, 2001; Kvashis,

1997; A.N. Golovistikova, 'Istoriya otmeny primeneniya smertnoi kazni v Rossiiskom gosudarstve', *Advokat*, 10 (2005). (My thanks to Dmitri Sergeev for supplying me with this last reference.)

32 Speakers included S. Razumov, Supreme Court judge, Fr Alexander Borisov, member of the Presidential commission for questions of clemency, L. Borogaz, lawyer, S. Vitsin, president of the Council for Judicial Reform, Yu. Stetsovsky, professor of Juridical science, and V. Surov, Federal judge for Pskov oblast. Borshchev and Rybakov, 1997, 136–140.

33 Borodin, 2001, 61.

34 Solov'ev's argument and condemnation, for example, was discussed by Pristavkin at the 1999 Conference.

35 Kvashis, 2000, 6–7.

36 Boikov, 1999, 36, 38.

37 Zhil'tsov and Mal'ko, 2001, 449, 432.

38 I.I. Karpets, 'Vysshaya Mera: za i protiv, *Sovetskoe GiP* 7 (1991), 52.

39 Kistyakovsky, 1867, 280–281, cited in Mikhlin, 2000, 173.

40 See Mikhlin, 2000, 24–25; Borodin, 2001, 56, who cites the virtually identical wording in the 1958 *Osnova ugolovnogo zakonodatel'stva Soiuza SSR* (Art. 22).

41 O. Mironov, 2000, cited in Zhil'tsov, and Mal'ko, 2001, 435.

42 With employees at the Ministry of the Interior totalling 96 per cent in favour of the death penalty and 100 per cent of ex-prisoners in favour (Pristavkin, *Vserossiiskaya Konferentsiya*..., 43). Pristavkin cites another journalist, Inna Rudenko, who gives only 40 per cent in favour of the death penalty on the basis of a survey conducted in Moscow and St Petersburg. However, given the concentration of well-educated people in the two cities, she found the poll results disquieting even if the figure might be explained as an offshoot phenomenon of the war in Chechnya (Pristavkin, 45).

43 Pristavkin, 38, 46.

44 Cited in Zhil'tsov and Mal'ko, 2001, 430.

45 Information from a conversation with Anatoly Naumov (November 2005), who pointed out that Putin nevertheless accepts that civilized society does not condone the practice, the reason for which he officially endorses a programme of abolition.

46 Cf. Borodin, 2001, 62.

47 Kvashis, 2000, 14.

48 Kvashis citing Sakharov, followed by his own views, ibid., 21–22.

49 Naumov, 1990, 59; Tsvetinovich, 1994, 53.

50 In May 1993, the Academy of the Ministry of the Interior ran a seminar on the problems of devising new criminal politics and criminal legislation. See Demidov and Engel'hardt, 1994. This was followed by other roundtable discussions, including Sovremennye tendentsii, *GiP*, 6 (1994), 44–76.

51 Article 2 of the Constitution reads: 'Human beings and human rights and freedoms shall be of the highest value. Recognition of, respect for, and protection of the human and civil rights and freedoms shall be the duty of the state.' Cited in Smith, 1996, 239. Guidelines for the Criminal Code were set out in a resolution by a Supreme Court Plenum (31/x/1995), 'O Nekotorykh voprosakh primeneniya izdanii Konstitutsii Rossiiskoi Federatsii pri osushchestvlenii pravosudiya'. Another key source for the Code was the 'Foundations for the Criminal Legislations of the Union of Soviet Socialist Republics' were completed in 1991 but which never came into effect as planned. Its 'modernized' structure, however, provided the basic template for the 1996 Code. See Konyakhin, 2002, 58. Konyakhin also signals more distant precursors for the 1996 Code in aspects of pre-Revolutionary legislation. According to Naumov, the 1991 'Foundations' played an important role in the process of individualizing criminal responsibility and punishment. Naumov, 2004, 115.

52 Cited in Pudovochkin and Pirvagshchov, 2003, 59.

53 S.G. Kelinga; Tsvetinovich, 1994, 46, 52. See also Solomon, 1980.

54 Naumov,1996, 24.
55 Tsvetinovich, 1994, 56–57.
56 S.N. Nikulin, Sovremennye tendentsii, 1994, 55. Though not a widely held view among lawmakers working in state institutions, particularly because it, somewhat misleadingly, invoked Soviet practices, one does come across acknowledgement of the place of religious morality in law in contemporary literature. See, for example, N.G. Ivanov of the Juridical Institute attached to the Ministry for Internal Affairs, Ivanov , 1998.
57 Cited from *Primernyi ugolovnyi kodeks (USA)* (Moscow, 1969), in Naumov, 1996, 30.
58 Tagantsev, *Russkoe ugolovnoe pravo* (SPb., 1902), vol. 1, 45, cited in Naumov, 1996, 32.
59 'Obshchie nachala naznacheniya nakazaniya.' See, for example, Borzenkov, 1997; Klenova, 1997; Kashepov, 2003; Nepomnyashchaya, 1999. 60. The full text of Article 21 reads:

> (1) The dignity of the individual shall be protected by the state. Nothing may serve as a justification for its diminution. (2): No person shall be subjected to torture, violence, or other cruel or degrading treatment or punishment. No person may be subjected to medical, scientific, or other experiments without his/her voluntary consent.

See also Articles 2 and, particularly, 17 of the Constitution, the gist of which complies with the European convention of human rights: 'In the Russian Federation the rights and freedom of man and citizen are recognized and guaranteed in accordance with the universally recognized principles and norms of international law, and in accordance with the current Constitution', in Smith, 1996, 244, 243, and 239.
61 See, for example, Zvecharovsky, 2001, Ch. 2: 'Printsipi prava i ikh otrazhenie v ugolovnom zakonodatel'stve; I. Bikeev, 'Aktual'nye problemy ucheniya o sub'ektivnoi storone prestupleniya', *Ugolovnoe Pravo*, 3 (2002), 9–13; Kashepov, 2003; Nepomnyashchaya, 1999 (see above, note 59); Borodin and Klebanov, 2002; Ivanov, 1998; Emel'yanov, 2002.
62 According to A.N. Krasikov, *lichnost'* connotes value, worth, rights, and freedom, whereas *chelovek* is a neutral generic term. This view, however, is not widely accepted: others have argued that, as far as the law is concerned, *lichnost'* is any man (*chelovek*) and citizen. See Borodin and Klebanov, 2002, 107.
63 Emel'yanov, 2002, 67. Emel'yanov refers to the 1891 edition of Kistyakovsky's textbook (*Elementarnyi uchebnik ugolovnogo prava*) and Belogritz-Kotlyarevsky, 1903.
64 Naumov, 1996, 28.
65 Nepomnyashchaya, 1999, 80–82. According to A.A. Evstifeev, between January 1997 and March 2002, some 1,500 articles had appeared on the topic. See Kostrova, 2002, 29.
66 Naumov, 'Problemy Sovershenstvovaniya ugolovnogo kodeksa rossiiskoi federatsii', *GiP*, 10 (1999), 45–51. This text was originally a paper read to a meeting of the Presidential Council in June 1999.
67 Kashepov, 2003, 17.
68 Naumov, 1999, 51.
69 Ibid., Kostrova, 2002.
70 Kostrova, ibid., 28–32.
71 Klenova, 1997, 56–57.
72 Kvashis 1997, 50. See above, note 31.
73 In St Petersburg and the Leningrad region, there were some 250 cot deaths in the year 2000, most of which were not reported. Borodin and Klebanov, 2002, 108. (Source of information concerning cot deaths not given.)
74 Ibid., 106.
75 Ibid., 105.

76 *Rossiiskaya Gazeta,* 19/iv/2002.
77 The project, backed by the President, for a federal law 'o vnesenii izmenenii i dopolnenii v Ugolovnyi Kodeks Rossiiskoi Federatsii', was passed by the Duma at its first reading in April 2003. See Aleksandrov, 2003, 395.

Afterword: post-Soviet legal culture and pre-revolutionary models

1 Naumov, 2004, 489; Aleksandrov, 2003, 240.
2 I am grateful to Anatoly Naumov for sharing his ideas on the question of intellectual resources in conversation with me (November 2005). On his intellectual affinity with Tagantsev, see Naumov's introduction to the new edition of Tagantsev's *Course*: 'Nikolai Stepanovich Tagantsev (1843–1923)', in Tagantsev, 2001, 7–16.
3 Naumov, 2004, 5.
4 Medvedev, in Kashepov *et al.*, 1998, 477.
5 See, for example, Zvecharovsky, 2001, Ch. 3: 'Ugolovno-pravovaya politika Rossii na sovremennom etape.'
6 See, for example, the rubric 'Stranitsy Istorii' in *Sovetskoe Gosudarstvo i Pravo.*
7 Koni, 2003, 342; N.V. Radutnaya, 'Zhizn' v pravosudii i pravosudie v zhizni. Vstupitel'naya stat'ya', in Koni, 2003, 29–30: Naumov mentions the importance of Koni's work for post-Soviet criminal law procedure, especially trial by jury. See Naumov, 2004, 316. See also Aleksandrov, 2003, 82.
8 Medvedev, 1998, 477.
9 Lebedev, President of the Supreme Court, 'Obrashchenie k molodym sudebnym deyatelyam Rossii', in Koni, 2003, 6; Radutnaya, 2003, 13–14.
10 See, for example, the forewords to volumes on Spasovich, Arsen'ev published in the series 'Yuridicheskoe nasledie', Tula, 'Avtograf', 2000, 2001 – both written by Koni.
11 Korol'kov, 1997, 6.
12 Lyublinsky, 1917.
13 E. Solov'ev, 'The Humanistic–Legal Problematic in Solov'ëv's Philosophical Journalism', *SEET,* 2 (2003), 121.
14 Ibid., 126.
15 Ibid., 119, 123.
16 For example, Pyatkina *et al.*, Foreword.
17 Aleksandrov, 2003, 7.
18 Ibid., 42.
19 Aleksandrov's argument draws on Solov'ev's *Law and Morality* as it appeared under the different title, 'Opredelenie prava v ego svyazi s nrastvennost'yu' in the collection, *Vlast' i pravo. Iz istorii russkoi pravovoi mysli* (Leningrad, 1990), 101.
20 Smith, 1996, 237.

Select bibliography

Published primary sources I have consulted comprise textbooks, research papers, and transcripts of conferences that appeared in the periodical press. Renewed interest in the pre-Revolutionary legacy of legal theory in post-Soviet Russia has, however, produced many new commented editions of works by individual authors, reprints, as well as anthologies intended for instructional purposes. Thus, where possible, I have also made use of these more readily available monographs and collections. Likewise, a large body of essays by Solov'ev on social questions has recently been translated into English, which I have used where appropriate.

Pre-Revolutionary Criminal legislation and the more comprehensive Digest of Laws exist in numerous editions. I made use of the following: *Svod Zakonov Rossiiskoi Imperii dopolnennyi po prodolzheniyam 1906, 1908, 1909 i 1910 gg* (pod red. A.A. Dobrovol'skogo, 2nd edn, SPb., 1913); *Ugolovnoe ulozhenie, vysochaishe utverzhdennoe 22 marta 1903 goda* (SPb., 1903); *Ugolovnoe ulozhenie. Proekt, izmennyi Ministrom yustitsii po soglashcheniyu s predsedatelem Vysochaishe uchrezhdennoi Redaktsionnoi Kommissii* (SPb., 1898); *Ugolovnoe ulozhenie. Proekt Redaktsionnoi Kommissii* (SPb., 1895); *Ulozhenie o nakazaniyakh ugolovnykh i ispravitel'nykh (dopolneno po Prodolzheniyu 1868 g i pozneishim uzakoneniyam)* (SPb., M., 1869); *Ulozhenie o nakazaniyakh ugolovnykh i ispravitel'nykh (dopolneno po Prodolzheniyu 1885g i pozneishim uzakoneniyam)* (8th edn, pod red. N.S. Tagantseva, SPb., 1895). References to the 1845 *Ulozhenie o nakazaniyakh ugolovnykh i ispravitel'nykh* are based on B.N. Mironov, *Sotsial'naya istoriya Rossii*, vol. 2 (SPb., 1999).

Background information relating to the history of reform in part relies on secondary literature and in part reflects the perceptions of pre-Revolutionary eyewitnesses, as these were recorded in essays and in polemical writings.

Published primary sources

[Anon] *Ugolovnoe Pravo (chast' obshchaya i osobennaya). Konspektivnyi kurs* (Kazan', 1911).

Al'bov, A.P., Maslennikov, D.B., Chislov, A.I., and Filippova, S.V. (eds), *Russkaya filosofiya prava: Filosofiya very i nravstvennosti* (SPb., 1997).

Aleksandrov, A.I., *Ugolovnaya politika i ugolovnyi protsess v Rossiiskoi gosudarstvennosti* (SPb., 2003).

Arsen'ev, K. Brokgaus-Efron *Entsiklopedicheskii Slovar'*, vol. XXXVIII (1899). Volume entitled 'Rossiya', headword: 'Ugolovnoe pravo'.

—— *Entsiklopedicheskii Slovar'*, vol. XXX (1900), headword: 'Smertnaya Kazn'.
—— *Entsiklopedicheskii Slovar'*, vol. XXXIVa (1902), headword: 'Ugolovnoe pravo'.
—— (ed.), *Glavnye deyateli i predshestvenniki sudebnoi reformy* (SPb., 1904).
—— *Svoboda sovesti i veroterpimost'. Sbornik Statei* (SPb., 1905).
—— 'Iz vospominanii', *Golos minuvshego*, 2 (1915).
—— *Za chetvert' veka (1871–1894). Sbornik Statei* (Pgd., 1915).
Baitin, M.I., *Sushchnost' prava: Sovremennoe normativnoe pravoponimanie na grani vekov* (Saratov, 2001).
Belogritz-Kotlyarevsky, L.S., 'Zadacha i metod nauki ugolovnogo prava', *Yuridicheskii Vestnik*, Sept. (1892), 41–51.
—— *Uchebnik Russkogo ugolovnogo prava. Obshchaya i osobennaya chasti* (Kiev, SPb., 1903).
Bikeev, I., 'Aktual'nye problemy ucheniya o sub'ektivnoi storone prestupleniya', *Ugolovnoe Pravo*, 3 (2002), 9–13.
Boikov, A.D., 'O Smertnoi Kazni', *Zakonnost'*, 8 (1999), 34–38.
Borodin, S. and Klebanov, L., 'Zashchita lichnosti v Rossii (Kriminologicheskii i ugolovno-pravovoi aspekty)', *Ugolovnoe Pravo*, 2 (2002), 105–111.
Borodin, S.V., 'Eshche raz o smertnoi kazni za ubiistvo', *GiP*, 4 (2001), 56–63.
Borshchev, V. and Rybakov, Y., 'Razgovor o smertnoi kazni', *Chelovek i Zakon*, 2 (1997).
Borzenkov, G.N., 'Novyi UK: Kakoi on? Naznachenie Nakazaniya', *Chelovek i Zakon*, 2 (1997), 37–43.
Bulgakov, S., 'Chto daet sovremennomu soznaniyu filosofiya Vladimira Solov'eva?' in *Ot Marksizma k idealizmu: Sbornik Statei, 1896–1903* (SPb., 1903).
Chubinsky, M.P., *Kurs ugolovnoi politiki* (SPb., 1905, 2nd edn, 1912).
Davydov, E.V., 'Kompromiss sotsial'noi kriminologii i dogmy ugolovnogo prava', *Zhurnal Ministerstva Yustitsii*, 5 (1900), 93–107.
Demidov, Yu. N. and Engel'hardt, A.A., 'Obsuzhdenie problem ugolovnoi politiki', *GiP*, 1 (1994), 145–148.
Dril', D., 'Obychai i Zakon', *Yuridicheskii Vestnik*, June–July (1883), 234–277.
—— *Prestupnost' i Prestupniki: Ugolovnye psikologicheskie etiudy* (SPb., 1895).
Emel'yanov, V.P., 'Kontseptual'nye aspekty issledovaniya ob'ekta prestuplaniya,' *Pravo i Politika*, 10 (2002), 61–72.
Esipov, V.V., 'Lichnoe sostoyanie prestupnosti, kak predmet nakazaniya', *Zhurnal Grazhdanskogo i Ugolovnogo Prava*, 10 (1893), 22–50.
—— *Grekh i prestuplenie, svyatotatstvo i krazha* (SPb., 1894).
—— *Nravstevennost' i Pravo* (Warsaw, 1907).
—— *Ukazatel' vazhneishei literatury po ugolovnomu pravu* [nl. ndg.].
Filippov, O., 'Smertnaya Kazn', *Russkoe Slovo*, 11 (1863), 121–144.
Foinitsky, I., 'Russkaya karatel'naya sistema', in *Sbornik Gosudartsvennikh Znanii*, vol. 1 (1874), 1–48, 97–144.
—— 'Neobkhodimost' reformy postanovlenii russkogo ugolovnogo zakonodatel'stva po voprosu o lishenii prav', *Zhurnal Grazhdanskogo i ugolovnogo prava* 5, Sept.–Oct. (1875), 160–194.
—— 'Ssylka ili Tiur'ma?', *Yuridicheskii Vestnik*, June (1881), 686–698.
—— *Kurs ugolovnogo sudoproizvodstva* (SPb., 1884).
—— *Uchenie o nakazanii v svyazi s tyur'movedeniem* (SPb., 1889).
—— *A.F. Kistyakovsky kak kriminalist* (Kiev, 1895).

Gernet, M.N., Gol'dovsky, O.B., and Sakharov, I.N. (eds), *Protiv smertnoi kazni* (Moscow, 1906, 2nd edn, 1907).
Gernet, M.N., Ustinov, V.M., and Novotsky, I.V., *Osnovnye poniatiya russkogo gosudarstvennogo, grazhdanskogo i ugolovnogo prava* (Moscow, 1906).
Gernet, M.N. (ed.), *O smertnoi kazni. Mneniya russkikh kriminologov* (Moscow, 1909).
Gernet, M.N., *Ugolovnoe pravo i sotsializm* (Moscow, 1908).
—— *Bibliograficheskie ukazateli po voprosam ugolovnogo prava* (SPb., 1913).
—— *Istoriya tsarskoi tiur'my*, vol. 3: 1870–1900 (3rd edn, Moscow, 1961).
—— *Smertnaya Kazn'* (Moscow, 1913).
—— *Ugolovnoe Pravo. Chast' Obshchaya* (Kherson, 1913).
Gessen, S.I., 'Filosofiya Nakazaniya', *Logos* (1912), kn. 2–3, 183–232.
Gogel', S.K., *Kurs ugolovnoi politiki v svyazi s ugolovnoi sotsiologii* (SPb., 3rd edn, 1910).
—— *Rol' obshchestva v dele bor'by s prestupnost'yu* (SPb., 1906).
—— *Voprosy ugolovnogo prava, protsessa i tyur'movedeniya* (SPb., 1906).
Gol'tsev, V., 'Nravstvennost' i pravo' po povodu polemiki V.S. Solov'eva s B.N. Chicherin', *Russkaia Mysl'*, 5 (1898), 47–56.
Gorodensky, N., 'Nravstvennaya filosofiya Vl.S. Solov'eva', *Bogoslovskii Vestnik*, 11 (1899), 287–321.
Ivanov, N.G., 'Paradoksy ugolovnogo zakona', *GiP*, 3 (1998), 50–57.
Karpets, I.I., 'Vysshaya Mera: za i protiv', *Sovetskoe GiP*, 7 (1991), 49–53.
Kashepov, V.P., 'O problemakh gumanizatsii ugolovnogo zakonodatel'stva pri ego obnovlenii', *Zhurnal Rossiiskogo Prava*, 6 (2003), 15–23.
Kashepov, V.P., Mitskevich, A.V., and Pyatkina, S.A. (eds), *Istoriya Russkoi pravovoi mysli. Biografii – dokumenty – publikatsii* (Moscow, 1998).
Kelinga, S. (ed.), *Kogda ubivaet gosudarstvo* (Moscow, 1989).
Kistyakovsky, A.F., *Issledovanie o smertnoi kazni* (Kiev, 1867).
—— *Elementarnyi uchebnik obshchego ugolovnogo prava* (Kiev, 1875).
—— 'Glavneishie momenty razvitiya ugolovnogo prava', *Universitetskie Izvestiya* (Kiev, 1876) [pamphlet].
—— 'Nekotorye cherty iz istorii smertnoi kazni v Rossii' (Kiev, 1879) [pamphlet].
Kistyakovsky, B.A., 'In Defence of Law', *Vekhi* [1909], in Marshall S. Shatz and Judith E. Zimmerman (trans. and ed.), *Vekhi-Landmarks: A Collection of Articles about the Russian Intelligentsia* (New York, 1994).
—— 'Metodologicheskaya priroda nauki o prave', in G. Radbrukh (ed.), *Vvedenie v nauku prava* (Moscow, 1915), v–xv.
Kizilov, A.Yu., *Smertnaya Kazn': Apologiya* (Moscow, 2003).
Klenova, T.V., 'Printsipi ugolovnogo prava i printsipi kodifikatsii v ugolovnom prave', *GiP*, 1 (1997), 54–59.
Kommentarii k Ugolovnomu Kodeksu Rossiiskoi Federatsii (pod red. i so vstup. stat. Prof. iur. nauk A.V. Naumova) (M., 1996).
Koni, A.F., 'Nravstennye nachala v ugolovnom protsesse', *Zhurnal Ministerstva Yustitsii*, 1 (1902), 1–44.
—— 'Vladimir Sergeevich Solov'ev', *VE*, 2 (1903), 651–689.
—— *Sobranie Sochineniya. Tom 8. Pis'ma 1868–1917* (Moscow, 1969).
—— *Ottsy i deti Sudenoi reformy* [1914] (repr., Moscow, 2003).
Korol'kov, A.A., 'Odukhtvorennaya nauka o prave', in *Russkaya filosofiya prava: Filosofiya very i nravstvennosti* (SPb., 1997).
Korsakov, D., *Konstantin Dmitrievich Kavelin. Ocherk zhizni i deyatel'nosti* (SPb., 1896).

Kostrova, M., 'Ugolovnyi kodeks Rossiiskoi Federatsii – pyat' let spustya: problemy i perspektivy sovershenstvovaniya norm ugolovnogo zakonodatel'stva', *Ugolovnoe Pravo*, 3 (2002), 28–32.

Kuchinsky, I.A., 'K voprosu o nravstvennom ispravlenii prestupnikov', *Zhurnal Ministerstva Yustitsii*, Dec. (1897), 147–157.

Kuz'min-Karavaev, V.D., Brokgaus-Efron *Entsiklopedicheskii Slovar'*, vol. XXXa (1900), headword: 'Smertnaya kazn' po voenno-ugolovnom zakonam.'

—— *Iz epokhi osvoboditel'nogo dvizheniya*, 2 vols (SPb., 1907).

Kvashis, V.E. (ed.), *Vserossiiskaya konferentsiya po probleman otmeny smertnoi kazni. Moskva, 3–4 iuinya 1999 goda* (Moscow, 2000).

——'"Smertnaya Kazn": Mifologicheskie predstavleniya i kriminologicheskie realii (vstupitel'naya stat'ya)', in Kvashis, V.E. (ed), *Vserossiiskaya konferentsiya po probleman otmeny smertnoi kazni. Moskva, 3-4 iuinya 1999 goda* (Moscow, 2000), 6–22.

—— 'Primenenie smertnoi kazni ne imeet kriminologicheskoi znachimosti', *Yuridicheskii Mir*, 5 (1997), 49–53.

Lebedev, V.M., 'Obrashchenie k molodym sudebnym deyatelyam Rossii', in A.F. Koni, *Ottsy i deti sudebnoi reformy* (rep., Moscow, 2003), Preface.

Lemke, M.K. (ed.), *M.M. Stasyulevich i ego sovremenniki v ikh perepiske*, 5 vols (SPb., 1911–1913).

Leventsim, A., *Sueverie i ugolovnoe pravo* (SPb., 1897).

Levitsky, G.A., *Russkie i Zapadnoevropeiskie uchenye XIX i nachala XX vv., ob ugolovnom zakone, prestuplenii i nakazanii,* Khrestomatiya (SPb., 2004).

Lyublinsky, P.I., *Svoboda lichnosti v ugolovnom protsesse (Mery, obezpechivayushchie neuklonenie obvinyaemogo ot pravosudiya)* (SPb., 1906).

—— 'Eticheskoe nachalo i svoboda lichnosti v ugolovnom protsesse', *Pravo*, 50 (1907).

—— 'O deistvii nakazaniya', *Novye idei v pravovedenii*, Sbk.1 (SPb., 1914), 1–27.

—— *Pamyati trekh russkikh kriminalistov: Foinitsky, Dril', Sergeevsky* (SPb., 1914).

—— 'Sud i prava lichnosti', in N.V. Davydov and N.N. Polyanskii (eds), *Sudebnaya Reforma*, vol. II (Moscow, 1915), 1–40.

—— *Na smenu starogo prava, Sbornik statei po voprosam tekushchei pravovoi zhizni* (Pgd., 1915).

—— *Osnovy grazhdanskoi svobody* (Lausanne: The Herzen Society for the People's Press, 1917) [pamphlet].

Malinovsky, I., *Russkie pisateli-khudozhniki o smertnoi kazni*, 2 vols (Tomsk, 1908, 1910).

Medvedev, A.M., 'Nikolai Stepanovich Tagantsev', in Kashepov, V.P., Mitskevich A.V., and Pyatkina, S.A. (eds), *Istoriya Russkoi pravovoi mysli*' (Moscow, 1998), 465–477.

Mikhailovsky, I.V., *Ocherki filosofii prava*, vol. 1 (Tomsk, 1914).

Mikhlin, A.S., *Vysshaya mera nakazaniya. Istoriya, sovremennost', budushchee* (Moscow, 2000).

Mironov, O.O., 'Doklad o deyatel'nosti upolnomochennogo po pravam cheloveka v Rossiiskoi federatsii v 1999 godu', in *Rossiiskaya Gazeta* (18 v 2000).

Mokrinsky, S.P., 'Etiko-politicheskoe napravlenie v ugolovnom prave', *Zhurnal Min. Yust*, March (1903).

—— *Nakazanie, ego tseli i predpolozhenie*, 3 vols (Moscow, 1902–1905).

—— 'Sistema i metody nauki ugolovnogo prava', in *Vestnik Prava*, kn3 (1906), 21–53.

Murav'ev, N.V., 'Obryad publichnoi kazni', *Yuridicheskii Vestnik*, 7–8 (1874), 67–128.

Nabokov, V.D., *Sbornik statei po ugolovnomu pravu* (SPb., 1904).

Naumov, A.V., 'Ugolovnyi zakon i prava cheloveka', *Sovetskoe GiP*, 1 (1990), 52–60.

—— 'Nikolai Stepanovich Tagantsev (1843–1923)', in *N.S. Tagantsev. Russkoe ugolovnoe pravo* (Tula, 2001), 7–16.

—— *Rossiiskoe ugolovnoe pravo. Kurs lektsii*, vol. I (3rd edn, Moscow, 2004).

Neklyudov, N., *Obshchaya chast' ugolovnogo prava* (SPb., 1875).

Nepomnyashchaya, T.V., 'Obshchie nachala, printsipy i kriterii naznacheniya nakazaniya', *Zhurnal Rossiiskogo Prava*, 12 (1999), 75–85.

Nikiforov, A.S., 'O smertnoi kazni', *GiP*, 4 (2001), 64–65.

Novgorodtsev, P., 'Ideya prava v filosofii Vl. S. Solov'eva' (Moscow, 1901) [pamphlet].

—— 'Nravstvennyi idealism v filosofii prava: k voprosu o vozrozhdenii estestvennogo prava', in *Problemy Idealizma* (Moscow, 1902), 236–296.

—— *Krizis sovremmenogo pravosoznaniya. Vvedenie v filosofiyu prava* (Moscow, 1909).

Petrazhitsky, L., *Vvedenie v izuchenie prava i nravstvennosti'* (SPb., 1905).

—— *Teoriya prava i gosudarstva v svyazi s teoriei prava i nravstvennosti*, 2 vols (SPb., 1907, 2nd edn, 1909–1910).

Pobedonostsev, K., *Reflections of a Russian Statesman* (Ann Arbor, 1965).

Povorinsky, A., *Sistematicheskii ukazatel' russkoi literatury po sudoustroistvu i sudoproizvodstvu grazhdanskomu i ugolovnomu*, I [npg., 1896].

Poznyshev, S.V., *Osnovnye voprosy ucheniya o nakazanii* (Moscow, 1904).

—— *Uchenie o karatel'nykh merakh* (Moscow, 1908).

—— *Zadachi obshchestvennikh nauk v svyazi s osnovami etiki* (Moscow, 1908).

—— 'Ob izuchenii prestupnika v nauke ugolovnogo prava', *Voprosy Prava*, kn VI–VIII (1911), 184–206; 40–71; 190–231.

—— *Osnovnye nachala nauki ugolovnogo prava* (Moscow, 1912).

Przheval'sky, V.V., 'Proekt ugolovnogo ulozheniya i sovremennaya nauka ugolovnogo prava', *Zhurnal Yuridicheskogo Obshchestva* (December 1896 and January 1897).

Pudovochkin,Yu.E. and Pirvagshchov, S.S., *Ponyatie, printsipi i istochniki ugolovnogo prava. Sravnitel'no-pravovoi analiz* (SPb., 2003).

Sal'nikov, V.P., Al'bov, A.P., and Maslennikov, D.P. (eds), *A.S. Yashchenko: Filosofiya prava Vladimira Solov'eva. Teoriya federalizma* (SPb., 1999).

Sbornik Gosudarstvennykh Znanii (T.I–VIII, 1874–1880).

Sbornik statei N.M. Korkunova (1877–1897) (SPb., 1898).

Sergeevsky, N.D., 'Lichenie zhizni, kak ugolovnoe nakazanie', *Yuridicheskii Vestnik*, 6 (1879), 829–860.

—— 'Prestuplenie i nakazanie, kak predmet yuridicheskoi nauki', *Yuridicheskii Vestnik*, 12 (1879), 877–904.

—— 'Anthropologicheskoe napravlenie v izsledovaniyakh o prestuplenii i nakazanii', *Yuridicheskii Vestnik*, 2 (1882), 209–221.

—— 'Sovremennye zadachi ugolovnogo zakonodatel'stva v Rossii', *Zhurnal Grazhdanskogo i Ugolovnogo Prava*, 3 (1883), 107–133.

—— *Russkoe ugolovnoe pravo (posobie k lektsiam)* (2nd edn, SPb., 1887).

—— 'Osnovnye voprosy nakazaniya v noveishei literature', *Zhurnal Grazhdanskogo i Ugolovnogo Prava*, IV (1893), 3–24.

Shershenevich, G.F., 'Po povudu knigi Vl.S. Solov'eva *Opravdanie Dobra*', in *Voprosy Filosofii i Psikhologii*, vol. 38 (1897), 456–474.

Shishov, O.F. and Paffenova, T.S. (eds), *Smertnaya Kazn'. Za i protiv* (Moscow, 1989).

Slominsky, L., 'Teoriya i praktika zakonnosti', *VE*, 1895 (1 and 2), 317–331; 768–794.

Solov'ev, V.S., 'Narodnaya beda i obshchestvennaya pomoshch', *VE*, 10 (1891).

—— 'Mnimye i deistvitel'nye mery k pod'emu narodnogo blagosostoyaniya', *VE*, 11 (1892), 353–361.

—— 'Spor o spravedlivosti', *VE*, 4 (1894), 785–797.
—— 'Nravstvennaya filosofiya, kak samostoyatel'naya nauka', *VE*, 11 (1894), 345–365.
—— 'Nravstvennye osnovy obshchestva', *VE*, 12 (1894), 802–817.
—— 'Printsip nakazaniya s nravtsvennoi tochki zreniya', *VE*, 3 (1895), 212–235.
—— 'Znachenie Gosudarstva', *VE*, 12 (1895).
—— *Opravdanie Dobra* (SPb., 1897).
—— *Pravo i Nravstevnnost'* (SPb., 1897).
—— 'Zamechaniya na Stat'yu prof. G.F. Shershenevicha', *Voprosy Filosofii i Psikhologii*, vol. 38 (1897), 475–484.
Sorochinsky, N., 'K Voprosu o prave nakazaniya', *Vestnik Prava*, June (1905), 27–59.
'Sovremennye tendentsii razvitiya ugolovnogo zakonodatel'stva i ugolovno-pravovoi teorii', *GiP*, 6 (1994), 44–76.
Spasovich, V., *Uchebnik ugolovnogo prava* (SPb., 1863).
—— *Sochineniia V.D. Spasovicha*, vol. 8: 'Poslednie raboty v devyanostykh godov' (SPb., 1896).
—— *V.D. Spasovich. Izbranniye trudy i rechi* (Tula, 2000).
Struve, P., *Na raznye temy (1893–1901)* (SPb., 1902).
Sudebnye Ustavy, 20 XI 1864 (za 50 let), 2 vols and suppl. (Pgd., 1914).
Tagantsev, N.S., 'Poslednee dvadtsatipiatiletie v istorii ugolovnogo prava (1867–1892)', *VE*, 12 (1892), 818–829.
—— *Lektsii po russkomu ugolovnomu pravu*, 4 vols (2nd edn, SPb., 1887–1892).
—— *Smertnaya Kazn'. Sbornik Statei* (SPb., 1913).
Tal'berg, D.B., *Russkoe ugolovnoe sudoproizvodstvo. Posobie k lektsiyam*, vol. 1 (Kiev, 1889).
Tarnovsky, F.V., *Uchebnik entsiklopedii prava* (Yurev, 1917).
Tol'stoi, L., 'Ne mogu molchat', [1908] in W. Gareth Jones (ed.), *I Cannot be Silent: Writings on Politics, Art and Religion by Leo Tolstoy* (The Bristol Press, 1989).
Tregubov, S.N., *Nastol'naya kniga kriminalista-praktika*, T.I. [npg., 1894–1908].
Trubetskoi, Evg., *Lektsii po entsiklopedii prava* (Moscow, 1909).
—— *Mirosozertsanie Vl. S. Solov'eva* (Moscow, 1913).
Ugolovnyi Kodeks Rossiiskoi Federatsii [UK RSFSR] (Moscow, 1996).
Ustav ugolovnogo sudoproizvodstva, compiled by Prof. M.N. Gernet (Moscow, 1916).
Viktorsky, S.I., *Istoriya smertnoi kazni v Rossii i sovremennoe ee sostoyanie* (Moscow, 1912).
Vladimirov, L.E., *Uchebnik russkogo ugolovnogo prava* (Kharkov, 1889).
—— 'Ugolovnyi zakonodatel' kak vospitatel' naroda' (Moscow, 1903) [pamphlet].
—— *Kurs ugolovnogo prava* (Moscow, 1908).
Vorotynsky, B.I., 'Biologicheskie i sotsiali'nye factory prestupnosti', *Zhurnal Mininsterstva Yustitsii*, 9 (1901), 1–34.
Vul'fert, A., 'Brokgaus-Efron' *Entsiklopedicheskii slovar'*, 20 (1897), headword: 'Nakazanie'.
Wozniuk, V., *Politics, Law, Morality. Essays by V.S. Solov'ev* (Yale University Press, 2000).
Zhil'tsov, V. and Mal'ko, A.V., *Smertnaya kazn' v Rossii; istoriko-teoreticheskoe issledovanie* (Tol'yatti, 2001).
Zhizhilenko, A.A., *Nakazanie. Ego ponyatie i otlichie ot drugikh pravookhranitel'nykh sredstv* (Pgd., 1914).
Zvecharovsky, I.E., *Sovremennoe ugolovnoe pravo Rossii: Poniatie, printsipy, politika* (SPb., 2001).

Secondary literature

Criminal justice, legal theory and culture

Adams, B.F., *The Politics of Punishment: Prison Reform in Russia, 1863–1917* (DeKalb, 1996).

—— Criminology in Russia, Wieczynski, J.L. (ed.), *The Modern Encyclopaedia of Russian and Soviet History* (Gulf Breeze, FL, 1988), vol. 47.

Baberowski, J., *Autokratie und Justiz: Zum Verhältnis von Rechtsstaatlichkeit und Rückständigkeit im ausgehenden Zarenreich 1864–1914* (Frankfurt am Main, 1996).

Balzer, M.M., *Russian Traditional Culture: Religion, Gender, and Customary Law* (New York, 1992).

Berman, H.J., *Law and Revolution: The Formation of the Western Legal Tradition* (Cambridge, Mass., 1983).

Bryner, C., 'The Issue of Capital Punishment in the Reign of Elizabeth Petrovna', *Russian Review*, 49 (1990), 386–416.

Burbank, J., *Russian Peasants go to Court: Legal Culture in the Countryside, 1905–1917* (Indiana University Press, 2004).

Confino, M., 'Russian Customary Law and the Study of Peasant Mentalities', *Russian Review*, 44 (1985), 1, 35–43.

Crisp, O. and Edmondson, L. (eds), *Civil Rights in Imperial Russia* (Oxford, 1989).

Daly, J., 'On the Significance of Emergency Legislation in Late Imperial Russia', *Slavic Review*, 54 (1995), 602–629.

—— 'Political Crime in Late Imperial Russia', *Journal of Modern History*, 74 (March, 2002), 62–100.

—— 'Russian Punishments in the European Mirror', in Susan P. McCaffray and Michael Melancon (eds), *Russia in the European Context, 1789–1914* (New York and Basingstoke, 2005), 161–188.

Emsley, C. and Knaffa, L. (eds), *Crime History and the History of Crime: Studies in the Historiography of Crime and Criminal Justice in Modern History* (London, 1996).

Engelstein, L., *The Key to Happiness: Sex and the Search for Modernity in Fin-de-siècle Russia* (Ithaca and London, 1992).

—— 'Combined Underdevelopment: Discipline and Law in Imperial and Soviet Russia', in Jan Goldstein (ed.), *Foucault and the Writing of History* (London, 1999), 220–236.

Evans, R., *Rituals of Retribution: Capital Punishment in Germany, 1600–1987* (London, 1997).

Frank, S., 'Popular Justice, Community, and Culture among the Russian Peasantry, 1870–1900', *Russian Review*, 46 (1987), 3, 239–265.

—— 'Narratives Within Numbers: Women, Crime and Judicial Statistics in Imperial Russia, 1834–1913', *Russian Review*, 55 (1996), 4, 541–565.

—— *Crime, Cultural Conflict, and Justice in Rural Russia, 1856–1914* (Los Angeles, 1999).

Frierson, C., 'Crime and Punishment in the Russian Village: Rural Concepts of Criminality at the End of the Nineteenth Century', *Slavic Review*, 46, 1 (1987), 55–69.

Fuller, W.C. Jr, 'Civilians in Russian Military Courts', *Russian Review*, 41, 3 (1982), 288–305.

Gantzel, H., *Wladimir Solowjews Rechtsphilosophie auf der Grundlage der Sittlichkeit* (Frankfurt am Main, 1968).

Gurvich, G., 'Die Zwei grössten russischen Rechtsphilosophen: Boris Tchitcherin und Wladimir Solowieff', *Philosophie und Recht*, 2 (1922–1923), 80–102.

—— 'Prof. P.I. Novgorodtsev, kak filosof prava', *Sovremmenye Zapiski*, 20 (1924), 389–393.

Ivanov, L.O., 'Izuchenie prestupnosti sotsiologicheskoi shkoloi ugolovnogo prava v Rossii', *Sovetskoe GiP*, 4 (1982), 98–102.

Kaiser, F.B., *Die Russische Justizreform von 1864: Zur Geschichte der Russischen Justiz von Katharina II bis 1916* (Leiden, 1972).

Konyakhin, V.P., 'Razvitie struktury obshchei chasti ugolovnogo kodeksca v ramkam kodifitsirovannogo ugolovnogo zakonodatel'stva Rossii (1845–1996)', *Pravo i Politika*, 3 (2002), 50–72.

Kucherov, S., 'Administration of Justice under Nicholas I of Russia', *American Slavic and East European Review*, 7 (2) 1948, 125–138.

—— *Courts, Lawyers, and Trials under the Last Three Tsars* (Westport, Conn., 1974).

Lentin, A., 'Beccaria, Shcherbatov, and the Question of Capital Punishment in Eighteenth-century Russia', *Revue Canadienne des Slavistes*, XXIV, 2 (June 1982), 128–137.

Marsh, C. and Gvosdev, N., *Civil Society and the Search for Justice in Russia* (Lanham, 2002).

Popkins, G., 'Popular Development of Procedure in a Dual Legal System. "Protective Litigation" in Russia's Peasant Courts, 1889–1912', *Journal of Legal Pluralism*, 43 (1999), 57–87.

—— 'Peasant Experiences of the Late Tsarist State: District Congresses of Land Captains, Provincial Boards and the Legal Appeals Process, 1891–1917', *SEER*, 78, 1 (Jan. 2000), 90–114.

—— 'Code versus Custom? Norms and Tactics in Peasant Volost Court Appeals, 1889–1917', *Russian Review*, 59 (2000), 408–424.

Potapchuk, I. (ed.), *K. K. Arsen'ev. Zametki o russkoi advokature* (Tula, 2001).

Rawson, D., 'The Death Penalty in Late Tsarist Russia: An Investigation of Judicial Procedures', *Russian History/Histoire Russe*, 11, 1 (Spring, 1984), 29–52.

Smith, G., *Reforming the Russian Legal System* (Cambridge, 1996).

Smolyarchuk, V.I., 'V.D. Spasovich: uchenyi-yurist, literator, sudebnyi orator', *Sovetskoe GiP*, 10 (1982), 93–99.

Solomon, P. Jr, 'Soviet Penal Policy, 1917–1934: A Reinterpretation', *Slavic Review*, XXXIX, 2 (1980), 195–217.

—— *Soviet Criminal Justice Under Stalin* (Cambridge, 1996).

—— (ed.), *Reforming Justice in Russia, 1864–1996: Power, Culture, and the Limits of Legal Order* (New York, 1997).

'Soviet Penal Policy, 1917–1934: A Reinterpretation', *Slavic Review*, XXXIX, 2 (1980), 195–217.

Solov'ev, E., 'Defitsit pravoponimaniya kak predmeta russkoi filosofii', *VF* (1988), 10.

—— 'The Humanistic–Legal Problematic in Solov'ev's Philosophical Journalism', *SEET*, 2, vol. 55 (2003), 115–139.

Sutton, J. (ed.), 'Conceptions of Legality and Ethics in Nineteenth and Twentieth Century Russian Thought', *SEET*, vol. 48, 2–4 (1996).

Szeftel, M., 'Personal Inviolability in the Legislation of the Russian Absolute Monarchy', *The American Slavic and East European Review*, XVII (1958), 1–24.

Timasheff, N.S., 'The Impact of the Penal Law of Imperial Russia on Soviet Penal Law', *American Slavic and East European Review*, XII, 4 (1953), 441–462.

Wagner, W.G., 'Tsarist Legal Policies at the End of the Nineteenth Century: A Study in Inconsistencies', *SEER*, LIV, 3 (1976), 371–394.

—— *Marriage, Property, and Law in Late Imperial Russia* (Oxford, 1994).

Waldron, P., 'States of Emergency: Autocracy and Emergency Legislation, 1881–1917', *Revolutionary Russia*, 8 (1995), 1–25.

Walicki, A., *Legal Philosophies of Russian Liberalism* (Oxford, 1987).

—— 'Nravstvennost' i pravo v teoriyakh russkikh liberalov kontsa XIX – nachala XX vekov', *Voprosy Filosofii*, 8 (1991), 25–40.

Wartenweiler, D., *Civil Society and Academic Debate in Russia 1905–1914* (Oxford, 1999).

Wheatcroft, S., 'Crisis of the Late Tsarist Penal System', *Challenging Traditional Views of Russian History* (Basingstoke, 2002), 27–54.

Wood, A., 'The Siberian Exile System in Tsarist Russia', *History Today*, 30 (Sept. 1980), 19–24.

—— 'Crime and Punishment in the House of the Dead', in Crisp, O. and Edmondson, L. (eds), *Civil Rights in Imperial Russia* (Oxford, 1989).

Wortman, R., *The Development of a Russian Legal Consciousness* (Chicago, Ill., 1976).

Wozniuk, V., 'Vladimir S. Solov'ev and the Politics of Human Rights', *Journal of Church and State*, 41 (Winter, 1999), 33–50.

Zagorodnikov, N.I., *Vydaiushchiisya russkii uchenyi-yurist N.S. Taganstev, 1843–1923* (Moscow, 1992).

Liberalism and Obshchestvennost'

Balmuth, D., *The Russian Bulletin, 1863–1917: A Liberal Voice in Tsarist Russia* (New York, 2000).

Balykin, D.A., *A.N. Pypin kak issledovatel' techenii russkoi obshchestvennoi mysli* (Briansk, 1996).

Brooks, J., *When Russia Learned to Read: Literacy and Popular Culture, 1861–1917* (Princeton, 1985).

Clowes, E., Kassow, S.D., and West, J.L. (eds), *Between Tsar and People. Educated Society and the Quest for Public Identity in Late Imperial Russia* (Princeton, 1991).

Eklof, B., Bushnell J., and Zakharova L. (eds), *Russia's Great Reforms, 1855–1881* (Bloomington, 1994).

Fischer, G., *Russian Liberalism: From Gentry to Intelligentsia* (Cambridge, Mass., 1958).

Gekker, N., 'M.M. Stasyulevich i staryi russkii liberalism', *Sovremennik*, 4 (1911), 230–253.

Kel'ner, V.E., *Chelovek svoego vremeni. M.M. Stasyulevich: izdatel'skoe delo i liberal'naya oppozitsiya* (SPb., 1993).

Leontovitch, V., *Geschichte den russischen Liberalismus* [1958].

Lincoln, W.B., *The Great Reforms: Autocracy, Bureaucracy, and the Politics of Change in Imperial Russia* (DeKalb, 1990).

McClelland, J., *Autocrats and Academics: Education, Culture and Society in Tsarist Russia* (Chicago, Ill., 1979).

Manning, R., *The Crisis of the Old Order: Gentry and Government* (Princeton, 1982).

Milyukov, P., *Iz istorii russkoi intelligentsii. Sbornik statei i etyudov*, 2nd edn (SPb., 1903).

Pirumova, N.M., *Zemskoe liberal'noe dvizhenie. Sotsial'nye korni i evoliutsiya do nachala XX veka* (Moscow, 1977).

Pogorelskin, A.E., 'N.I. Kostormarov and the Origins of the Vestnik Evropy Circle', *Oxford Slavonic Papers*, XI (1971), 84–100.

Pustarnakov, V.F. and Khudushuna, I.F. (eds), *Liberalizm v Rossii* (Moscow, 1996).

Riasanovsky, N., *A Parting of Ways: Government and the Educated Public in Russia, 1801–55* (Oxford, 1976).

Schrooyen, P., *Vladimir Solov'ev in the Rising Public Sphere: A Reconstruction and Analysis of the Concept of Christian Politics in the* Publitsistika *of Vladimir Solov'ev* [Phd., Nijmegen, 2006].

Shelokhaev, V.V., Gorshkov, M.K., Zhuravlev, V.V., Pustarnikov, V.F., and Sorokin, A.K. (eds), *Russkii Liberalism. Istoricheskie sud'by i perspektivy* [Materialy mezhdunarodnoi nauchnoi konferentsii, Moskva, 27–29 Maia, 1998g] (Moscow, 1999).

Sutton, J., 'Vladimir Solov'ev, Moral Philosophy and "Sound Politics"', *SEET*, 52, 4 (December 2000), 309–326.

Taranovski, T. (ed.), *Reform in Modern Russian History. Progress or Cycle?* (Cambridge, 1995).

Timberlake, C.E., *Essays on Russian Liberalism* (Columbia, 1972).

—— (ed.), *Religious and Secular Forces in Late Tsarist Russia: Essays in Honour of D.W. Treadgold* (Seattle, 1992).

Wcislo, F.W., *Reforming Rural Russia: State, Local Society, and National Politics, 1855–1914* (Princeton, 1990).

Zimmerman, J., 'Russian Liberal Theory, 1900–1917', *Canadian American Slavic Studies*, 14, 1 (Spring 1980), 1–20.

Background

Billington, J., *The Icon and the Axe. An Interpretive History of Russian Culture* (New York, 1970).

Borisova I. and Kozyrev, A. (eds), *Solov'evskii Sbornik: Materialy mezhdunarodnoi konferentsii 'V.S. Solov'ev u ego filosofskoe nasledie'* (Moscow, 2001).

Brown, A., *The Gorbachev Factor* (Oxford, 1997).

Brown, A. and L. Shevtsova, L. (eds), *Gorbachev, Yeltsin and Putin: Political Leadership in Russia's Transition* (Carnegie Endowment for International Peace, 2001).

Byrnes, R.F., *Pobedonostsev: His Life and Thought* (Bloomington, 1968).

Dallin, A. (ed.), *The Gorbachev Era* (New York, 1992).

Daly, J., *Autocracy under Siege: Security Police and Opposition in Russia, 1866–1905* (DeKalb, 1998).

Daniels, R. (ed.), *Soviet Communism from Reform to Collapse* (Lexington, 1995).

de Courten, M., *History, Sophia and the Russian Nation: A Reassessment of Vladimir Solov'ev's Views on his History and his Social Commitment* (Bern, 2004).

Emel'yanov, Yu.N. (ed.), *Moskovskii Universitet v vospominaniiakh sovremennikov, 1755–1917* (Moscow, 1989).

Evtuhkov, C., *The Cross and the Sickle. Sergei Bulgakov and the Fate of Russian Religious Philosophy* (Ithaca, 1997).

Fleron, F.J. Jr. and Hoffmann, E.P. (eds), *Post-Communist Studies in Political Science* (Boulder, 1993).

Freeze, G.L., 'The Soslovie (Estate) Paradigm and Russian Social History', *American Historical Review*, vol. 91 (1986), 1, 11–36.

Frierson, C., *Peasant Icons: Representations of Rural People in Late Nineteenth Century Russia* (Oxford, 1993).

Gaidenko, P., '*Landmarks* – An Unheard Warning', *Russian Studies in Philosophy* (Summer, 1993), 16–46.

—— 'The Problem of Freedom in Nikolai Berdiaev's Existential Philosophy', *SEET*, vol. 46 (Sept. 1994), 153–186.

Gaut, G., 'Can a Christian be a Nationalist? Vladimir's Solov'ev's Critique of Nationalism', *Slavic Review*, vol. 57, 1 (Spring, 1998), 77–94.

Golubev, A.N., 'Ponyatie lichnosti v etike Vladimira Solov'eva', *VF*, 3 (1978), 125–136.

Hosking, G., *Russia and the Russians* (London, 2002).

Hosking, G. and Service, R. (eds), *Russian Nationalism Past and Present* (London, 1998).

Kaiser, D.H., *The Growth of the Law in Medieval Russia* (Princeton, 1980).

Koyre, A., *Etudes sur l'histoire de la pensée philosophique en Russie* (Paris, 1950).

Miller, J., *Mikhail Gorbachev and the End of Soviet Power* (Basingstoke, 1993).

Mironov, B.N., *Sotsialnaya istoriya Rossii* (SPb., 1999), 2 vols.

Mosse, W.E., *Alexander II and the Modernization of Russia* (New York, 1992)

Nahirny, V.C., *The Russian Intelligentsia: From Torment to Silence* (London, 1983).

Sakwa, R., *Gorbachev and his Reforms, 1985–1990* (New York, 1990).

Sutton, J., *The Religious Philosophy of Vladimir Solov'ëv: Towards a Reassessment* (Basingstoke, 1988).

Tolz, V., *Russia. Inventing the Nation* (London, 2001).

Valliere, P., *Modern Russian Theology. Bukharev, Soloviev, Bulgakov: Orthodox Theology in a New Key* (Michigan, 2000).

van den Bercken,W., de Courten, M., and van der Zweerde, E. (eds), *Vladimir Solov'ev: Reconciler and Polemicist* [Selected Papers of the International Vladimir Solov'ev Conference, Nijmegen, Sept., 1998] (Leuven, Paris, Sterling, Virginia, 2000).

van der Zweerde (ed.), 'Vladimir Solov'ev – Russian European Thinker', *SEET*, vol. 55, 2 (2003) [Special Issue].

White, S., *Gorbachev and After* (Cambridge, 1992).

—— *After Gorbachev* (Cambridge, 1993).

Index

Printed in Great Britain
by Amazon

80934353R00129